Adobe® InDesign For Dummies®

D1758912

Common Command Shortcuts

Command	Mac Shortcut	Windows Shortcut	Command	Mac Shortcut	Windows Shortcut
Save	⌘+S	Ctrl+S	Check Spelling	⌘+I	Ctrl+I
Place	⌘+D	Ctrl+D	Bring to Front	⌘+Shift+]	Ctrl+Shift+]
Print	⌘+P	Ctrl+P	Bring Forward	⌘+]	Ctrl+]
Undo	⌘+Z	Ctrl+Z	Send Backward	⌘+[	Ctrl+[
Redo	⌘+Shift+Z	Ctrl+Shift+Z	Send to Back	⌘+Shift+[	Ctrl+Shift+[
Paste Into	⌘+Option+V	Ctrl+Alt+V	Group	⌘+G	Ctrl+G
Find/Change	⌘+F	Ctrl+F	Ungroup	⌘+Shift+G	Ctrl+Shift+G
Snap to Guides	⌘+Shift+ semicolon (;)	Ctrl+Shift+ semicolon (;)			

Type Style Shortcuts

Type Style	Mac Shortcut	Windows Shortcut
Normal	⌘+Shift+Y	Ctrl+Shift+Y
Bold	⌘+Shift+B	Ctrl+Shift+B
Italic	⌘+Shift+I	Ctrl+Shift+I
All caps	⌘+Shift+K	Ctrl+Shift+K
Small caps	⌘+Shift+H	Ctrl+Shift+H
Superscript	⌘+Shift+ equal (=)	Ctrl+Shift+ equal (=)
Subscript	⌘+Shift+Option+ equal (=)	Ctrl+Shift+ Alt+equal (=)
Underline	⌘+Shift+U	Ctrl+Shift+U
Strikethrough	⌘+Shift+slash (/)	Ctrl+Shift+ slash (/)

Palette Shortcuts

Palette	Mac Shortcut	Windows Shortcut
Align	F8	F8
Character	⌘+T	Ctrl+T
Character Styles	Shift+F11	Shift+F11
Color	F6	F6
Layers	F7	F7
Links	⌘+Shift+D	Ctrl+Shift+D
Pages	F12	F12
Paragraph	⌘+M	Ctrl+M
Paragraph Styles	F11	F11
Stroke	F10	F10
Swatches	F5	F5
Tabs	⌘+Shift+T	Ctrl+Shift+T
Text Wrap	⌘+Option+W	Ctrl+Alt+W
Transform	F9	F9

Alignment Shortcuts

Alignment	Mac Shortcut	Windows Shortcut
Flush left	⌘+Shift+L	Ctrl+Shift+L
Centered	⌘+Shift+C	Ctrl+Shift+C
Flush right	⌘+Shift+R	Ctrl+Shift+R
Justified	⌘+Shift+J	Ctrl+Shift+J
Force justified	⌘+Shift+F	Ctrl+Shift+F

IDG BOOKS WORLDWIDE

...For Dummies®: Bestselling Book Series for Beginners

Adobe® InDesign For Dummies®

Type Size and Leading Shortcuts

Operation	Mac Shortcut	Windows Shortcut
Increase type size 2 points*	⌘+Shift+>	Ctrl+Shift+>
Decrease type size 2 points*	⌘+Shift+<	Ctrl+Shift+<
Increase type size 10 points*	⌘+Shift+Option+>	Ctrl+Shift+Alt+>
Decrease type size 10 points*	⌘+Shift+Option+<	Ctrl+Shift+Alt+<
Increase leading 2 points*	Option+up arrow	Alt+up arrow
Decrease leading 2 points*	Option+down arrow	Alt+down arrow
Increase leading 10 points*	⌘+Option+up arrow	⌘+Alt+up arrow
Decrease leading 10 points*	⌘+Option+down arrow	Ctrl+Alt+down arrow
Enable auto leading	⌘+Shift+Option+A	Ctrl+Shift+Alt+A

*Assuming default Preference settings

Kerning Shortcuts

Operation	Mac Shortcut	Windows Shortcut
Kern letters together 0.02 em space*	Option+left arrow	Alt+left arrow
Kern letters apart 0.02 em space*	Option+right arrow	Alt+right arrow
Kern letters together 0.1 em space*	⌘+Option+left arrow	Ctrl+Alt+left arrow
Kern letters apart 0.1 em space*	⌘+Option+right arrow	Ctrl+Alt+right arrow
Clear all manual kerning and tracking	⌘+Shift+Q	Ctrl+Shift+Q

*Assuming default Preference settings

Navigation Shortcuts

Operation	Mac Shortcut	Windows Shortcut
Scroll document	Spacebar+drag	Spacebar+drag
Scroll document when text is selected	Option+drag	Alt+drag
Move to previous page	Shift+Page Up	Shift+Page Up
Move to next page	Shift+Page Down	Shift+Page Down
Move to first page	⌘+Shift+Page Up	Ctrl+Shift+Page Up
Move to last page	⌘+Shift+Page Down	Ctrl+Shift+Page Down
Zoom in	⌘+plus (+)	Ctrl+plus (+)
Zoom out	⌘+minus (−)	Ctrl+minus (−)
Zoom to 100%	⌘+1	Ctrl+1
Fit page in window	⌘+0	Ctrl+0
Fit spread in window	⌘+Option+0	Ctrl+Alt+0
View entire pasteboard	⌘+Shift+Option+0	Ctrl+Shift+Alt+0
Switch between current and previous views	⌘+Option+2	Ctrl+Alt+2

...For Dummies®: Bestselling Book Series for Beginners

TM

...For Dummies References for the Rest of Us!®

BESTSELLING BOOK SERIES

Are you intimidated and confused by computers? Do you find that traditional manuals are overloaded with technical details you'll never use? Do your friends and family always call you to fix simple problems on their PCs? Then the *...For Dummies*® computer book series from IDG Books Worldwide is for you.

...For Dummies books are written for those frustrated computer users who know they aren't really dumb but find that PC hardware, software, and indeed the unique vocabulary of computing make them feel helpless. *...For Dummies* books use a lighthearted approach, a down-to-earth style, and even cartoons and humorous icons to dispel computer novices' fears and build their confidence. Lighthearted but not lightweight, these books are a perfect survival guide for anyone forced to use a computer.

> *"I like my copy so much I told friends; now they bought copies."*
>
> — *Irene C., Orwell, Ohio*

> *"Quick, concise, nontechnical, and humorous."*
>
> — *Jay A., Elburn, Illinois*

> *"Thanks, I needed this book. Now I can sleep at night."*
>
> — *Robin F., British Columbia, Canada*

Already, millions of satisfied readers agree. They have made *...For Dummies* books the #1 introductory level computer book series and have written asking for more. So, if you're looking for the most fun and easy way to learn about computers, look to *...For Dummies* books to give you a helping hand.

IDG BOOKS WORLDWIDE

1/99

ADOBE®
INDESIGN™
FOR
DUMMIES®

by Deke McClelland and
Amy Thomas Buscaglia

IDG Books Worldwide, Inc.
An International Data Group Company

Foster City, CA ◆ Chicago, IL ◆ Indianapolis, IN ◆ New York, NY

Adobe® InDesign™ For Dummies®

Published by
IDG Books Worldwide, Inc.
An International Data Group Company
919 E. Hillsdale Blvd.
Suite 400
Foster City, CA 94404
www.idgbooks.com (IDG Books Worldwide Web site)
www.dummies.com (Dummies Press Web site)

Library of Congress Catalog Card No.: 99-65873

ISBN: 0-7645-0599-8

Printed in the United States of America

10 9 8 7 6 5 4 3 2 1

1O/QS/QZ/ZZ/IN

Distributed in the United States by IDG Books Worldwide, Inc.

Distributed by CDG Books Canada Inc. for Canada; by Transworld Publishers Limited in the United Kingdom; by IDG Norge Books for Norway; by IDG Sweden Books for Sweden; by IDG Books Australia Publishing Corporation Pty. Ltd. for Australia and New Zealand; by TransQuest Publishers Pte Ltd. for Singapore, Malaysia, Thailand, Indonesia, and Hong Kong; by Gotop Information Inc. for Taiwan; by ICG Muse, Inc. for Japan; by Intersoft for South Africa; by Eyrolles for France; by International Thomson Publishing for Germany, Austria and Switzerland; by Distribuidora Cuspide for Argentina; by LR International for Brazil; by Galileo Libros for Chile; by Ediciones ZETA S.C.R. Ltda. for Peru; by WS Computer Publishing Corporation, Inc., for the Philippines; by Contemporanea de Ediciones for Venezuela; by Express Computer Distributors for the Caribbean and West Indies; by Micronesia Media Distributor, Inc. for Micronesia; by Chips Computadoras S.A. de C.V. for Mexico; by Editorial Norma de Panama S.A. for Panama; by American Bookshops for Finland.

For general information on IDG Books Worldwide's books in the U.S., please call our Consumer Customer Service department at 800-762-2974. For reseller information, including discounts and premium sales, please call our Reseller Customer Service department at 800-434-3422.

For information on where to purchase IDG Books Worldwide's books outside the U.S., please contact our International Sales department at 317-596-5530 or fax 317-596-5692.

For consumer information on foreign language translations, please contact our Customer Service department at 1-800-434-3422, fax 317-596-5692, or e-mail rights@idgbooks.com.

For information on licensing foreign or domestic rights, please phone +1-650-655-3109.

For sales inquiries and special prices for bulk quantities, please contact our Sales department at 650-655-3200 or write to the address above.

For information on using IDG Books Worldwide's books in the classroom or for ordering examination copies, please contact our Educational Sales department at 800-434-2086 or fax 317-596-5499.

For press review copies, author interviews, or other publicity information, please contact our Public Relations department at 650-655-3000 or fax 650-655-3299.

For authorization to photocopy items for corporate, personal, or educational use, please contact Copyright Clearance Center, 222 Rosewood Drive, Danvers, MA 01923, or fax 978-750-4470.

About the Authors

Deke McClelland is a contributing editor for *Macworld* and *Publish* magazines. He has authored more than 50 books on electronic publishing and the Macintosh computer, and his work has been translated into more than 20 languages. He started his career as artistic director at the first service bureau in the United States.

Deke won a Society of Technical Communication Award in 1994, an American Society for Business Press Editors Award in 1995, and the Ben Franklin Award for Best Computer Book in 1989. He is also a five-time recipient of the prestigious Computer Press Award.

Deke is the author of the following books published by IDG Books Worldwide, Inc.: *Photoshop 5 Bible,* Gold Edition; *Macworld Photoshop 5 Bible; Photoshop 5 for Windows Bible; Web Design Studio Secrets*, and *Photoshop Studio Secrets,* Second Edition. He is also the author of *Real World Illustrator 8* and *Real World Digital Photography* from Peachpit Press. The first edition of *Photoshop Studio Secrets* won the Computer Press Award for the best advanced how-to book of 1997.

Amy Thomas Buscaglia is a writer and editor specializing in electronic publishing and computer graphics. She frequently writes for Adobe's Web site, www.adobe.com, and has contributed to other books from IDG Books, including *Photoshop 5 Bible,* Gold Edition, and *CorelDRAW 8 For Dummies.* She began her career with Cambridge University Press in New York and now lives and works in Santa Barbara, California.

ABOUT IDG BOOKS WORLDWIDE

Welcome to the world of IDG Books Worldwide.

IDG Books Worldwide, Inc., is a subsidiary of International Data Group, the world's largest publisher of computer-related information and the leading global provider of information services on information technology. IDG was founded more than 30 years ago by Patrick J. McGovern and now employs more than 9,000 people worldwide. IDG publishes more than 290 computer publications in over 75 countries. More than 90 million people read one or more IDG publications each month.

Launched in 1990, IDG Books Worldwide is today the #1 publisher of best-selling computer books in the United States. We are proud to have received eight awards from the Computer Press Association in recognition of editorial excellence and three from Computer Currents' First Annual Readers' Choice Awards. Our best-selling *...For Dummies®* series has more than 50 million copies in print with translations in 31 languages. IDG Books Worldwide, through a joint venture with IDG's Hi-Tech Beijing, became the first U.S. publisher to publish a computer book in the People's Republic of China. In record time, IDG Books Worldwide has become the first choice for millions of readers around the world who want to learn how to better manage their businesses.

Our mission is simple: Every one of our books is designed to bring extra value and skill-building instructions to the reader. Our books are written by experts who understand and care about our readers. The knowledge base of our editorial staff comes from years of experience in publishing, education, and journalism — experience we use to produce books to carry us into the new millennium. In short, we care about books, so we attract the best people. We devote special attention to details such as audience, interior design, use of icons, and illustrations. And because we use an efficient process of authoring, editing, and desktop publishing our books electronically, we can spend more time ensuring superior content and less time on the technicalities of making books.

You can count on our commitment to deliver high-quality books at competitive prices on topics you want to read about. At IDG Books Worldwide, we continue in the IDG tradition of delivering quality for more than 30 years. You'll find no better book on a subject than one from IDG Books Worldwide.

John Kilcullen
Chairman and CEO
IDG Books Worldwide, Inc.

Steven Berkowitz
President and Publisher
IDG Books Worldwide, Inc.

IDG is the world's leading IT media, research and exposition company. Founded in 1964, IDG had 1997 revenues of $2.05 billion and has more than 9,000 employees worldwide. IDG offers the widest range of media options that reach IT buyers in 75 countries representing 95% of worldwide IT spending. IDG's diverse product and services portfolio spans six key areas including print publishing, online publishing, expositions and conferences, market research, education and training, and global marketing services. More than 90 million people read one or more of IDG's 290 magazines and newspapers, including IDG's leading global brands — Computerworld, PC World, Network World, Macworld and the Channel World family of publications. IDG Books Worldwide is one of the fastest-growing computer book publishers in the world, with more than 700 titles in 36 languages. The "...For Dummies®" series alone has more than 50 million copies in print. IDG offers online users the largest network of technology-specific Web sites around the world through IDG.net (http://www.idg.net), which comprises more than 225 targeted Web sites in 55 countries worldwide. International Data Corporation (IDC) is the world's largest provider of information technology data, analysis and consulting, with research centers in over 41 countries and more than 400 research analysts worldwide. IDG World Expo is a leading producer of more than 168 globally branded conferences and expositions in 35 countries including E3 (Electronic Entertainment Expo), Macworld Expo, ComNet, Windows World Expo, ICE (Internet Commerce Expo), Agenda, DEMO, and Spotlight. IDG's training subsidiary, ExecuTrain, is the world's largest computer training company, with more than 230 locations worldwide and 785 training courses. IDG Marketing Services helps industry-leading IT companies build international brand recognition by developing global integrated marketing programs via IDG's print, online and exposition products worldwide. Further information about the company can be found at www.idg.com. 1/24/99

Dedications

When all is memory and more is forgot,

I'll see how you were, my love.

We're so very small, but you were my world.

I'm your number-one fan, EP.

— Deke

To Ted, my love, my joy, my soulmate

— now, forever, and whatever comes after that.

— Amy

Authors' Acknowledgments

Deke and Amy wish to thank all the folks who helped make this book a reality. We are especially grateful to our most excellent project editor, Susan Pink (a.k.a. "spink"), and to Tim Cole, the world's greatest technical editor for all things InDesign. Thanks also to Whitney McCleary for sharing her vast product knowledge.

Publisher's Acknowledgments

We're proud of this book; please register your comments through our IDG Books Worldwide Online Registration Form located at `http://my2cents.dummies.com`.

Some of the people who helped bring this book to market include the following:

Acquisitions, Editorial, and Media Development

Project Editor: Susan Pink

Acquisitions Editor: Andy Cummings

Associate Acquisitions Editor: Steven H. Hayes

Technical Editor: Tim Cole

Editorial Manager: Mary C. Corder

Media Development Manager: Heather Heath Dismore

Editorial Administration: Constance Carlisle

Production

Project Coordinator: E. Shawn Alysworth

Layout and Graphics: Angela F. Hunckler, Brent Savage, Janet Seib, Michael A. Sullivan, Mary Jo Weis, Dan Whetstine

Proofreaders: Nancy Price, Marianne Santy, Susan Sims

Indexer: Lori Lathrop

Special Help
James Russell

General and Administrative

IDG Books Worldwide, Inc.: John Kilcullen, CEO; Steven Berkowitz, President and Publisher

IDG Books Technology Publishing Group: Richard Swadley, Senior Vice President and Publisher; Walter Bruce III, Vice President and Associate Publisher; Steven Sayre, Associate Publisher; Joseph Wikert, Associate Publisher; Mary Bednarek, Branded Product Development Director; Mary Corder, Editorial Director

IDG Books Consumer Publishing Group: Roland Elgey, Senior Vice President and Publisher; Kathleen A. Welton, Vice President and Publisher; Kevin Thornton, Acquisitions Manager; Kristin A. Cocks, Editorial Director

IDG Books Internet Publishing Group: Brenda McLaughlin, Senior Vice President and Publisher; Diane Graves Steele, Vice President and Associate Publisher; Sofia Marchant, Online Marketing Manager

IDG Books Production for Dummies Press: Michael R. Britton, Vice President of Production; Debbie Stailey, Associate Director of Production; Cindy L. Phipps, Manager of Project Coordination, Production Proofreading, and Indexing; Tony Augsburger, Manager of Prepress, Reprints, and Systems; Laura Carpenter, Production Control Manager; Shelley Lea, Supervisor of Graphics and Design; Debbie J. Gates, Production Systems Specialist; Robert Springer, Supervisor of Proofreading; Kathie Schutte, Production Supervisor

Dummies Packaging and Book Design: Patty Page, Manager, Promotions Marketing

◆

The publisher would like to give special thanks to Patrick J. McGovern, without whom this book would not have been possible.

◆

Contents at a Glance

Cartoons at a Glance

By Rich Tennant

"NO, THAT'S NOT A PIE CHART, IT'S JUST A CORN CHIP THAT GOT SCANNED INTO THE DOCUMENT."

page 71

"Remember, your Elvis should appear bald and slightly hunched - nice Big Foot, Brad.- Keep your two-headed animals in the shadows and your alien spacecrafts crisp and defined."

page 7

"Of course graphics are important to your project, Eddy, but I think it would've been better to scan a picture of your worm collection."

page 165

"...and here's me with Cindy Crawford. And this is me with Madonna and Celine Dion..."

page 233

"THAT'S A LOVELY SCANNED IMAGE OF YOUR SISTER'S PORTRAIT. NOW TAKE IT OFF THE BODY OF THAT PIT VIPER BEFORE SHE COMES IN THE ROOM."

page 297

Fax: 978-546-7747 • E-mail: the5wave@tiac.net

Table of Contents

Introduction

● ●

*H*ello and welcome to *Adobe InDesign For Dummies*, the one book tailored for beginners and new users of Adobe InDesign. Given that InDesign is a new product, a lot of new users are out there — just about everyone, in fact, with the exception of a handful of beta users and Adobe programmers — so we've worked hard to make sure you are well served.

What is InDesign? Nothing less than the most ballyhooed piece of software to hit the design market in a decade. Originally code-named K2, InDesign is the first major desktop publishing application written from the ground up in the 1990's — and the last such program devised in the 20th century.

K2 created a sensation in September 1998 during a keynote address at a Seybold conference conducted by Apple's Steve Jobs. At the time, rumors were flying about a half-baked bid from the privately held Quark to take over the publicly traded Adobe, whose stock was at an all-time low. So imagine the crowd's surprise when right on the heels of a gushy testimonial to Apple from Quark's Tim Gill, Adobe was invited on stage to demonstrate its upcoming "Quark killer." It may have been the closest thing to a sting operation in the history of electronic design. Talk of the takeover bid vaporized almost instantly, replaced by, "Will K2 really destroy QuarkXPress?"

The jury is still out on that question, but the odds are against it. QuarkXPress is too entrenched a standard to be knocked off its perch so easily. That said, InDesign is a decidedly capable page-layout program, uniquely suited to the essential chores of formatting text and importing graphics, as you discover as you read this book. Furthermore, although InDesign boasts a comparatively modest collection of features, it's one of the most elegant and logical applications in recent memory. For day-to-day tasks, it earns high marks indeed.

But perhaps the biggest factor in InDesign's favor, and the reason the program has a fighting chance to make a dent in the 15-year-old desktop publishing market, is that many in the design business hate Quark. The company's technical support is widely regarded as some of the worst in the industry. Quark creates departments only to kill them as quickly as six months later, leaving customers in the lurch. One highly positioned Quark official is well known for his public outbursts of temper, most often directed at the press. (Buy a beer for just about any computer journalist and he or she will tell you a story.) And perhaps most damning, at least one ex-Quark employee has shared stories of what can only be called a high degree of contempt toward customers fostered by the management.

So there you have it. Reasonably strong first-version program, well-known company in back of it, and everyone hates the competition. Sounds like a recipe for success to us.

About This Book

As we said at the outset, this book is for beginners. But just because you're a beginner at InDesign doesn't mean you're inexperienced with desktop publishing in general. Many of you are coming from other programs — some from XPress, others from PageMaker, and even a few from Microsoft Publisher.

What we're trying to say is, don't worry. Whether you've never touched a page-layout program before or you're simply switching teams, we have you covered. If you're a novice, rest assured we don't assume any prior knowledge. And for those of you who are experienced, we make specific comparisons to XPress and PageMaker. Regardless of whether you use a Mac or a PC, we cover everything you need to know, from the simplest feature to the most complex. Beginners won't get lost and even savvy designers will find the information useful and authoritative.

Why Should You Believe Us?

Together, Deke and Amy bring to bear nearly 25 years of design and publishing experience. Deke has been working in desktop publishing since its earliest days in 1985. Amy cut her teeth in the academic publishing world and recently has contributed a wealth of material to Adobe's official Web site, *www.adobe.com.*

Deke's early entry into the electronic design world started as a fluke. In college, he drew a comic strip called *Cereal*. After fooling around with one of the first Macintosh computers in 1984, he printed some patterns he had created in MacPaint and integrated them into a week of strips. One of those comics is shown here. (Okay, so it's not all that funny — what do you want? Deke had finals that week.) The newspaper decided he was a computer expert and hired him to start their electronic design department. This led to a job as art director at one of the first service bureaus in the United States, which led to some early and pretty inept books, which led to some better books, which led to a cable television show, which led to . . . well, you get the idea. It was all dumb luck.

The reason we mention this story — besides to make you think, "Wait a second, *I* can do that!"— is to introduce you to a character who pops up several times throughout the figures in this book, one Shenbop the frog.

One of the cartoons that got Deke his first computer design job.

Shenbop is in fact a dead frog, stuffed and equipped with a mechanical voice box. A second and funnier comic strip from a year earlier tells the story of his origin. For those of you who are thinking, "This is dumb," we'll have you know that Shenbop snagged a prestigious "Maggie" for Best How-To Article of 1999 from the Western Publications Association when he popped up in an article for *Publish* magazine. As you might imagine, we're all very proud of him.

The origin of Shenbop, the dead but cordial frog who populates many of the figures in this book.

How to Use This Book

Like any computer book, this one uses a few conventions that make it easier for us to explain stuff and easier for you to follow along. They go something like this:

- ✔ The first time we introduce a term that you may or may not be familiar with, we *italicize* it and follow it up with a definition. How's that for easy?

- ✔ Menu commands are listed like this: File⇨Place, which translates to "Please click on the File menu (with your mouse, of course) and kindly choose the Place command."

✔ Keyboard shortcuts look like this: ⌘+S or Ctrl+S. This means if you're using a Mac, press and hold the ⌘ key, press the S key, and then release both keys. If you're using a PC running Windows, press and hold the Ctrl key, press the S key, and then release both keys.

✔ Occasionally, we refer you to a Web site where you can find up-to-date information on a particular topic. In those instances, URLs (Uniform Resource Locators) are presented like this: *www.adobe.com.*

How This Book Is Organized

Every ...*For Dummies* book is divided into several parts, which are explained in two places, both here in the introduction and later on the opening page to each part (on the flip side of the Rich Tennant comics). We whine and rebel, but what can we do? We're just lowly authors. So here are the real descriptions of each part. The discussions on the opening page to each part are complete nonsense. (We're serious about this — don't read the first pages of the parts — they are *complete* nonsense.)

Part I: InDesign in an Afternoon

The four chapters in the first part of the book introduce you to InDesign, provide a quick overview of the interface, and tell you how to make, save, and open documents. Then we close things out with a discussion of rulers, guides, and grids. Nothing particularly challenging in these chapters — just the basics.

Part II: Type Is Thicker than Gravy

We forget why we called this section, "Type Is Thicker than Gravy." Probably because "gravy" struck us as a funny word at the time. Hee hee. It still does. These chapters explain everything you need to know about text, from creating simple frames to applying character and paragraph formatting. We end with a discussion of style sheets, which may do more to save you time and effort than any other feature in InDesign.

Part III: Pictures on the Paper Trail

There was a time when we were taught that picture books were for kids. Now even the most educated adults expect their pages to be filled with a heaping helping of graphics. Chapter 10 gets the ball rolling by showing how to import and modify graphics created in other applications. Then we explain how to color graphics, edit clipping paths, and mix type and graphics together.

Part IV: InDesign for Einsteins

As promised, this book explains the simple stuff and the complex stuff alike. Luckily, the complex stuff turns out to be pretty easy. These chapters tell you how to add and delete pages, make the most of master pages and libraries, and manage links to imported text and graphics. You'll also discover the ins and outs of printing and exporting to the all-important Portable Document Format.

Part V: The Part of Tens

"The Part of Tens" is our chance to flick the lights on and off and say, "Closing time, please take your purchases to the register," without altogether kicking you out of the joint. Here you'll find the most essential shortcuts, some very cool tips and techniques, and our take on the best typefaces on the market. After that, the book really does end and we will have to kick you out of the joint.

Icons in This Book

We spent a lot of time on this book, so we'd naturally like to think that you'll read every word from beginning to end. But we understand that some of you skim. That's why we've provided the following six helpful margin icons — to stop you in your tracks and say, "Not so fast, look at this."

We hate computer jargon, but sometimes we *have* to use it because there's no word for this stuff in normal, everyday, conversational English. This icon warns you that something nerdy is coming your way.

If ever an icon didn't need explaining, this is it. It's a tip, for crying out loud. Follow our guidelines and make your life happier.

This icon calls your attention to special little reminders of things we've mentioned in the past or things we want you to bear in mind for the future.

InDesign is a fairly tame program, but it can turn wild on you under certain conditions. The Warning icon tells you when to keep an eye out for trouble.

Every once in a while, we feel compelled to share something that has nothing much to do with your understanding InDesign or any other computer program. Feel free to skip it if you must.

Now that InDesign has murdered your old layout program, it's time to pick up the pieces and move on. XPress survivors and PageMaker casualties alike should look to this icon for transitioning assistance.

Where to Go from Here

If you have questions about the content of this book, feel free to jot us a line. You can reach Amy at *amythomas@worldnet.att.net*. To reach Deke, visit his Web site at *www.dekemc.com* and click on the Contact Deke button. We ask you to limit your questions and comments to issues pertaining to this book. Please don't write us to ask why InDesign or some other program isn't behaving the way it's supposed to on your machine — this is the job of Adobe's technical support team and they're far better qualified to help you with these questions than we are.

Oh, and by the way, on Deke's Web site you can also find the Shenbop documents pictured in various figures throughout the book. So sometime when you have a few minutes to spare, we encourage you to stop by for a visit.

Best of luck with InDesign. We sincerely hope we make getting to know this program an efficient and enjoyable experience.

Part I
InDesign in an Afternoon

The 5th Wave   By Rich Tennant

"Remember, your Elvis should appear bald and slightly hunched - nice Big Foot, Brad - keep your two-headed animals in the shadows and your alien spacecrafts crisp and defined."

In this part . . .

Don't you love those books that promise to teach you some ridiculously complex topic in an amazingly brief period of time? Like *Learn Quantum Physics in Three Days*. Or *Master Supply-Side Economics in 20 Minutes with a 5-Minute Break for Milk and Cookies*. And who can forget *Teach Yourself the Meaning of Life in Less Time than It Takes to Comb Your Hair*? Sure, you know it's impossible, but you still hold out hope that you can discover the world's secrets without expending the slightest effort.

Well, get ready to hope some more. For in this part, you'll find out the purpose of InDesign, how the program works, how to make new documents, and how to set up guides and grids. And because we skimp on pages, it won't take you long to read. No fooling! In fact, we're so confident that you'll be able to breeze through these chapters in a single afternoon that we're prepared to offer this guarantee: *Master InDesign fast or receive nothing!* That's right, if it takes you more than one afternoon to read the chapters in this part, send us the UPC symbol from the back cover along with a notarized videotape showing you reading in front of a Cesium-atomic clock for verification. In return, we'll send you nothing — not even an empty envelope — for absolutely free! We will, in fact, completely ignore you — we're *that* confident.

Even if you elect not to participate in our exciting offer, these chapters provide you with an overview of InDesign that will get you up and running with the program in record time. Chapter 1 even goes so far as to compare InDesign to rivals QuarkXPress and PageMaker, so you know exactly what the program can and can't do. So, get ready for one of the most productive afternoons of your life!

Chapter 1

Why Use InDesign?

In This Chapter
▶ Understanding page layout and how it differs from word processing
▶ Getting acquainted with InDesign's basic capabilities
▶ Deciding where to create text and graphics
▶ Comparing InDesign to QuarkXPress and PageMaker

Chances are, you already have at least a vague idea of what InDesign is all about. If you didn't, you probably wouldn't be reading this. But just so we're all clear, the basic purpose of InDesign is to create professional-looking documents.

If InDesign marks your first encounter with a page-layout program, you might be wondering why you need it. After all, you can create documents in your word processor just fine. Well, InDesign isn't about creating ordinary, everyday documents like those you'd create in Microsoft Word, Corel WordPerfect, or some other popular word processor. It's for designing documents with a little more oomph and pizazz — ones that include multiple columns, graphics, colors, and other stuff that help make documents easy to read and interesting to look at.

This chapter begins with a brief introduction to how InDesign differs from a word processor and when you should use which. Then we zoom in to take a closer look at InDesign and how it compares to the popular page-layout programs QuarkXPress and PageMaker, so that if you're a migrant from one of these two camps, you'll be prepared for the changes that await you.

What the Heck Is Page Layout, Anyway?

Grab a copy of your favorite magazine — *Newsweek*, *People*, *Mad Magazine*, any one will do. Now flip through a few pages. Look at the way text, graphics, page numbers, figure captions, and other elements are arranged on each page. The positioning of those elements constitutes the *page layout*.

So a page-layout program, such as InDesign, is first and foremost a tool for assembling all your graphics and text and making them look the way you want them to appear in your final document.

When it comes to laying out pages, InDesign is your friend, helpmate, and partner in crime. It includes scads of features that give you precise control over your document's look and feel. It also makes the whole layout process relatively simple and sometimes — dare we say it — even fun.

Can't I Just Use My Word Processor?

Although most popular word processors can perform basic layout tasks, their primary purpose is to make it easy to create and edit text — in other words, to process words. In general, a word processor alone is adequate for creating documents such as memos, letters, faxes, and long single-column documents that don't include high-quality graphics, color, or sophisticated layout and formatting. If your document's layout needs are simple, process away. But it you're creating more complex documents such as newsletters, brochures, catalogs, and advertisements, you should do your layout work with InDesign.

Meeting InDesign's Multiple Personalities

If InDesign were to seek out counseling, it would surely be diagnosed as having multiple personalities — enough, in fact, to earn a spot on *Oprah* for sure or maybe even the *Jenny Jones* show. You see, although InDesign is primarily a page-layout program, it's also a capable word processing, typesetting, drawing, and image manipulation tool. This begs the question: "Which tasks should I perform in my word processor and graphics applications and which should I do in InDesign?"

Where to create and edit text

You can create and edit text directly in InDesign or in a word processor. Most of the time, you'll want to do a little of both. Here are some guidelines to help you decide what kinds of text to create where:

✔ Create your main body text in a word processor and import it into your InDesign document. (Importing text is explained in Chapter 5.) Why? Because this is precisely what a word processor is designed for. Entering text is fast and editing it is simple. Besides, it's much easier to focus on the content of your text when you're not distracted by layout elements.

✔ Enter special text and make adjustments in InDesign. For example, it doesn't make much sense to write a bunch of headlines for articles in your word processor and then import them into InDesign. For one thing, it's more work to import many small pieces of text than it is to just type the text directly in an InDesign document. For another, you'll probably need to rewrite or edit most headlines to fit within your layout anyway.

Where to create graphics

InDesign provides several drawing tools that are useful when you need to create simple shapes, such as starbursts, or draw lines on the fly. But for anything beyond basic shapes and lines, you should create and prepare graphics in a dedicated graphics program (such as Adobe Photoshop, Illustrator, or Macromedia FreeHand) and then import them into your InDesign documents, as explained in Chapter 10.

Where to do everything else

Where should you do everything else? In InDesign, of course. Here's a quick hit list of some of InDesign's most basic capabilities, all of which are discussed in detail in future chapters:

✔ **Working with multiple columns:** InDesign lets you create columns in a flash and then drag to resize them. You can easily create different numbers of columns on the same page and run text and graphics within or across column boundaries (as shown in Figure 1-1) using text and graphics frames.

✔ **Formatting text:** Sure, you can do basic text formatting in a word processor, such as choosing a font and making text bold or italic. But when it comes to dealing with stuff such as leading, kerning, drop caps, paragraph spacing, and alignment (all explained in Chapters 7 and 8), InDesign gives you far greater control than any word processor.

✔ **Importing and manipulating graphics:** InDesign lets you import the most popular graphics formats and then scale, skew, rotate, reshape, and crop graphics with just a few clicks and drags of the mouse. You can even wrap text around the exact shape of a graphic, as shown in Figure 1-2.

Don't try this in your word processor. You're likely to suffer strange side effects, such as uncontrollable body tics and the urge to run from your computer screaming, "It's pure evil!"

Figure 1-1:
InDesign makes it easy to create different numbers of columns on the same page and position text and graphics within or overlapping column boundaries.

Figure 1-2:
InDesign lets you wrap text around the exact shape of a graphic.

✔ **Precisely positioning page elements:** InDesign offers a host of tools that make it a snap to position items anywhere on a page by simply dragging them. You can even position text and graphics before you place them on a page by using frames as placeholders.

✔ **Defining and applying colors:** Create and save custom colors on the fly or add colors from one of InDesign's built-in swatch libraries. Then apply them to objects with a few mouse clicks.

✔ **Automating layout and formatting tasks:** You can use InDesign's master pages, libraries, and paragraph and character styles to make laying out pages and formatting text faster and easier.

✔ **Printing high-resolution color documents:** If you want to print professional looking color documents on a high-resolution printer, InDesign has you covered.

The Killer Bares Its Fists

So now we're all clear about the most basic stuff we can do in InDesign. But a larger question looms. How does InDesign compare to the popular page-layout programs QuarkXPress and Adobe PageMaker? Whether InDesign represents your first foray into desktop publishing or a recent migration from another page-layout program, you've likely heard the hype about this new heavyweight contender and are curious to know just how powerful a punch it really packs.

Ten features worth cheering about

InDesign delivers some powerful new features you won't find in XPress or PageMaker — or any other page-layout program, for that matter. It even provides a few features that make transitioning from XPress or PageMaker a little easier. The following list highlights ten of the most notable new capabilities that InDesign has to offer:

✔ **Smarter hyphenation and justification:** Feel free to jump up and down, wave your arms, and scream wildly, because this is one of the most exciting features InDesign introduces. The Multi-line Composer enables InDesign to consider multiple (rather than single) lines in a paragraph when determining how to adjust spacing and hyphenate words to create line breaks. Don't worry if this sounds like Greek to you. Chapter 8 makes everything crystal clear. For now, just take comfort in knowing that you'll get more attractive text with less effort.

 ✔ **Superior automatic kerning controls:** *Kerning* is the process of adjusting the amount of space between two adjacent letters. Both XPress and PageMaker can kern characters automatically using a font's built-in kerning pairs, but InDesign goes one better. Sure, you can use built-in kerning pairs in InDesign, but you can also use optical kerning (explained in Chapter 7) to kern *all* letter pairs automatically based on their appearance, which often results in better looking type. If you're skeptical, check out Figure 1-3. The top example uses regular automatic kerning, which you find in XPress and PageMaker. It looks good enough until you compare it to the more even spacing between the letters in the bottom example, which uses optical kerning.

Figure 1-3:
The
automatic
kerning
used in
XPress and
PageMaker
(top) often
doesn't
measure
up to
InDesign's
automatic
optical
kerning
(bottom).

Washington

Washington

 ✔ **Flexible guides and grids:** XPress and PageMaker let you create ruler guides and baseline grids to help you align graphics and text on a page, and so does InDesign. But InDesign also lets you quickly create custom grids using guides and then copy and paste them onto different pages, even in different documents. You can also set up document grids that work like graph paper laid down over your page. See Chapter 4 for the full scoop.

 ✔ **Better master pages:** Master pages help automate basic layout tasks. In InDesign, you can create master pages based on other master pages, so when you make changes to the "based-on" master, the others are updated automatically. This feat is simply not possible in XPress or PageMaker. Chapter 15 has all the delightful details.

 ✔ **Direct export to PDF:** Adobe's Portable Document Format (PDF) is a great way to preserve documents for distribution over the Web or through e-mail. Although you can export XPress and PageMaker files to PDF using Acrobat Distiller, InDesign lets you export files *directly* to PDF — no distilling required. For more on this juicy feature, see Chapter 18.

✔ **Consistency with Photoshop and Illustrator:** Photoshop and Illustrator are two of the most powerful and popular graphics programs around, and there's a good chance you use at least one of them. If you do, you're in for a treat. Not only does InDesign sport many cool features Photoshop and Illustrator users know and love, it lets you import or drag and drop native Photoshop and Illustrator files directly onto pages in your documents, as discussed in Chapter 10. And when you drag and drop Illustrator files, you can edit them directly in InDesign.

✔ **Multiple undo and redo capability:** Both XPress and PageMaker let you undo and redo the last operation you perform, but InDesign truly takes the pain out of making mistakes by letting you undo and redo multiple steps — up to 300, in fact. So feel free to make a mess of things; until you save changes, you can always undo them. Chapter 3 contains more information.

✔ **Capability to open QuarkXPress and PageMaker files:** If you're transitioning to InDesign from QuarkXPress 3.3 – 4.0 or PageMaker 6.5, you can bring your work with you. The document conversion process isn't flawless — documents are likely to require somewhere between a little and a lot of reworking after conversion — but it sure beats the heck out of having to recreate documents from scratch. See Chapter 3 to find out more about opening XPress and PageMaker documents in InDesign.

✔ **Editable shortcuts:** Here's another feature likely to be of particular interest to former XPress and PageMaker users. InDesign lets you create custom sets of keyboard shortcuts, so you can continue to work in familiar ways. InDesign even includes a predefined set of XPress-compatible shortcuts, which you can put into effect with a few clicks of the mouse. Chapter 2 explains all.

✔ **Easy zooming and navigation:** When it comes to zooming and navigating your way around pages, InDesign leaves XPress and PageMaker in the dust. To find out how to zoom and navigate like nobody's business, read Chapter 3.

These aren't the only InDesign features worth cheering about, but we can't possibly cover them all in this chapter. Besides, our mothers taught us that good things come to those who wait. So we'll hold off for a few more pages.

A few reasons not to cheer

InDesign isn't just one big, raucous page layout party, however. Like any newborn, it can be cranky. It also has plenty of room to grow. If you're accustomed to working in XPress or PageMaker, you're likely to go hunting for some features that simply don't exist — at least, not as we write this. Here are a few of the most conspicuous absentees:

✔ InDesign doesn't include many of the long document features found in XPress and PageMaker for building books, indexes, and tables of contents.

✔ If you're accustomed to whipping up text on a path in XPress, don't bother trying in InDesign because you can't.

✔ Although InDesign is a capable word processing tool, PageMaker users are likely to mourn the loss of the convenient Story Editor. InDesign doesn't include a comparable feature.

On the bright side, chances are good that third-party vendors will develop plug-ins to fill some of these holes. In fact, Adobe has specifically designed InDesign to give third-party vendors an unprecedented amount of power to build new features and enhance the capabilities of existing ones. A company called Virginia Systems (*www.virginiasystems.com*), for example, has already announced plans to produce an InDesign plug-in for creating indexes and tables of contents, but it wasn't available as of this writing. For the latest information on third-party plug-ins, visit Adobe's Web site at *www.adobe.com*.

Chapter 2

The Killer's Kisser

*N*ow it's time to meet the famed Killer face to face. Aw, don't be scared; this killer is more likely to kiss than bite (in our experience, anyway). If you're new to desktop publishing programs, this chapter introduces you to the basic stuff you need to know before you can start making pages.

If you're familiar with Adobe Photoshop or Illustrator, you'll no doubt feel right at home in InDesign. But give this chapter the once-over anyway. Who knows? You might actually discover something new.

Preparing for Lift-off

InDesign is no lightweight program, so it needs some room to work. Computers provide this room in the form of *random access memory* (known as *RAM*), which is measured in *megabytes* (MB). You know the saying "less is more?" Well, we've never been quite sure what that means, but when it comes to RAM, it certainly doesn't apply. You need at least 20 to 22MB of RAM to run InDesign on the Mac (depending on your system) and 15MB of RAM to run it under Windows. The more the better.

Under Windows, programs simply gobble up as much available RAM as they need. On the Mac, programs ask the system for RAM when they start up, and then use that amount while they're running. Being the considerate program that it is, InDesign might not ask for as much RAM as it really wants, so you need to take matters into your own hands. Here's how you assign memory to InDesign on the Mac:

1. **Start your computer.**

   If your computer is already on, quit any applications that are running.

2. **From the Apple menu, choose About This Computer.**

   The Apple menu is in the top-left corner of your screen.

3. **Jot down the Largest Unused Block value.**

   This tells you how much RAM is left after the operating system loads. We'll use 69.4 as an example.

4. **Multiply that value by 0.75 and round it off to the nearest whole number.**

   In our example, $69.4 \times 0.75 = 52.05$, which we round off to 52. This represents the amount of free RAM we'll assign to InDesign (about 75 percent).

   Depending on the amount of RAM installed on your system and the number and type of other programs you generally want to have running at the same time, you might want to assign a higher or lower percentage of RAM to InDesign.

5. **Locate and open the Adobe InDesign folder.**

   If you have trouble finding the folder, try choosing File⇨ Find from the menu bar (or press ⌘+F). Then type the word **InDesign** and press the Return key. After you locate the folder, double-click on it to open it.

6. **Click on the InDesign icon to select it.**

   It's the one with the butterfly.

7. **Choose File⇨Get Info⇨Memory.**

   This brings up the Info dialog box.

8. **In the Preferred Size option box, enter the value from Step 4.**

   The Preferred Size value is measured in K (*kilobytes*) instead of MB, so you need to add three zeros to the end of it. Our value from Step 4, for example, would be 52000.

9. **Click on the box in the upper-left corner to close the dialog box.**

   That's it. Now you're ready to get started.

Firing Up InDesign

The process of launching InDesign is a little different depending on whether you're using a Mac or a PC running Windows. Here's how it works on the Mac:

1. **Start your computer.**

   Because you just finished assigning RAM, we figure you have this step covered. If you still need to assign RAM, see the previous section.

2. **Locate and open the Adobe InDesign folder.**

   Again, this step is already old hat.

3. **Double-click on the InDesign icon.**

   This launches the program.

4. **Wait and see if it works.**

   If you see the InDesign splash screen, you're good to go. If you see a message that says "There is not enough memory available to open InDesign" or something like that, you basically have two options: 1) run around in a blind panic, cursing your blasted machine; or 2) quit one or more applications to free some space for the program to work.

To launch InDesign in Windows, click on the Start button in the lower-left corner of the screen to display the Start menu. Move your cursor over the Programs item to display a submenu showing all your program groups. Next, move your cursor over the Adobe item to display yet another submenu listing all your Adobe programs. Then move your cursor over the InDesign item to display (you guessed it) another submenu and, finally, click on the Adobe InDesign item. Phew!

The Anatomy of a Killer

At this point, you should be looking straight at the interface of the reputed Killer. See it's not so bad. A toolbox, a few palettes — it's quite unassuming really. But then you know what they say about killers. They always seem so nice and normal, just like the program next door.

To get the full picture, you need to open a new document (also known in some circles as a *publication*). We cover all the basics of creating a new document in Chapter 3. For now, just choose File⇨New or press ⌘+N on the Mac or Ctrl+N under Windows. When the New Document dialog box appears, click on OK. Figure 2-1 shows how your screen will look on the Mac. It looks pretty much the same under Windows, with a few exceptions, which are noted throughout this section.

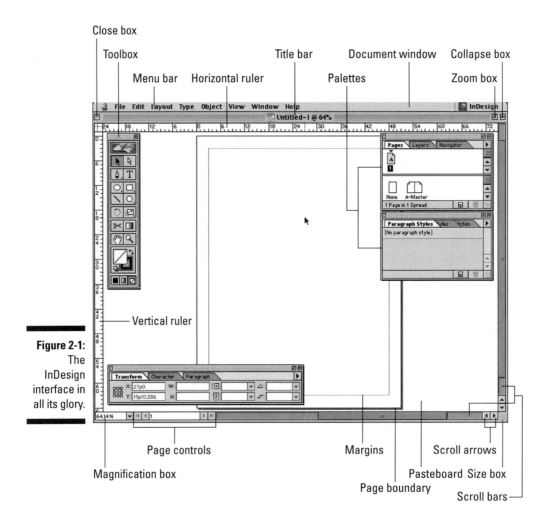

Figure 2-1:
The
InDesign
interface in
all its glory.

Many of the items labeled in Figure 2-1 are common to all Mac and Windows programs, but just in case you're new to the whole computer thing (or you're simply the forgetful type), we explain them all, blow by blow:

✔ The *menu bar* gives you access to InDesign's eight menus, which contain lists of commands that perform various operations. Menus are pretty darn important, which is why they're the topic of the next section.

✔ The *document window* is the large window below the menu bar. At the top of the document window is a *title bar* that displays the name of the document. You can move the document window by dragging the title bar.

✔ Click on the *close box* in the upper-left corner (or the *close button* in the upper-right corner under Windows) to close the document.

✔ Drag the *size box* in the lower-right corner to reduce or enlarge the window manually.

✔ On the Mac, click on the *zoom box* on the right side of the title bar to expand the window to fill the entire screen. Click on the zoom box again to restore the window to its previous size. Click on the *collapse box* next to the zoom box to collapse the window so that only the title bar is displayed. Click on it again to redisplay the document window.

The Windows equivalent to the collapse box is the *minimize button*, which is the button with a line in it on the right side of the title bar. Click on the minimize button to reduce the document to display only a portion of the title bar just above the Windows taskbar. Click on the button again to redisplay the document window. Similarly, the Windows equivalent to the zoom box is the *restore/maximize button*, located between the minimize and close buttons on the title bar. Click on the restore button (a button with two boxes in it) to shrink the window so that you can see other open windows. Click on the maximize button (a button with just one box) to make the window fill the entire screen again.

✔ Beneath the title bar is the *horizontal ruler*. Along the left edge of the document window is the *vertical ruler*. You use the rulers to position elements on a page, as discussed in Chapter 4.

✔ Along the right and bottom edges of the document window are *scroll bars*. Click on the up-pointing *scroll arrow* or down-pointing scroll arrow to move the on-screen display up or down. Click on the left- or right-pointing scroll arrows to move the view of the document to the left or right. To move in bigger increments, click in the gray area of a scroll bar. Drag the large tab in a scroll bar to move the document manually.

✔ The big rectangle in the center of the document window represents a *page*. The purple and pink lines inside the page show the left, right, top, and bottom page *margins*.

✔ The area outside the page boundary is the *pasteboard*. It's like a holding tank for graphics and other elements you may or may not want to use in your document. Items on the pasteboard aren't included when you print the document.

✔ The *page controls* at the bottom of the document window provide a way to move between various pages in a multipage document. Type a page number in the option box and press Return or Enter to go to a specific page. Click on the inner left- and right-pointing arrows to move to the previous or next page in a document. Click on the outer left- and right-pointing arrows to move to the first or last page in a document.

✔ The *magnification box* shows the current view size of a document. To change the view size, double-click inside the box, type a new zoom percentage, and press Return or Enter. Or click on the down arrow to the right of the magnification box and choose a zoom percentage from the resulting pop-up menu. Actually, InDesign offers countless ways to change the view size of a document, which we discuss in detail in Chapter 3.

✔ *Palettes* are like little on-screen command posts that give access to some of InDesign's most commonly used options and commands. They are also the subject of an upcoming section in this chapter.

✔ In the upper-left corner of the document window is the all-important *toolbox*. It contains the various gizmos you'll use to create, place, manipulate, and otherwise fiddle with text and graphics, and it's discussed in detail later in this chapter.

Making Your Way through Menus

Like all Macintosh and Windows programs, InDesign houses a good portion of its brains in the menu bar (labeled in Figure 2-1). Each word in the menu bar gives you access to a list of commands you can use to perform all kinds of operations, from opening, closing, and saving documents to wrapping text around graphics.

We discuss how to boss InDesign around throughout the book. But first, we thought we'd share a little information on how menus work:

✔ To choose a command from a menu, click on the menu name and then click on the command name. Alternatively, you can click and hold on the menu name, drag down to the command name and release the mouse button.

✔ Some commands bring up additional menus called *submenus*. For example, if you choose File➪Preferences, you display a submenu offering still more commands. So if we ask you to choose File➪Preferences➪General, you choose the Preferences command from the File menu and then choose the General command from the resulting submenu.

✔ If you're a Windows user and prefer keyboards to mice, you can choose commands by pressing *hot keys* in combination with the Alt key. The hot key for a command is indicated by an underlined letter in the command name. For example, to the display the File menu, press Alt+F. To choose the Preferences command from the File menu, press F again (without the Alt key this time). If you then want to choose the General command from the Preferences submenu, just press G. You can also use hot keys to access options inside dialog boxes, as we explain later in this chapter.

▶ Here's a tip both Mac and Windows users can enjoy. You can access many commands by pressing *keyboard shortcuts*. For example, to initiate the File⇨New command, you can press the keyboard shortcut ⌘+N on the Mac or Ctrl+N under Windows — that is, press and hold the ⌘ key on the Mac or the Ctrl key under Windows, press the N key, and then release both keys.

Most keyboard shortcuts for commands are listed along the right side of a menu. But there are also loads of keyboard equivalents that select tools, insert special characters, or perform other functions. You can even create your own shortcuts using InDesign's Edit Shortcuts dialog box, as discussed later in this chapter. Memorizing even a few can save you lots of time. That's why we keep you up to speed on relevant keyboard shortcuts throughout the book and devote all of Chapter 19 to a discussion of the most essential ones.

InDesign offers another convenient way to access some commands. On the Mac, if you press and hold the Control key and then click inside a document window, you display a *context-sensitive menu*, which is a mini-menu that contains commands related to the current tool, palette, document, or selected item, as shown in Figure 2-2. Under Windows, simply right-click—that is, click the right mouse button—to display a context-sensitive menu.

Context-sensitive menu

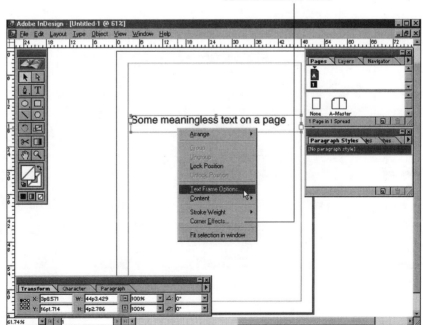

Figure 2-2:
Context-
sensitive
menus give
you access
to com-
mands
related to
the task at
hand.

Dealing with Dialog Boxes

Some menu commands spark immediate action, but others require some further input from you through a *dialog box*. Figure 2-3 shows the various options you encounter in dialog boxes.

- ✔ A box in which you can enter numbers or text is called an *option box*. Double-click in an option box to highlight its contents and then enter new information from the keyboard.

- ✔ Multiple-choice options often appear in *pop-up menus*. Click on the double-pointing arrow on the Mac or the down-pointing arrow under Windows to display a menu of options. Then click on the option to choose it, just as you would choose a command from a standard menu.

- ✔ You can turn some options on or off by clicking on a *radio button*. To select a radio button, click on the button or the name next to it. A black dot appears in the radio button when it is selected. You can turn on only one radio button at a time in a group of radio buttons.

- ✔ Click on a *check box* or the name that follows it to turn the corresponding option on or off. A check mark in the box indicates that the option is turned on. Unlike radio buttons, you can select as many check boxes in a group as you like.

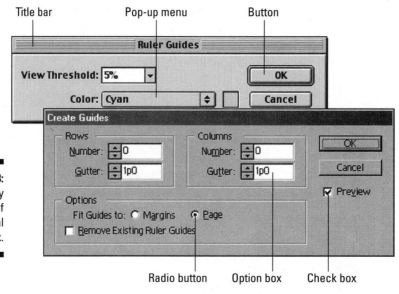

Figure 2-3:
The many
elements of
a typical
dialog box.

✔ Regular old *buttons* let you close the current dialog box or display others to access more options. For example, click on the Cancel button to close the dialog box and cancel the command. Click on OK to close the dialog box and initiate the command. Click on a button with an ellipsis (three dots) to display another dialog box.

You can move around and select options inside dialog boxes using the keyboard, just as you can with menus. The following shortcuts work in most dialog boxes:

✔ To advance from one option to the next, press the Tab key. To back up, press Shift+Tab.

✔ Under Windows, you can also select an option by pressing Alt plus the hot key (remember, that's the underlined letter in the option's name) for the option.

✔ Press Return or Enter to select the button surrounded by a heavy outline (such as the OK button in Figure 2-3).

✔ Press the up arrow key or down arrow key to make the value in the option box one higher or lower, respectively. Press Shift+up arrow and Shift+down arrow to raise and the lower the value in larger increments.

✔ If you haven't already saved your changes, you can return to the settings that were in effect when you first opened a dialog box. In most dialog boxes, pressing and holding the Option or Alt key changes the Cancel button to a Reset button. Click on the Reset button to restore the original settings.

If a dialog box is blocking your view of a document, you can move the dialog box out of the way by dragging its title bar.

Working with Palettes

Palettes are basically free-floating dialog boxes that you can hide or display on-screen while you work. They provide easy access to options and controls that affect the performance of tools, change the appearance of text and graphics, and otherwise help you get around and do stuff in your documents. InDesign offers more than a dozen palettes in all, which we'll cover throughout the book. For now, here's a brief introduction to how palettes work:

✔ As shown in the top example in Figure 2-4, some palettes contain a lot of the same kinds of options as dialog boxes — pop-up menus, option boxes, and so on.

✔ By default, many palettes (like those shown in Figure 2-4) are displayed in groups within one palette window. To switch to a different palette in a palette window, click on its tab.

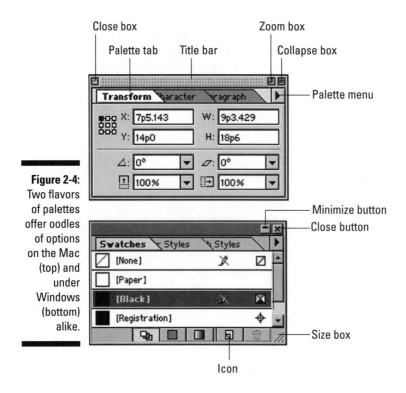

Figure 2-4:
Two flavors
of palettes
offer oodles
of options
on the Mac
(top) and
under
Windows
(bottom)
alike.

✔ To close a palette, click on the close box, which is located in the upper-left corner on the Mac, or on the close button in the upper-right corner on a PC. To make the palette reappear, you need to choose its name from the appropriate menu. We'll talk more about this later.

If you're accustomed to choosing palettes from the View menu in QuarkXPress or the Window menu in PageMaker, InDesign's palette locations will take a little getting used to. Although most palettes live in the Window menu, others call the File, Type, or Object menu home.

✔ Press Tab to hide all open palettes and the toolbox. Press Tab again to redisplay them. Press Shift+Tab to hide or display the palettes but leave the toolbox visible. This tip doesn't work under the following circumstances: when a text insertion point (a blinking cursor) is visible; when text is selected (highlighted); or when an option box in a palette is active. In these cases, the Tab key affects the text or palette option. To deselect text or deactivate an option box, click outside the palette or active text with any tool except the type tool. (Tools? Who said anything about tools? We will, and in the very next section.)

✔ Some palettes contain icons that perform specific functions when you click on them. For example, clicking on the icon labeled in Figure 2-4 would create a copy of the highlighted black swatch.

✔ If you're not sure what a particular item in a palette is or does, hover your cursor over the item to display a hint.

✔ If you want to move a palette, just drag its title bar.

✔ Some palettes have a size box (labeled in the bottom example of Figure 2-4) that you can drag to resize the palette. To return a palette to its default size, double-click on its palette tab.

✔ Click on the zoom box on the Mac or the minimize button under Windows to shrink a palette so that only the tabs are displayed. Click on the zoom box or the maximize button again to redisplay all the options.

To move quickly between tab only view and full palette view, double-click on the palette's title bar.

✔ Click on the right-pointing arrow on the right side of a palette to display a palette menu offering a slew of commands related to the currently selected palette.

✔ Some palette menus include a Show/Hide Options command. Choose the Hide Options command to display an abbreviated view of a palette that shows only one or more essential options. Choose the Show Options command to restore the palette to full view.

If a palette offers the Show/Hide Options command, you can simply double-click on the palette tab to cycle between the tab only, abbreviated, and full palette views.

✔ You can drag a palette tab out of its current window to give it a window of its own, as shown in Figure 2-5. You can also combine palettes into a single palette window by dragging a tab from one palette window to another. This technique is great for rearranging palettes to save screen real estate and to better suit the way you work.

Figure 2-5:
Drag a palette tab out of its window (left) to give it a home of its own (right).

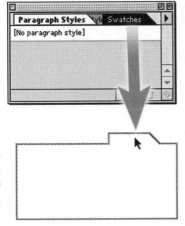
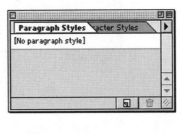
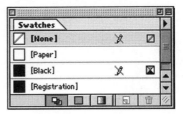

✔ Just as in dialog boxes, you can raise and lower values in palette option boxes using the arrow keys. Press the up arrow and down arrow keys to raise and lower a value by one, respectively. Press Shift+up arrow and Shift+down arrow to raise and lower values in larger increments.

Tackling the Toolbox

InDesign's toolbox doesn't contain a hammer and nails, and it won't help build your bathroom shelves, but it is chock full of tools you can use to build pages. As Figure 2-6 shows, the toolbox contains two categories of items: tools and color controls.

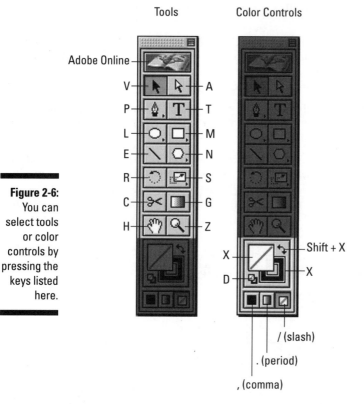

Figure 2-6:
You can select tools or color controls by pressing the keys listed here.

We explain how to use all the tools and controls in other chapters. For now, here's a quick look at how the toolbox is organized and how you can find and select stuff:

- ✔ The top part of the toolbox is home to a variety of tools you can use to create and lay out text and graphics. To select a tool, click on its icon. Then click or drag in the document window to put the tool to work.

- ✔ If a tool icon contains a small right-pointing triangle, more tools are tucked away behind it. To reveal the hidden tools, press and hold the mouse button on the icon to display a *flyout* menu. Drag across the flyout menu until the tool you want appears depressed (as in pressed down, not forlorn) and then release the mouse button.

- ✔ Click on the open book at the top of the toolbox to display the Adobe Online welcome screen. If you have a Web browser, such as Netscape Navigator or Internet Explorer, and an Internet connection, you can click on the Refresh button on this screen to connect to Adobe's Web site, where you'll find up-to-date information about InDesign.

- ✔ You can access any tool or color control also by pressing its keyboard shortcut (labeled in Figure 2-6). To select a tool on a flyout menu, press Shift plus the shortcut key. For example, to select the rectangle tool, you press the M key. To select the rectangle frame tool, which shares a flyout menu with the rectangle tool, you press Shift+M.

If you're familiar with Illustrator, InDesign's tool shortcuts will make a lot of sense. But they bear no resemblance to the ones in QuarkXPress or PageMaker. We suggest you take a few minutes to memorize InDesign's shortcuts; once you get the hang of them, they're faster. If you're reluctant to change your ways, however, you can change any of InDesign's shortcuts using the Edit Shortcuts dialog box, which is the topic of the next section in this chapter.

- ✔ If you can't remember the name of a tool or a color control, just hover your cursor over its icon to display the name of the tool and its keyboard equivalent.

One tool merits immediate introduction. The arrow tool, which is located in the top-left corner of the toolbox, is the most common laborer among tools. You use it to select, move, and resize elements on your pages. InDesign calls this tool the selection tool. But it looks like an arrow, so by golly we call it an arrow.

Changing Shortcuts

As you've probably noticed by now, InDesign is loaded with *shortcuts* that let you perform various tasks directly from the keyboard. The cool thing about shortcuts is that they enable you to work much faster. The not-so-cool thing about them is that you have to know what they are to use them. If you just migrated over to InDesign from QuarkXPress, PageMaker, or some other page-layout program, you're probably not thrilled by the idea of having to memorize a whole new set of shortcuts. Well, guess what? You don't have to.

Making like Quark

InDesign sports a shortcut editor that lets you change InDesign's shortcuts to match those of QuarkXPress with just a few clicks of the mouse. Just choose File⇨Edit Shortcuts to display the Edit Shortcuts dialog box, as shown in Figure 2-7. Then from the Set pop-up menu, choose Set For QuarkXPress 4.0, and click on OK. That's it. InDesign replaces its default shortcuts with QuarkXPress shortcuts wherever applicable.

Changing InDesign's keyboard shortcuts doesn't change its features. You can press ⌘+Option+I on the Mac or Ctrl+Alt+I under Windows until your fingers fall off, but you'll never get the QuarkXPress Index palette to appear in InDesign. The feature simply doesn't exist — at least not for now.

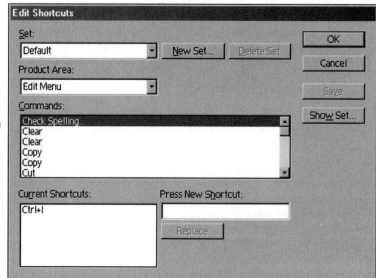

Figure 2-7: The Edit Shortcuts dialog box lets you create and apply new keyboard shortcuts.

Making like any other program

If you want to use keyboard shortcuts from PageMaker or any other program, you can do that too, but it's quite a chore. You need to create a new shortcuts set and manually enter the new keyboard shortcut for each command. If you think you're up to the task, here's how:

1. **Choose File⇨Edit Shortcuts.**

   The dialog box shown in Figure 2-7 appears.

2. **Click on the New Set button.**

   The New Set dialog box appears.

3. **In the Name option box, type a name for your new shortcuts set.**

   For example, if you are creating a set to match PageMaker's shortcuts, you might name it PageMaker Set.

4. **In the Based On Set pop-up menu, tell InDesign what current set to use as the basis for the new one, and then click OK.**

   The first time you create a new set, it's usually best to choose Default.

5. **In the Product Area pop-up menu, choose a menu name or a topic to display a related list of commands.**

   If you choose File Menu, for example, you see a list of commands in the File menu, as shown in Figure 2-8.

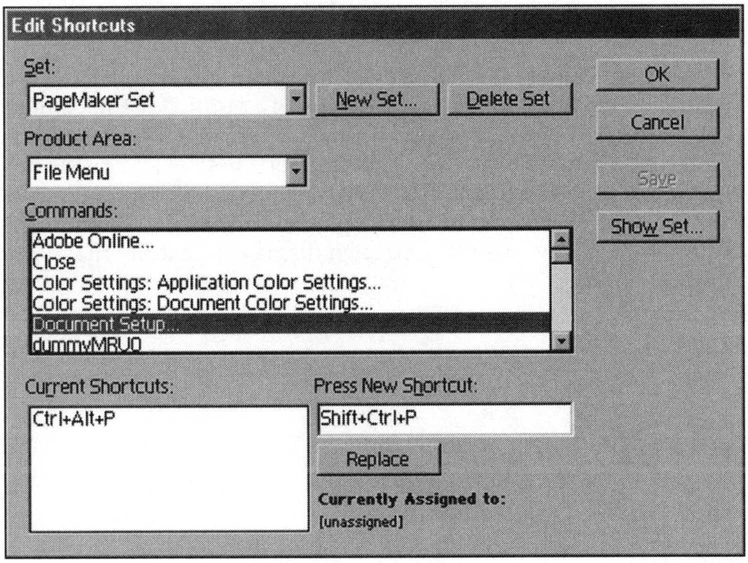

Figure 2-8:
Enter new keyboard shortcuts in the Press New Shortcut box.

6. **Click on a command whose shortcut you want to change.**

   Here's the bummer: You need to manually select each command and enter the new shortcut. When you select a command, the default short-cut (if any) for that command is listed in the Current Shortcuts box.

7. **Click in the Press New Shortcut box and press the keys for the new shortcut you want to define.**

   In Figure 2-8, we entered the keyboard shortcut for the Document Setup command in PageMaker for Windows (Ctrl+Shift+P). If the new shortcut you entered is currently being used by another command, that com-mand will be displayed under Currently Assigned To. If overriding that command's shortcut is okay with you, proceed to Step 8. Otherwise, enter a new shortcut in the Press New Shortcut box.

8. **Click on the Assign or Replace button to save your new shortcut to your new set.**

   If the command you chose doesn't have a predefined shortcut, you will see an Assign button below the Press New Shortcut box. If the command already has a shortcut assigned, you'll see a Replace button. Click on either button to save your new shortcut.

9. **Repeat Steps 6 to 8 for every new shortcut you want to define. When you're finished, click on OK.**

   The dialog box closes and your new shortcut set is put into effect.

You can also use the Edit Shortcuts dialog box to quickly find shortcuts for specific commands. Just choose the menu or topic for the command from the Product Area pop-up menu and then click on the name of the command in the resulting Commands list. The Current Shortcuts list shows the keyboard equivalent to the command. To view all shortcuts for an entire set, choose the name of the set from the Set pop-up menu and click on the Show Set button. After a few seconds, InDesign displays a text file that lists all the shortcuts for that set.

Chapter 3

It's a Page!

Dialog boxes, palettes, menus, tools, blah, blah, blah. Sure, they're neat and all, but they don't let you do squat until you open a document. It's like having a pen, a protractor, and some magic markers, but no paper — not even a tissue or a candy wrapper. It's all just a bunch of stuff taking up space.

That's why this chapter shows you how to open documents and set up pages. Then it explains the nearly endless ways you can move around and view your document on-screen. You'll also find out how to undo mistakes and save your work to avoid mind-numbing catastrophes.

You're here to create pages, darn it, and you're not getting any younger. So let's get to it.

Opening a New Document

To open a new document, choose File⇨New or press ⌘+N on the Mac or Ctrl+N under Windows. InDesign responds by serving up the New Document dialog box, shown in Figure 3-1. This is where you give InDesign the information it needs to set up the most basic elements of your document: the number, size, and margins of pages; the number of columns and space between them; and whether your document has single-sided or double-sided pages. If that last sentence was enough to give you heartburn, don't go looking for the Tums just yet. The following few subsections dice up this dialog box into easily digestible pieces. You'll have your new document on-screen in no time.

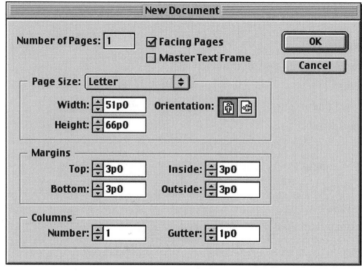

Figure 3-1:
The options
in this dialog
box tell
InDesign
how to set
up your new
document.

Here's another word of comfort. Although it's best to have at least some idea about how you want your final document to look, you don't need to have your entire layout planned at the start. You can change most settings at any time using the Document Setup and Margins and Columns commands, as discussed later in this chapter.

Your first page options

The first option in the New Document dialog box is a no-brainer. Enter the number of pages you want in your document in the Number of Pages option box. You can create documents from 1 to 9,999 pages long, so feel free to go nuts.

If you want your document to be double-sided and contain left and right pages (called *verso* and *recto*, respectively, in publishing lingo), select the Facing Pages check box. As shown in Figure 3-2, InDesign displays facing pages (also known as a *spread*) next to each other on-screen, just as they would appear in an open book. When you move from a left-hand page to a right-hand page in a spread, you scroll across rather than down. We'll talk more about scrolling and other viewing options later in this chapter.

Immediately below the Facing Pages check box is the Master Text Frame option. We explain this option later in this chapter.

Figure 3-2:
The Facing
Pages
check box
places left
and right
pages side
by side to
form a
spread.

Choosing page size settings

The page size settings determine the size and orientation of the pages in your document. Choose an option from the Page Size pop-up menu, which offers ten preset page sizes (including Letter, Legal, and other common sizes) and a Custom option. The dimensions of the page size you select appear measured in *picas* and *points* in the Width and Height option boxes. Picas and points are standard units of measurement in publishing, and InDesign uses them by default. Just in case they're new to you, 12 points are in a pica and 6 picas are in an inch. So a standard letter-size page is 8½ x 11 inches or 51 x 66 picas. In dialog boxes, InDesign displays measurements in picas and points like this: 51p0. That means 51 picas and 0 points.

If you just aren't comfortable with the whole points and picas thing, you can quickly change InDesign's default settings to use another unit of measurement. Click on Cancel to close the New Document dialog box. Make sure no document is open, and then choose File⇨Preferences⇨Units & Increments to display the Units & Increments Preferences dialog box. Then choose a new unit of measurement (such as Inches) from the Horizontal and Vertical Ruler Unit pop-up menus. Press ⌘+N on the Mac or Ctrl+N under Windows to redisplay the New Document dialog box. Now the Width and Height boxes display your new unit of measurement.

You never need to choose the Custom option from the Page Size pop-up menu. To specify a page size other than one of the preset options, just enter the dimensions in the Width and Height option boxes.

The last page size option is Orientation. Click on the button that shows a person standing upright if you want the long side of the page to go from top to bottom. This option is called *portrait* in many programs because that's how portrait paintings are oriented. Click on the button that shows a person sideways if you want the long side of the page to go from side to side. This option is often called *landscape* because that's how paintings of landscapes are oriented. Most documents and publications, such as letters, brochures, magazines, and most books, use the portrait orientation.

All pages in a document must have the same orientation. So if you want to include both portrait and landscape pages in your layout, you need to create separate documents — one for your portrait pages and one for your landscape pages.

Making margins

The Margins settings determine the size of the margins on all four sides of a page: Top, Bottom, Left, and Right. Larger values create larger margins, and smaller values create smaller ones. (Like you needed us to tell you that.) If you selected the Facing Pages check box, the Left and Right options change to Inside and Outside. With facing pages, the inside margin is the right margin on a left-hand page and the left margin on a right-hand page (as you can see in Figure 3-2). If your document will be bound (like a book, for example), you can make the inside margin slightly larger than the outside margin to account for the amount of space lost in the binding.

Setting up columns

The Columns settings let you specify the number of columns in your document and the amount of space between them (called a *gutter*). Enter the number of columns in the Number option box and the amount of space you want between them in the Gutter option box.

Chances are, you'll use columns in most of your documents. See Chapter 4 for more details on working with columns.

Back to Master Text Frame

We explain what text frames are and how they work in Chapter 5, but here's a quick introduction. In InDesign, text is always contained in a *frame*, which is basically just a box that holds stuff on a page. If you select the Master Text Frame check box, InDesign automatically places a text frame within the margins and columns of every page of your document. Any text you enter with the type tool or import from another program automatically flows between the text frames on each page. If your document is mostly text with few or no graphics, this option can be very handy.

When you've finished entering all your new document settings, click on OK or press Return or Enter. Your new document is displayed in a document window with the catchy title "Untitled-1."

Opening a Used Document

What if you want to open an existing document? That's a cinch. Not only can InDesign open saved InDesign documents, it can open PageMaker 6.5 and QuarkXPress 3.3 to 4.04 files. So if you've been using one of those programs, you can continue to work with your existing documents without missing a beat.

To open an existing document, choose File⇨Open or press ⌘+O on the Mac or Ctrl+O under Windows to display the Open A File dialog box. Figure 3-3 shows how this dialog box appears on the Mac (top) and under Windows (bottom).

Choose the folder that contains the document you want from the pop-up menu at the top of the dialog box. Then locate the file in the list in the center of the dialog box and double-click on it. Here are a few helpful hints:

✔ If you don't see the file you want, choose All Files from the Show pop-up menu on the Mac or from the Files of Type pop-up menu under Windows. This displays all files stored in the selected folder — even files InDesign can't open — as shown in the bottom example of Figure 3-3. On a PC, you can also choose to display only PageMaker 6.5 or QuarkXPress 3.3 to 4.04 files.

✔ If you choose the Open Copy radio button (Mac) or the Copy radio button (Windows), InDesign opens a copy of the selected document. This option is useful if you want to experiment with a document without affecting the original.

✔ Select the Open Original radio button (Mac) or the Original radio button (Windows) to open a *template* file for editing. Templates are simply documents that you can't save over (unless you select the Open Original or Original radio button when you first open them). They are great starting points for documents you produce regularly. For example, if you prepare a newsletter every month, you can create a template that contains the basic layout, text, and graphics of a typical issue.

You can open as many documents at a time as you like, until your computer runs out of memory.

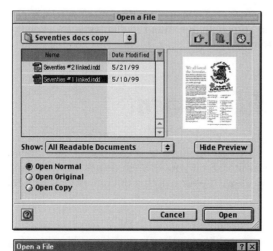

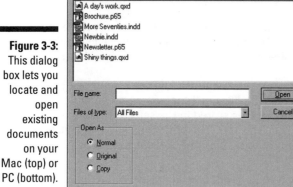

Figure 3-3: This dialog box lets you locate and open existing documents on your Mac (top) or PC (bottom).

What happened to my document?

When InDesign opens a QuarkXPress or PageMaker file, it has to convert the document to its own format. It does its best to preserve elements such as text attributes, embedded profiles in images, and so on, but you may find that some aspects of your document have been modified. Unfortunately, that means you may need to make some adjustments to your document after InDesign opens and converts it. But fortunately, InDesign notifies you about any changes it needs to make during conversion by displaying the Conversion Warnings dialog box.

You should take note of the warnings in this dialog box so that you can check any elements that have changed.

The folks at Adobe say they plan to produce special kits that will help you manage the conversion process. None were available as of this writing, but you may want to keep an eye out for them on Adobe's Web site at *www.adobe.com*.

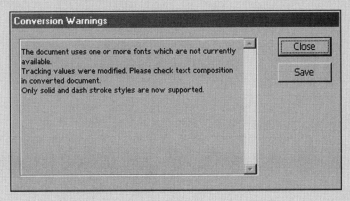

Changing Your Basic Layout Settings

So you have your document nicely displayed on the screen, and now you decide you want to make some changes. You need five pages instead of three, and letter-size paper just won't do. You can access the options you encountered back in the New Document dialog box through two separate commands: the Document Setup command and the Margins and Columns command.

Changing your page settings

To change the page settings in your open document, choose File⇪Document Setup or press ⌘+Option+P (or Ctrl+Alt+P under Windows) to display the Document Setup dialog box shown in Figure 3-4.

Figure 3-4:
You can
change your
document's
page set-
tings in the
Document
Setup dialog
box.

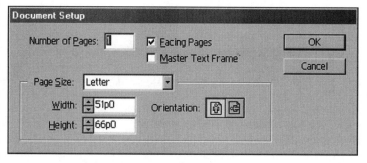

The options in this dialog box work just like the ones in the top half of the New Document dialog box.

✔ Enter a number in the Number of Pages option box to add or remove pages from your document. Pages are added or deleted from the end of your document.

✔ Select the Facing Pages check box to change a single-sided document to a double-sided document, so that left and right pages form a spread. Deselecting the check box changes a double-sided document to a single-sided one.

✔ If you choose the Document Setup command when a document is open, the Master Text Frame option appears dimmed. That's because you can't add or delete a Master Text Frame in an existing document.

✔ You can change the size of your pages by choosing an option in the Page Size pop-up menu or entering new values in the Width and Height option boxes. To change the orientation of your pages from portrait to landscape or vice versa, click on the appropriate Orientation button.

✔ When a document is open, any changes you make in the Document Setup dialog box are applied to the entire document and affect its layout. The results can be alarming to an unsuspecting novice. For example, if you have entered text or graphics in a portrait-oriented document and then change the orientation to landscape, your content will run off the top and bottom of your pages, creating a big mess. Fortunately, InDesign provides a command called Layout Adjustment that can help you avoid such surprises. We discuss this command in Chapter 4.

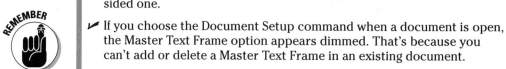

Any changes you make inside the Document Setup dialog box when no document is open become the default settings for all future documents. This is super-handy if you typically create documents of the same page size, orientation, and so on, and InDesign's built-in defaults don't fit the bill.

But it also means you can change default settings accidentally if you're not paying attention. If this happens, don't panic. You can easily restore InDesign's built-in defaults. Simply quit the program and find and delete the files named InDesign Defaults and InDesign SavedData. They're located in the program folder called Adobe InDesign on the Mac or InDesign under Windows. The next time you start the program, InDesign reestablishes its built-in defaults.

Modifying margins and columns

To access margin and column settings, choose Layout⇨Margins and Columns to display the dialog box shown in Figure 3-5. We should warn you that changing margin and column settings for all pages in an open document is not as straightforward as changing page settings in Document Setup. The problem is that the Margins and Columns command affects only the currently selected page or spread. That's fine if you're working in a small document, but what if you're working on a document of 100 pages or more? You can change margin and column settings for an entire document using a feature called *master pages*, which are the topic of Chapter 15.

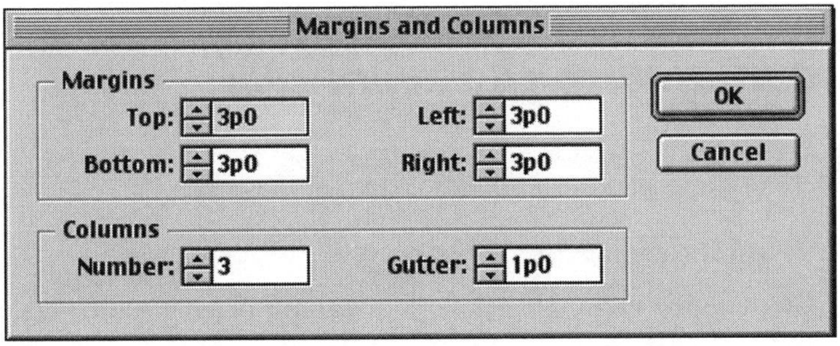

Figure 3-5: Use this dialog box to change your margin and column settings.

For now, you should know a couple of things about the Margins and Columns dialog box. First, any changes you make to margin or column measurements while a document is open are applied to the currently selected page or spread and any new pages you add to your document. Second, just as is the case in the Document Setup dialog box, when no document is open, any changes you make become the default settings for all future documents.

Moving around Your Document

InDesign gives you about a billion ways to move around and view your document, a process called *navigating* by adventuresome types. The InDesign toolbox includes a hand tool, which lets you move around inside the document window with more speed and control than the scroll bars allow. The toolbox also sports a zoom tool, which lets you move closer to or farther away from a page.

And that's not all. The Navigator palette gives you another convenient way to scroll and zoom your document. Throw in a few View commands and magnification controls and you have something to talk about, which is precisely what we do next.

Getting handy with the hand tool

Select the hand tool by clicking on the icon in the toolbox that looks like a hand. Now click on a spot in your document and drag in any direction. The document moves with the hand cursor.

You can also select the hand tool by pressing the H key. To temporarily access the hand tool when another tool is selected (and there's no text insertion point), press and hold the spacebar. Releasing the spacebar returns you to the selected tool. If a blinking cursor is inside a block of text, pressing the spacebar enters spaces in your text, so you need to press Option or Alt and then click to temporarily access the hand tool.

Zooming with the zoom tool

If you want your page to get closer to you, get closer to it using the zoom tool. Here's an example of how the zoom tool works:

1. **Select the zoom tool.**

   Click on the tool in the toolbox that looks like a magnifying glass, or press the Z key.

2. **Click somewhere on a page in your document.**

   The page is magnified to the next preset zoom size (75 percent to 100 percent, and so on) as shown in the second example in Figure 3-6. InDesign centers the zoomed view at the point where you clicked. In Figure 3-6, for example, we clicked on Shenbop's mouth.

3. **Keep clicking to continue zooming.**

   The more you click, the more you zoom. You can keep zooming until the plus sign (+) in the zoom cursor disappears. That means you're at maximum magnification.

It may take a lot of clicks with the zoom tool to reach maximum magnification. That's because InDesign lets you magnify your view up to a whopping 4000 percent. That's 3200 percent more than you can zoom in QuarkXPress 4 and 3600 percent more than you can zoom in PageMaker. Way to go InDesign!

Figure 3-6:
Click with
the zoom
tool to
magnify a
page in
preset
increments.

Here are several other ways to use the zoom tool:

- ✔ Option+click on the Mac or Alt+click under Windows with the zoom tool to zoom out from your page in preset increments (100 percent to 75 percent to 50 percent, and so on). Note that the little plus sign in the center of the zoom tool changes to a minus sign.

- ✔ Drag with the zoom tool to draw a dotted rectangle (called a *marquee*) around a portion of a page you want to magnify. InDesign zooms in to display only the marquee area in the document window.

- ✔ You can also zoom in and out using keyboard shortcuts. Press ⌘+plus (+) on the Mac or Ctrl+plus (+) under Windows to zoom in. Press ⌘+minus (–) on the Mac or Ctrl+minus (–) under Windows to zoom out.

- ✔ You can quickly switch between the current and previous view sizes by pressing ⌘+Option+2 on the Mac or Ctrl+Alt+2 under Windows.

- ✔ To temporarily access the zoom tool while another tool is selected, press ⌘+spacebar on the Mac or Ctrl+spacebar under Windows to activate the zoom in tool. Press ⌘+Option+spacebar on the Mac or Ctrl+Alt+spacebar under Windows to activate the zoom out tool. When you release the keys, you return to the previously selected tool.

- ✔ Zooming doesn't affect the size at which a page prints. It simply changes the size at which you view the page on screen.

- ✔ InDesign displays the current *zoom percentage* in the title bar and in the magnification box (discussed shortly) in the bottom left corner of the document window.

- ✔ Double-click on the zoom tool in the toolbox to quickly change the zoom percentage to 100 percent.

Viewing by the menu

In addition to using the zoom tool, you can use several commands in the View menu to change the view size:

- ✔ You can pretty much ignore the first two commands in the View menu — Zoom In and Zoom Out. You can zoom faster using keyboard shortcuts and more precisely using the zoom tool.

- ✔ Choose View⇨Fit Page In Window or press ⌘+0 on the Mac or Ctrl+0 under Windows to display the current page so that it fits within the document window. You can also just double-click on the hand tool to access this command.

- ✔ Choose View⇨Fit Spread In Window to display an entire spread in the document window. (Remember, a spread consists of two or more facing pages, as shown back in Figure 3-2.) If a single page is currently selected, choosing this command will fit the page in the window just as if you chose the Fit Page In Window command. You can also press ⌘+Option+0 on the Mac or Ctrl+Alt+0 under Windows to choose this command.

✔ Choose View➪Actual Size or press ⌘+1 on the Mac or Ctrl+1 under Windows to display a page at full size (100 percent).

✔ To quickly access the Actual Size view, you can double-click on the zoom tool.

✔ To see the entire pasteboard on the screen, choose View➪Entire Pasteboard. You can also press ⌘+Shift+Option+0 on the Mac or Ctrl+Shift+Alt+0 under Windows.

Using the magnification box

If you want more control over your zoom percentages, the magnification box is the way to go. Located in the lower-left corner of the document window, it lets you enter precise zoom values. Simply double-click on the magnification box, enter a zoom percentage, and press Return or Enter. If you want to experiment with different zoom percentages, enter a value and press Shift+Return or Shift+Enter. InDesign zooms according to your instructions but keeps the magnification box value highlighted so you can change it without having to reselect it.

To quickly select the magnification box value, press ⌘+Option+5 on the Mac or Ctrl+Alt+5 under Windows. (Be sure to press the 5 key on the main keyboard. This trick doesn't work if you use the number keypad.)

Click on the down-pointing arrow next to the magnification box to display a pop-up menu of preset zoom percentages ranging from 5 percent to 4000 percent. To choose a zoom value, just click on it.

The Navigator

Being the important person that you are, your time is valuable. That's why you'll want to get acquainted with the Navigator palette. It makes zooming and scrolling fast, easy, and even a little fun. It's especially useful when you're working with large page sizes and doing lots of detail work. It's also handy when you want to zoom way out to view a bunch of pages in your document at once.

To display the Navigator palette, choose Window➪Navigator. Or press F12 to display the Pages palette (if it's not already visible), and then click on the Navigator palette tab. Here's how the palette works:

✔ As shown in Figure 3-7, the Navigator palette displays a thumbnail view of one or more pages in your document. To view all the pages in your document, click on the right-pointing arrow in the upper-right corner to display the palette menu and choose the View All Spreads command.

✔ The view box (labeled in Figure 3-7) surrounds the portion of your document that's visible in the document window. As you drag the box, InDesign scrolls your document in the document window to correspond to the area within the box. You can also click anywhere in the thumbnail to move the view box over that portion of the document. To view only the page or pages the view box is touching, choose the View Active Spread command from the palette menu.

Figure 3-7:
The
Navigator
palette
gives you
an easy way
to scroll
and zoom
around your
document.

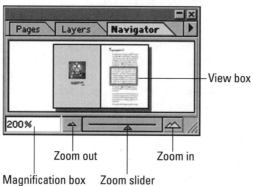

View box

Zoom out Zoom in

Magnification box Zoom slider

✔ The magnification box works just like the one in the document window, except it doesn't have a pop-up menu of preset zoom percentages. Just enter a zoom percentage and press Return or Enter.

✔ To zoom in or out in preset increments, click on the zoom in or zoom out buttons. Alternatively, you can drag the zoom slider to the left to zoom out or to the right to zoom in.

✔ Drag the size box to make the palette bigger or smaller.

✔ The view box is red by default. If you'd rather choose your own color, go right ahead. Choose the Palette Options command from the palette menu. Then choose a color from the Color pop-up menu.

Flipping through pages

You *can* scroll between pages in your document, but please don't. If your document contains more than a few pages, scrolling between them takes forever. Besides, as the following sections explain, much better ways to move from page to page are available.

Paging from the Layout menu

The Layout menu contains six commands that let you jump through pages in a jiffy. Here's how they work:

- ✔ Choose Layout⇨First Page to go to the first page in your document. You can also press ⌘+Shift+Page Up on the Mac or Ctrl+Shift+Page Up under Windows. If the First Page command appears dimmed, you're currently viewing the first page of your document.

- ✔ To move back one page in your document, choose Layout⇨Previous Page or press Shift+Page Up. This command appears dimmed when you are currently viewing the first page.

- ✔ Choose Layout⇨Next Page or press Shift+Page Down to move one page forward in your document. This command appears dimmed when you are viewing the last page.

- ✔ To go to the last page in your document, choose Layout⇨Last Page. You can also press ⌘+Shift+Page Down on the Mac or Ctrl+Shift+Page Down under Windows. If this command appears dimmed — you guessed it — you're already viewing the last page.

- ✔ The last two commands work like the Back and Forward buttons in a Web browser. You can move to the page you last viewed by choosing Layout⇨Go Back or by pressing ⌘+Page Up on the Mac or Ctrl+Page Up under Windows. To move forward one page in the sequence of pages you've viewed, choose Layout⇨Go Forward or press ⌘+Page Down on the Mac or Ctrl+Page Down under Windows.

Using the page controls

The page controls, located to the right of the magnification box in the bottom left corner of the document window, provide another way to move from page to page in your document. (You also meet the page controls in Chapter 2.) To go to a specific page, press ⌘+J on the Mac or Ctrl+J under Windows to highlight the page number option box, type a number, and then press Return or Enter. Click on the inner left- and right-pointing arrows to move to the previous or next page. Click on the outer left- and right-pointing arrows to move to the first or last page.

You can also go to a specific page by double-clicking on its icon in the Pages palette, which we discuss in detail in Chapter 14.

Multiplying your views

You can create multiple views of a single document by choosing Window➪New Window. InDesign creates a second document window on top of the first. This is not a copy of the document; it's simply a second view. You can choose the New Window command again to create a third view, and again to create a fourth view, and so on. Choose Window➪Tile to display all views of your document side by side.

Why would you want to do this? It's especially useful in tracking how changes you make in one place in your document affect the overall design. You can zoom in on particular details for easy editing while keeping an eye on the big picture. When you no longer need the additional windows, just close them.

Doing, Undoing, and Redoing Stuff

No matter how brilliant, careful, and precise you are, chances are you make mistakes sometimes. We all do from time to time. Some mistakes in life can't be fixed — like the time you told your mother she was starting to look old, or the time you left the winning lottery ticket in your favorite pair of jeans and it disintegrated in the wash. Man, that hurt.

Well, lucky for us all, you can't do much in InDesign that you can't undo. InDesign gives you more control to correct mistakes than any other page-layout program on the market today. The keywords are multiple undo and redo. The following sections explain all.

Undoing mistakes

If you use just about any other Macintosh or Windows program, you're probably familiar with the concept of undo. As in most programs, you can negate the last operation you performed by choosing Edit➪Undo or pressing ⌘+Z on the Mac or Ctrl+Z under Windows. For example, if you move a graphic on your page and then decide that you want to put it back where it was, you can just choose Edit➪Undo Move Item or press ⌘+Z or Ctrl+Z to return the graphic to its original location. Pretty simple stuff.

Now suppose you move that same graphic and rotate it 90 degrees (rotating graphics is discussed in Chapter 10), and then decide you want to return it to its original position. You could either press ⌘+Z on the Mac or Ctrl+Z under

Windows twice, or choose Edit⇨Undo Rotate Item followed by Edit⇨Undo Move Item to negate in order the last two operations you performed. That's an example of multiple undo. Notice that the name of the action you are undoing is displayed after the word Undo in the command name, so you can always keep track of the operations you're undoing. Here's a list of several other things you should know about undoing what you did:

- ✔ When you save a document, the Undo command is reset. So you can't undo actions you performed before saving.

- ✔ You can undo up to 300 consecutive operations depending on the amount of RAM available to InDesign. After you reach the maximum number of undos, the Undo command appears dimmed.

- ✔ You can quickly perform a whole bunch of undos by pressing and holding ⌘+Z on the Mac or Ctrl+Z under Windows. After a few seconds, you'll see your document dissemble right before your eyes.

- ✔ To undo all changes you made since the last time you saved, choose File⇨Revert. If you haven't made any changes since you last saved your document or if you've never saved it, the Revert command appears dimmed.

- ✔ To stop an operation in progress, press the Escape key.

- ✔ With all these options at your disposal, you might start thinking you can undo every little move you make. But the Undo command doesn't apply to certain actions, such as scrolling, zooming, and selecting palettes and dialog boxes.

Redoing what you've undone

What if you want to redo your undos? No problema, amigos. (Oh, we didn't tell you this is a bilingual book? Back to English then.) To redo something you've undone, choose Edit⇨Redo. You can also press ⌘+Shift+Z on the Mac or Ctrl+Shift+Z under Windows. You can choose Redo only if the Undo command was the most recent operation performed. Otherwise, the Redo command is dimmed.

Just as you can undo multiple operations quickly by pressing and holding ⌘+Z on the Mac or Ctrl+Z under Windows, you can redo up to 300 undos by holding ⌘+Shift+Z on the Mac or Ctrl+Shift+Z under Windows.

Saving Your Work to Disk

Save, save, save, save. You've heard it countless times — and with good reason. But let's make a deal right now: We won't bore you with tired old stories about how much work we've lost by not saving files often enough, if you promise to make ⌘+S on the Mac or Ctrl+S under Windows a standard part of your keystroke repertoire. That means you need to press ⌘+S or Ctrl+S every few minutes and after every significant change you make to your document. Promise? Good.

Your very first save

Now that we have that out of the way, it's time to get down to the business at hand: saving your document. Here's how to save your new document for the first time:

1. **Choose File⇨Save.**

   You can instead press ⌘+S on the Mac or Ctrl+S under Windows. This displays the Save As dialog box, shown in Figure 3-8.

2. **From the pop-up menu at the top of the dialog box, choose the folder in which you want to store your document.**

   This is called the Save In pop-up menu under Windows.

3. **In the Name option box on the Mac or the File Name option box under Windows, type a name for your document.**

   Attention Mac users! This tip is very important. Always add the file extension .indd at the end of your file names, as shown in Figure 3-8. Without it, Windows folks won't be able to open your files. Even if you seldom swap files between platforms, it's best to get in the habit of including the .indd extension. You never know when you might be stuck with a Mac file and a Windows machine — without the extension, the file would be worthless.

4. **From the Format pop-up menu on the Mac or the Save as Type pop-up menu under Windows, choose a file type.**

   These pop-up menus offer two options that allow you to save your document as a normal InDesign file or as a template. To save your document as a normal document file, which is what you'll want to do most of the time, choose the InDesign Document option from the Format or Save As Type pop-up menu. To save it as a template, choose the Stationery Option from the Format pop-up menu on the Mac or the InDesign Template option from the Save As Type pop-up menu under Windows.

Choosing the Stationery Option on the Mac displays another dialog box. Select the Stationery radio button and click OK to confirm that you want to save the file as a template. (Template files carry the .indt extension. Okay Mac users, you know what to do.)

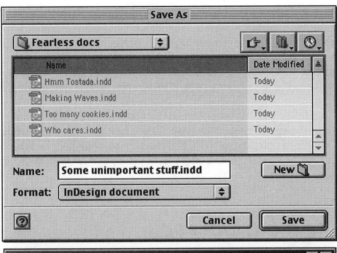

Figure 3-8: The Save As dialog box as it appears on the Mac (top) and under Windows (bottom).

A template is like a document shell. It can contain as many or as few elements as you like, but the idea is that it holds a basic layout that you can use over and over again. If you create documents in the same design on a recurring basis, templates are the way to go.

5. Click on the Save button or press Return or Enter.

Congratulations! Your document is now saved.

The name in the document title bar will change to the name you specified in the Save As dialog box. From now on, when you press ⌘+S on the Mac or Ctrl+S under Windows, InDesign will save your document without displaying the Save As dialog box because you've already told it everything it needs to know.

InDesign files can get darn big, especially when they contain embedded graphics. You can drastically reduce the size of your files — which are measured in K or MB — by saving them using the Save As command, as explained in the next section.

Saving a backup copy

Even a saved file can perish. So if losing your document would be a disaster or just inconvenient, make a backup copy. (See, no stories here.) Choose File⇨Save As to display the Save As dialog box. Enter a new file name and click on the Save button. InDesign closes the original file and displays the newly saved version on-screen. Alternatively, you can choose File⇨Save A Copy and enter a new file name in the Save As dialog box. When you choose this command, InDesign continues to display the original version of the document on-screen and saves a copy of it on disk.

Recovering from a system failure

Sometimes computers crash unexpectedly. We usually don't know why. We just have to accept it and do what we can to protect ourselves from losing our work. The Save, Save As, and Save A Copy commands are our best course of action, but InDesign tries to help us out too, with its automatic recovery feature. No, it's not a support group; it's better. You see, every once in awhile InDesign saves your work automatically and stores it in an invisible file. You won't even know it's happening.

Now suppose a power failure makes your system crash, or some other myste-
rious phenomenon causes your computer to unexpectedly shut down. After
you finish cursing, you restart your computer and start InDesign. The program finds the last file you were working on and displays a dialog box asking
whether you want to update the document with the recovered data. Click on
the Yes button to include any automatically recovered changes you made
after you last saved the document using one of the save commands. InDesign
opens the document, complete with the unsaved changes that it automatically recovered. The word *Recovered* appears after the file name in the title
bar, letting you know that it worked.

Chapter 4

Rulers, Guides, and Other Shackles

● ●

In This Chapter

▶ Setting up rulers

▶ Working with margins and columns

▶ Specifying measurements inside palettes and dialog boxes

▶ Adjusting and using the document grid

▶ Adding and modifying guides

▶ Understanding and using the Snap To commands

▶ Enabling automatic layout adjustment

● ●

*R*emember that semester you studied poetry in your sophomore English class? No? Too bad, it was exciting stuff. For instance, we learned that a sonnet has fourteen lines and, depending on whether it's the Shakespearean or Petrarchan variety, is divided into three quatrains and a couplet or an octave and a sestet. "So," you ask as your eyes glaze over, "what does this have to do with InDesign?" Good question. Our point is this: Page design is sort of like poetry. Just as the sonnet form provides the structure for a poem, the layout of a page provides the structure for a document.

What's that? You say Charles Bukowski is your favorite poet? Hey, even free verse has structure. Think about it — every line has to break somewhere, even for a barfly.

This chapter is your personal guided tour through the layout tools that will hold your pages together like poetry. You learn about lots of things with straight edges, including rulers, margins, columns, guides, and grids. We even cover such thrilling topics as choosing a measurement system and doing math inside dialog boxes. So put on your party hat and venture forth for some fun.

Making Rulers Work for You

When you first open a document, you see rulers along the top and left sides of the document window. Now you might be thinking, "Yeah, yeah, boooring." But these aren't ordinary, everyday rulers. They have special powers designed to make it easy for you to precisely position text and graphics on your pages. For one, the rulers display *tracking lines* to monitor the position of your cursor in the document window. (Imagine trying to get a regular ruler to show you where your pencil is.)

If the rulers aren't displayed on screen, choose View⇨Show Rulers or press ⌘+R on the Mac or Ctrl+R under Windows. Most of the time, you'll want to keep the rulers visible. But if you want to hide them temporarily to get a slightly larger view of a page, choose View⇨Hide Rulers or press ⌘+R or Ctrl+R again.

Choosing measurement units

The rulers use picas as the default unit of measurement (unless you changed the default measurement units as described in Chapter 3). But you can change to another measurement unit at any time by opening the Units & Increments panel of the Preferences dialog box, which is shown in Figure 4-1. Choose File⇨Preferences⇨Units & Increments. Or press ⌘+K on the Mac or Ctrl+K under Windows and then choose Units & Increments from the pop-up menu at the top of the dialog box.

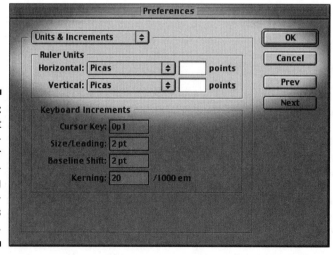

Figure 4-1: Set the unit of measurement for your document using the top portion of this dialog box.

The Horizontal and Vertical pop-up menus in the top part of the dialog box let you choose from seven preset measurement units. The options you choose will determine the measurement system used not only in the rulers but throughout your layout, including in dialog boxes, palettes, and so on. For most documents, you'll probably choose inches or picas, but you can also choose other standard units of measure such as points, millimeters, centimeters, and ciceros (a standard unit in European publishing).

You can also choose Inches Decimal, which makes the rulers display inches in increments that correspond to decimals (which are in base 10) rather than to fractions (which are in base 12).

The Custom option lets you define your own ruler measurement units in terms of points. For example, if you type **10** in a Points option box, the ruler displays the number 5 at the 50-point mark, the number 10 at the 100-point mark, and so on. You might want to use this option to align increments on the vertical ruler with a baseline grid. For more on using a baseline grid, see Chapter 8.

You can also change a ruler's measurement unit on the Mac by pressing the Control key and clicking on the ruler to display a pop-up menu listing the same options available in the Units & Increments panel of the Preferences dialog box. Under Windows, simply right-click on the ruler to display the pop-up menu.

Ruling the position of rulers

In addition to changing the unit rulers measure in, you can change the place the rulers measure from, called the *zero point*. By default, the zero point of the horizontal and vertical rulers is located at the upper-left corner of the page or spread. To change the zero point, click on the square box where the rulers meet (called the *ruler origin box*) and drag to the position where you want the zero point to be, as shown in the top example in Figure 4-2. When you release the mouse button, the zero point moves to the new location as shown in the bottom example in Figure 4-2. The new zero point also becomes the basis for the X and Y coordinates in the Transform palette, which is explained in Chapter 10.

Changing the zero point makes it easy to measure the size or distance between items on a page. For example, you can drag the zero point to line up with the upper-left corner of a graphic so you can quickly see its exact height and width.

To reset the zero point to its default position, double-click on the ruler origin box.

Ruler
origin box

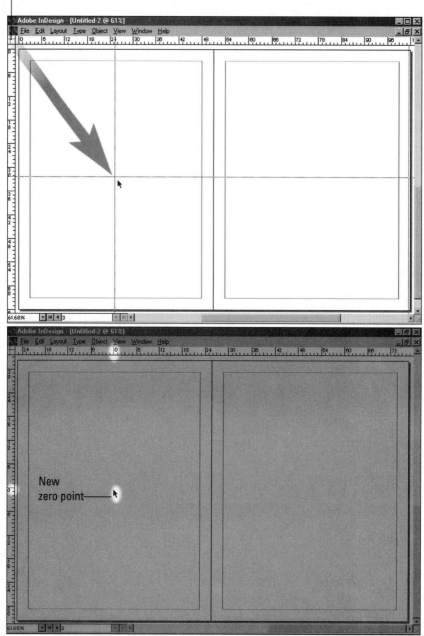

Figure 4-2:
Drag from
the ruler
origin box
(top) to
change the
position of
the zero
point
(bottom).

Margins and Columns and Gutters, Oh My!

The most basic elements of any page layout are margins and columns. The concept behind margins is simple: they keep your text and graphics from running off the edges of your page. You can't do much with margins, nor would you need to. You just set their sizes (as explained in Chapter 3), and that's it.

Columns, on the other hand, are flexible and dynamic. Their primary purpose is to organize text on a page so that people can actually read it. Here's the basic stuff you need to know about working with columns:

✔ Columns are displayed on-screen as nonprinting *column guides*, as shown in Figure 4-3. The space between two adjacent columns is called the *gutter*.

Column guides   Gutter

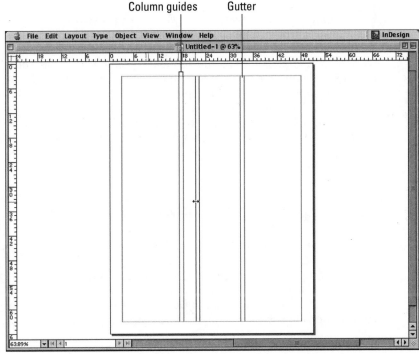

Figure 4-3: Drag a column guide to change the width of a column.

- You can specify the number of columns on a page in the New Document dialog box or by choosing Layout⇨Margins and Columns.

- By default, InDesign creates columns of equal size spaced evenly across a page. You can change the width of a column by dragging its column guide, as shown in Figure 4-3. When you resize a column in this way, the size of the gutter remains the same.

- When you import text created in a word processor (as explained in Chapter 5), you can *pour* it directly into a column just like you would pour a cool, refreshing beverage into a glass. The column guides act as boundaries to keep text from spilling all over the place. If your document includes a master text frame (described in Chapter 3), your text will automatically flow from column to column.

- You can run text across columns, create different numbers of columns on the same page, and create columns within columns using text frames, which are discussed in Chapter 5.

- To hide column guides, choose View⇨Hide Guides or press ⌘+semicolon (;) on the Mac or Ctrl+semicolon under Windows. This also hides margins and ruler guides (explained later in this chapter). To redisplay all guides, choose View⇨Show Guides or press ⌘+semicolon or Ctrl+semicolon again.

By default, margin guides are magenta and column guides are blue, but you can change their colors if you like. Choose File⇨Preferences⇨Guides and choose a color from the Color pop-up menus in the Margins and Columns sections of the dialog box. You can also double-click on the color swatch next to each of the Color pop-up menus to create a custom color in the Color Picker on the Mac or the Color dialog box under Windows. When you're finished, press Return or Enter to put your new colors into effect.

Making Changes by the Numbers

As mentioned previously in this chapter, the unit of measurement you specify in the Units & Increments panel of the Preferences dialog box (or the ruler pop-up menu) becomes the measurement system for your entire layout, including dialog boxes and palettes. But you can still enter values in dialog boxes and palettes using any of InDesign's measurement units. You just need to type the value using the appropriate notation, as shown in Table 4-1.

Table 4-1	Measurement Systems	
Measurement unit	*Notation*	*Example*
Points	p (then value)	p6=6 points
Picas	(value then) p	2p=2 picas or 2p6=2 picas, 6 points
Inches	in	1in=1 inch or 1.25in=1¼ inches
Centimeters	cm	2cm=2 centimeters
Millimeters	mm	14mm=14 millimeters
Ciceros	c	4c=4 ciceros

For example, suppose you set inches as your main unit of measurement in a one-page document containing three columns with a .25 inch gutter. Then you decide you want to change the gutter to 1 pica, which is 0.1667 inches. Choose Layout⇨Margins and Columns to display the Margin and Columns dialog box. Then double-click to highlight the value in the Gutter option box, type **1p**, and press Return or Enter. InDesign resizes the gutters to 1 pica, or 0.1667 inches.

You can also perform simple math in any option box. For example, if a measurement is set to 12p and you want to add 2 centimeters, you can simply type **+2cm** after the current value and press Tab, Return, or Enter. InDesign then calculates and updates the value for you. You can also subtract (–), multiply (*), and divide (/) values in the same manner.

Setting Up a Document Grid

In addition to margins and columns, InDesign offers two kinds of *grids* to help you align and position elements on a page. The *baseline grid* (explained in Chapter 8) lets you precisely align lines and columns of text, and the *document grid* provides an easy way to align graphics and other page elements.

The document grid looks like graph paper and serves the same basic purpose. But unlike graph paper, it does some of your alignment work for you. It's sort of like graph paper on steroids (not the illegal variety, of course). Here's how to set up a document grid:

1. Choose File➪Preferences➪Grids.

Or press ⌘+K on the Mac or Ctrl+K under Windows, and choose Grids
from the pop-up menu at the top of the Preferences dialog box. Either
way, the dialog box shown in Figure 4-4 will greet you. For now, just
ignore all the Baseline Grid options in the top portion of the dialog box.

Figure 4-4:
Set up a
document
grid using
the settings
highlighted
in this
dialog box.

> **Preferences**
>
> Grids ⬦
>
> OK
>
> **Baseline Grid**
> Cancel
> Color: Light Blue ⬦
> Start: 3p0
> Prev
> Increment every: 1p0
> Next
> View Threshold: 75% ⬇
>
> **Document Grid**
> Color: Light Gray ⬦
> Gridline every: 3p0
> Subdivisions: 4

**2. Choose a color from the Color pop-up menu in the Document Grid
panel of the dialog box.**

This sets the color of the grid lines. You can also double-click on the
color swatch next to the Color pop-up menu to create a custom color in
the Color Picker on the Mac or the Color dialog box under Windows.

It's best to choose a light color for grid lines so that they aren't too distracting when displayed on the screen.

**3. In the Gridline Every option box, enter a value to define the distance
between major grid lines.**

For example, if you enter **3p**, InDesign places a major (thick) grid line
every three picas, both horizontally and vertically.

**4. In the Subdivisions option box, enter a value to specify how many
squares (or subdivisions) occur between two major grid lines.**

InDesign creates the number of subdivisions you specify by placing
minor (thin) grid lines between major grid lines. For example, if you
enter **4** in the Subdivisions option box, InDesign creates 3 minor grid
lines between every 2 major grid lines to create 4 subdivisions.

5. **Press Return or Enter.**

   Or click on OK to close the dialog box. "Hey," you shout, "where's the darn grid?" Don't worry, it's there. You just have to tell InDesign to display it on-screen, which is what you do in the next step.

6. **Choose View⇨Show Document Grid.**

   Or press ⌘+apostrophe (') on the Mac or Ctrl+apostrophe under Windows. The document grid appears in the document window, as shown in Figure 4-5. But wait, there's one more important step.

7. **Choose View⇨Snap to Document Grid.**

   You can also press ⌘+Shift+apostrophe (') on the Mac or Ctrl+Shift+apostrophe under Windows. When this command is turned on, any text or graphics that you place or create will gravitate — *snap* — to grid lines. If you turn off the Snap to Document Grid command (by choosing View⇨Snap to Document Grid again), you can still see the grid on the screen, but it won't have any effect on your page elements. (We explain more about snapping later in this chapter.)

Major grid line

Minor grid line

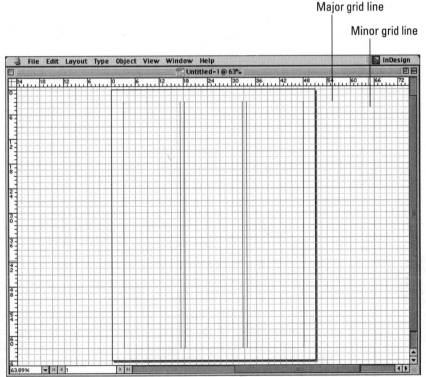

Figure 4-5:
A healthy
document
grid
reminiscent
of geometry
class.

Elements can snap to the document grid even when it's not visible, provided the Snap to Document Grid command is active. To hide the grid, choose View➪Hide Document Grid or press ⌘+apostrophe (') on the Mac or Ctrl+apostrophe under Windows.

You can't move or resize grid lines by dragging them as you can with column guides. To change the size of the grid (in other words, the frequency of grid lines), choose File➪Preferences➪Grids and change the values in the Gridline Every and Subdivisions option boxes.

Aligning by Guides

Grid lines are great for aligning page elements, but let's face it, they're not the most flexible tools around. You can't move them. You can't delete them. And frankly, they can be a bit tough on the eyes. That must be why the gods created *ruler guides*, also known simply as *guides*. You can create as many guides as you want, and because guides exist as items on a page, you can move, copy, or delete them. They even come in two flavors. *Page guides* appear on the page on which you create them — and nowhere else. *Spread guides* appear across all pages in a spread and on the pasteboard. Here's the lowdown on working with guides:

✔ To create a page guide, drag from a ruler onto a page, as shown in Figure 4-6. To create a spread guide, ⌘-drag on the Mac or Ctrl-drag under Windows from a ruler, or double-click on a ruler increment. Dragging from the horizontal ruler produces horizontal guides, and dragging from the vertical ruler gives you vertical guides.

✔ If you don't see a guide when you drag, choose View➪Show Guides or press ⌘+semicolon (;) on the Mac or Ctrl+semicolon under Windows.

✔ To move a page guide, simply drag it. To move a spread guide, drag a part of the guide that appears on the pasteboard. (Dragging the guide within the page boundary converts a spread guide to a page guide.) To move multiple guides at the same time, Shift-click on each guide to select it and then drag. (Guides change color slightly when selected.)

✔ To move a guide so that it snaps to ruler increments, press Shift while you drag. No matter what unit of measurement you select for the rulers, guides snap to the nearest visible ruler increment.

✔ When you have a bunch of guides set up just right on a page or spread, you can save time by copying and pasting them to other pages and spreads. Simply select all the guides you want to copy (by Shift-clicking on them), and press ⌘+C on the Mac or Ctrl+C under Windows. (You can quickly select all guides by pressing ⌘+Option+G on the Mac or Ctrl+Alt+G under Windows.) Then go to the desired page or spread and press ⌘+V or Ctrl+V.

Page guides

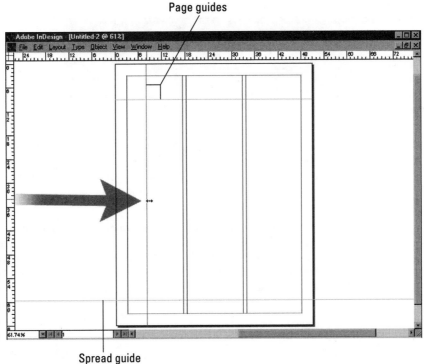

Figure 4-6:
Drag from
a ruler
to create
a guide.

Spread guide

- ✔ To delete a guide, click on it and press Delete. Under Windows, you can also press Backspace.

- ✔ Like grid lines, guides have magnetic powers only if the snapping function is turned on. Choose View⇨Snap to Guides to turn snapping on and off. You can also press ⌘+Shift+semicolon (;) on the Mac or Ctrl+Shift+semicolon under Windows. A check mark next to the command name means it's turned on.

- ✔ If all your guides are in place, you can avoid moving them accidentally by locking them. Choose View⇨ Lock Guides or press ⌘+Option+semicolon (;) on the Mac or Ctrl+Alt+semicolon under Windows. You cannot move, copy, or delete guides when they are locked.

- ✔ By default, ruler guides are cyan, but you can change their color by choosing Layout⇨Ruler Guides to display the dialog box shown in Figure 4-7. Then choose a color from the Color pop-up menu or double-click on the color swatch to create a custom color.

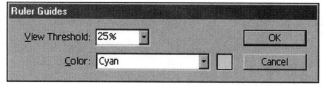

✔ The Ruler Guides dialog box also lets you set the magnification percentage below which guides are not visible on-screen. This is called the *view threshold*. For example, if you choose 25% from the View Threshold pop-up menu, ruler guides will not be visible when you view your document at 25 percent or less of its actual size.

✔ By default, ruler guides appear in front of all other page elements, including margins and column guides. If you find they're getting in your way, you can send them to the back of the stacking order. Just choose File➪Preferences➪Guides and select the Guides In Back check box at the bottom of the dialog box, as shown in Figure 4-8.

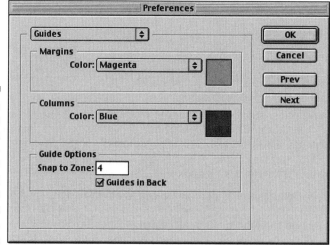

Creating a custom grid using guides

You can even create a custom page grid that you can modify on-the-fly using guides. The Create Guides command lets you set up rows and columns of evenly spaced page guides, without so much as a single drag. Just follow these steps:

1. **Choose Layout⇨Create Guides.**

   This displays the dialog box shown in Figure 4-9.

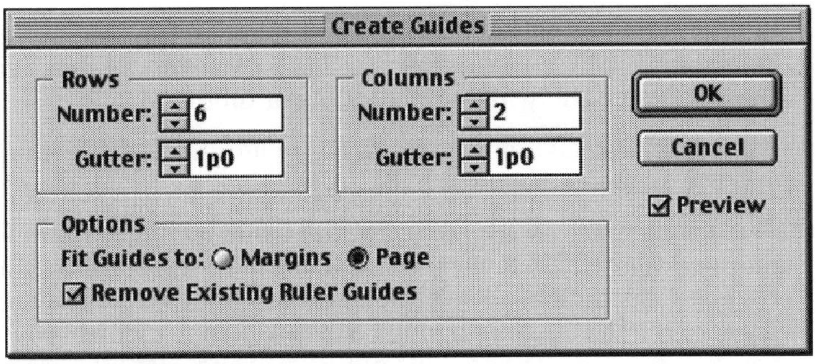

Figure 4-9:
Use the
options in
this dialog
box to
quickly
create a set
of evenly
spaced
guides.

2. **In the Number option box under Rows and also under Columns, spec-ify the number of rows and columns your grid will have.**

   If you want to experiment with different settings, you can select the Preview check box to see how your choices look on-screen.

3. **In the Gutter option boxes, type a value.**

   This creates a gutter between each set of guides. If you don't want a gutter, just type 0.

4. **Select the Margins or Page radio button.**

   If you want the guides to fit within the margins, select Margins. If you want them to extend to the edges of the page, select Page.

5. **If you want to delete any existing guides on a page, select the Remove Existing Ruler Guides check box.**

   This step is optional. If you want to keep existing guides, by all means do.

6. **Press Return or Enter.**

   Then sit back and enjoy your handiwork.

Making your work snap to it

As we've mentioned several times in this chapter, grids and guides take on a magnetic power when you enable the Snap To commands in the View menu. The purpose of these commands is to help you precisely align elements on a page without having to eyeball measurements on the rulers and painstakingly try to release the mouse button at just the right moment in a drag. When the

Snap To commands are turned on, the edges of items are actually pulled toward a grid or guide as they approach it. For example, if you drag a graphic near a guide, the graphic snaps into alignment with the guide. Here are a few other things you should know about snapping:

- ✔ Guides must be visible (that's ⌘+semicolon on the Mac or Ctrl+semi-colon under Windows) for items to snap to them. But items can snap to the document grid whether it's visible or hidden.

- ✔ When you drag an item near both a grid line and a guide, the grid line exerts a stronger magnetic pull.

- ✔ The distance at which a guide begins to pull an item toward it is called the *snap zone*. By default, the snap zone is set to 4 points, but you can change it. Just choose File⇨Preferences⇨Guides to display the Guides panel of the Preferences dialog box, as shown in Figure 4-8. Then enter a new value in the Snap To Zone option box and press Return or Enter.

To see how all this snapping business helps in laying out pages, take a look at Color Plate 4-1. It shows a layout with page items snapped to margins, columns, and ruler guides.

Letting InDesign Adjust Your Layout

Now that you're a brainiac about all things layout, let's take a brief trip into the future. Imagine that you've long since set up all your margins, columns, grids, and guides, and most of your text and graphics are in place. Then you decide that you really need to change your two-column document to a three-column layout, which will require repositioning text, graphics, guides, frames, and other elements on your pages. Before you head off to the Margins and Columns dialog box, you should pay a quick visit to the Layout Adjustment dialog box (shown in Figure 4-10) by choosing Layout⇨Layout Adjustment. This command lets you tell InDesign to handle many of those tedious layout adjustment tasks for you automatically.

The following list explains how the various options in the Layout Adjustment dialog box work:

- ✔ Select the Enable Layout Adjustment check box to tell InDesign to auto-matically adjust the layout whenever you change settings such as page size, orientation, margins, and columns.

- ✔ Enter a value in the Snap Zone option box to specify how close an item must be to a margin, a column, or a ruler guide to be anchored to that guide when the layout is adjusted.

Figure 4-10:
Use this
dialog box
to tell
InDesign
how to
make
adjustments
to your
layout for
you.

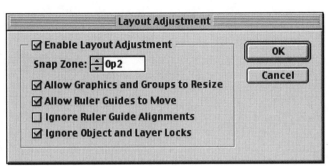

Changing the Snap Zone in the Layout Adjustment dialog box does not affect the Snap To Zone setting in the Guides panel of the Preferences dialog box.

✔ Select the Allow Graphics and Groups to Resize check box to tell InDesign to scale graphics, groups, and frames during layout adjustment. If you don't like the idea of letting InDesign make these decisions for you then turn this option off.

✔ If you want your ruler guides repositioned during layout adjustment, select the Allow Ruler Guides to Move check box. If items in your document aren't snapped to ruler guides or if your layout contains lots of guides that aren't being used for alignment, select the Ignore Ruler Guide Alignments check box.

If your document contains extraneous layout tools, such as unused column and ruler guides, and items don't adhere to margins and guides, you probably shouldn't use the layout adjustment feature. The results are sure to be disappointing. Better yet, go back and tighten up your layout; then go ahead and enable layout adjustment.

✔ Select the Ignore Object and Layer Locks check box if you want InDesign to be able to move items that are locked. This option makes more sense after you read Chapter 10.

Part II
Type is Thicker than Gravy

The 5th Wave   By Rich Tennant

"NO, THAT'S NOT A PIE CHART, IT'S JUST A CORN CHIP THAT GOT SCANNED INTO THE DOCUMENT."

In this part . . .

Text is the life-blood of page layout, so it's fitting that words flow through InDesign's columns like so many corpuscles sloshing through your veins. The difference, of course, is that the words don't move on their own — you have to push, pack, and prod them. That's one difference, anyway. I suppose we could come with others if we thought about it. Words aren't microscopic, for example. They don't stain, either. And they don't squirt out all over the place in boxing matches and other contact sports. Then there's that whole coagulation thing — words just don't scab.

Okay, so it's a stupid analogy, but the point remains the same. Text in InDesign is altogether liquid, flowing from one page to the next in response to your edits and adjustments. You can modify the size and shape of letters, tweak the spacing between lines, manage such subtleties as alignment and justification, and otherwise control the way every single word appears on the page. You are the word's master.

You can't do any of that with blood, so again, our apologies. This is exactly the kind of stuff that the editor should be catching, too. If we were working for that newspaper in the movie *The Front Page*, Walter Matthau would be slapping us silly. So would Cary Grant and Adolphe Menjou. The good news is, the text looks good. See? And that's what InDesign is all about. Any monkey can write the text, but if it looks good on the page, your job is secure.

Chapter 5

Rock Yer Blocks Off

● ●

In This Chapter

▶ Typing text directly in InDesign

▶ Getting familiar with text blocks

▶ Editing your text

▶ Importing text from a word processor

▶ Flowing text in multiple blocks

▶ Checking spelling

▶ Using the dictionary

▶ Finding and changing text

● ●

Did you ever have to hack out a term paper on a typewriter? Perhaps you were wearing a leisure suit at the time? Okay, never mind about the leisure suit, but if the typewriter part sounds familiar, you're sure to remember the first time you cut and pasted some text in a word processor. "I'll be darned! This is amazing!"

If you thought word processors were the best thing to happen to the written word since ballpoint pens, working with text in InDesign is sure to rock your world. You see, in InDesign, you enter or place text in frames to create blocks that you can move, connect, and otherwise manipulate. This chapter explains all the basics of creating, editing, importing, and flowing text on your pages. You also get the scoop on InDesign's spell-check and find-and-change features. So read on — you'll be rockin' with your text blocks in no time.

Typing Text inside InDesign

You may be thinking, "Uh, hello? I already *know* how to type. Jeesh." Well, don't get us wrong, we're sure you're an outstanding typist. But typing text directly into an InDesign document is a little different than typing in a word processor, so it requires some explanation. Here's how to create some text in a document that doesn't include a master text frame:

1. **Click on the type tool or press T.**

   When you select the type tool, the cursor changes from an arrow to the text cursor (labeled in Figure 5-1).

2. **Drag to create a box.**

   This box is called a *text frame,* and it will hold your text. Text frames are explained in the very next section. For now, just click on the spot where you want the text to begin and drag to create a rectangle, as shown in Figure 5-1. Don't worry about making the rectangle the right size; you can resize it at any time, as explained later in this chapter.

   When you release the mouse button, you'll see a rectangular box with light blue borders and a blinking cursor (called a *text insertion point*) in the top-left corner.

3. **Type away.**

   The text stays inside the edges of the frame, as shown in Figure 5-2. A frame with text inside it is called a *text block.*

If your document contains a master text frame, you don't need to create another text frame to type text. Just press and hold ⌘+Shift on the Mac or Ctrl+Shift under Windows and click anywhere inside the margins on your page to select the master text frame. Click again with the type tool to get a text insertion point in the top-left corner of the page. Then you can begin typing.

Type tool   Text cursor

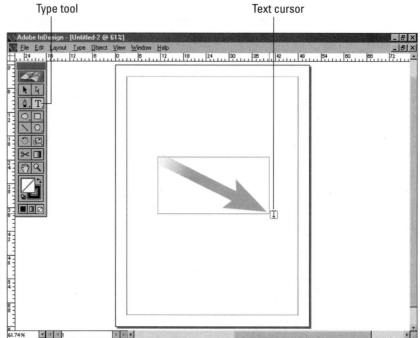

Figure 5-1:
Drag with
the type tool
to create a
text frame.

Text insertion point

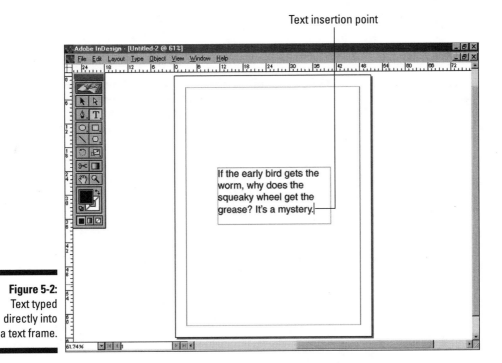

Figure 5-2:
Text typed
directly into
a text frame.

Learning to Love Text Blocks

So why do you have to type text into a frame to create a text block? It's not
because the folks at Adobe think words look better in boxes. No, text blocks
are much more than attractively framed words; they're like well-trained sol-
diers ready to jump at your every command. But before you can start barking
orders, you need to select a text block with the arrow tool. InDesign displays
the text block complete with the various gizmos shown in Figure 5-3.

In port   Handles

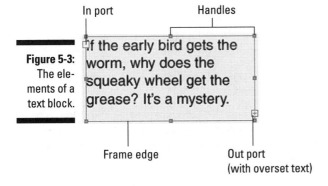

Figure 5-3:
The ele-
ments of a
text block.

Frame edge   Out port
(with overset text)

Here's what you can do:

- To move a text block, click with the arrow tool inside the text block or on the *frame edge*. Then drag to a new location.

- You can also move a text block using the keyboard. Press the up or down arrow key to move it up or down one point, a process called *nudging*. Press the left or right arrow keys to move it to the left or right one point. Press Shift plus an arrow key to move the text block in ten-point increments.

- You can change the nudge increment by choosing File⇨ Preferences⇨ Units & Increments. Then enter a new value in the Cursor Key option box and press Return or Enter.

- To move a selected text block to a precise position based on ruler units, press the F9 key to display the Transform palette. Then enter new horizontal and vertical coordinates in the X and Y option boxes, respectively, and press Return or Enter. The top left corner of the text block moves to the specified location. (For more on the Transform palette, see Chapter 10.)

- To select multiple text blocks at the same time, click on the first text block with the arrow tool. Then Shift-click to select additional text blocks. If you Shift-click on a text block that is already selected, it becomes deselected.

- Another way to select multiple text blocks is to *marquee* them. Click and drag with the arrow tool to create a dotted rectangular outline. Any text blocks or other objects that fall within the outline (even just partially) are selected when you release the mouse button. Marquee selecting is especially useful when you want to select a bunch of adjacent text blocks.

- To resize a selected text block, drag one of the frame *handles*. You can drag horizontally, vertically, or diagonally.

- You can also change the shape of a text block using the hollow arrow tool, as explained in Chapter 13.

- The *in port* and *out port* are controls for working with connections to other text blocks. A red plus sign in the out port means there's not enough room in the text block for all the text. The text you can't see is called *overset* text. To make overset text visible, you can either make the text block bigger by dragging a frame handle or click on the red plus sign and place the overset text in another text frame, as explained later in this chapter.

- To delete a text block, select it with the arrow tool and press Delete or Backspace. You can also choose Edit⇨Clear. Assuming the text block isn't threaded to other blocks (as discussed shortly), both the frame and the text inside it disappear.

✔ To hide a text block's frame, make sure the text block isn't selected and choose View➪Hide Frame Edges or press ⌘+H on the Mac or Ctrl+H under Windows.

This is just the tip of iceberg. You can also do loads of other things with text blocks, many of which are discussed in the upcoming section "Flowing, Threading, and Other Activities."

Editing Text

When you're working with text, there's always one thing you can count on: You'll need to make changes. Fortunately, editing text in InDesign is a lot like editing in a word processor. To begin, select the type tool (remember, you can just press T):

✔ To insert text, click to position the text insertion point at the spot where you want to add the text. As you type, InDesign moves the text that falls after the insertion point to the right to make room.

✔ You can move the insertion point around your text using the arrow keys. Press the right and left arrow keys to move the insertion point to the right or left one character, respectively. Press the up and down arrow keys to move it up or down one line. To move the insertion point to the beginning of the previous word, press ⌘+left arrow on the Mac or Ctrl+left arrow under Windows. To move it to the beginning of the next word, press ⌘+right arrow or Ctrl+right arrow. Press ⌘+up arrow on the Mac or Ctrl+up arrow under Windows to move the insertion point to the beginning of the previous paragraph; press ⌘+down arrow or Ctrl+down arrow to move the insertion point to the beginning of the following paragraph.

✔ To select individual characters, drag to highlight them. To select an entire word, double-click on it. Triple-click to select an entire paragraph.

✔ You can also select a range of text by clicking at the start of the text you want to select, pressing Shift, and then clicking at the end of the text.

✔ Press Delete or Backspace to delete selected text.

✔ To replace selected text, just type over it.

✔ You can also cut, copy, and paste text just as you would in a word processor. Press ⌘+X on the Mac or Ctrl+X under Windows to remove selected text from your document and send it to the Clipboard. Or press ⌘+C on the Mac or Ctrl+C under Windows to copy text to the Clipboard. To paste the text into another text frame, click in the frame and press ⌘+V or Ctrl+V.

✔ To display hidden characters in your text — such as spaces, tabs, and paragraph returns — choose Type⇨Show Hidden Characters. You can also press ⌘+Option+I on the Mac or Ctrl+Alt+I under Windows. Choose Type⇨Show Hidden Characters (or press the keyboard shortcut) again to rehide them.

Importing Text

More often than not, you'll prepare most of your text in a word processor and then copy it into your InDesign document for layout. The best way to get a text file into an InDesign document is to import it using the File⇨Place command, as follows:

1. **Choose File⇨Place.**

   You can also press ⌘+D on the Mac or Ctrl+D under Windows. InDesign displays the Place dialog box. Figure 5-4 shows the dialog box as it appears on the Mac and under Windows.

2. **Find and select the text file you want to import.**

   Use the pop-up menu at the top of the dialog box to find and open the folder that contains the file. Then click on the file to select it

   The Place dialog box lists only the files that InDesign can import. If you don't see the text file you want, you can most likely save it in another format that InDesign supports, such as rich text (.rtf) or text-only (.txt). See Table 5-1 for a list of supported text file formats.

3. **Select import and formatting options.**

   To keep most formatting you've performed in your text file, such as paragraph styles and character-level formatting, select the Retain Format check box. If you want InDesign to convert straight quotes (") and apostrophes (') into smart quotes (" and ") and apostrophes ('), select the Convert Quotes check box.

   InDesign won't necessarily retain *all* formatting applied in a text file. For example, if your text file includes italicized words in a font that doesn't actually include an italic type style — such as Charlemagne — your italics will be lost during import. So if you place a text file that includes much formatting, it's best to proof the text in your InDesign document against the original. For the full story on how type styles work in InDesign, see Chapter 7.

   If you want to see additional import options, select the Show Import Options check box. When you press Return or Enter, InDesign displays an Import Options dialog box that lists options specific to the type file you're placing. For example, if you're importing a Word, WordPerfect, or RTF file, you can select options to import tables of contents as tabbed text or preserve user-defined page breaks.

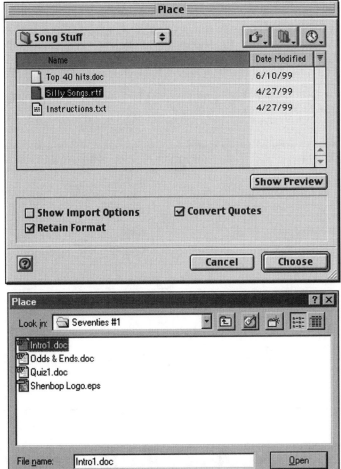

Figure 5-4:
The Place
dialog box
as it
appears on
the Mac
(top) and
under
Windows
(bottom).

4. **Press Return or Enter.**

InDesign displays a progress box letting you know that the text is being imported. When InDesign has finished importing, the cursor changes to a loaded place cursor that looks like a paragraph with an arrow in the upper-left corner.

5. Click on the spot where you want to place the text.

If you click in a column that has an existing text frame, InDesign simply places the text into the frame. If you click in a column that doesn't have a frame, InDesign automatically creates one that's the width of the column and begins at the spot where you clicked.

If your document contains a master text frame, everything inside the page margins is part of a frame.

Table 5-1	Supported Text File Formats
Type of File	*Its File Extension*
MS Word 4.0 – 5.0 (Mac only)	.doc
MS Word 6.0 – 7.0	.doc
MS Word 97 – 98	.doc
MS Excel 4.0	.xls
MS Excel 5.0/95	.xls
MS Excel 97 – 98	.xls
WordPerfect 6.1 – 9.0	.doc
Rich Text Format	.rtf
Text only	.txt

Flowing, Threading, and Other Activities

In addition to typing or importing text into a single column, you can flow text through multiple columns in connected blocks. Text that flows through multiple blocks is called a *story* — like a story in a newspaper. The process of flowing text between connected text blocks is called *threading* — also known as linking in some page layout programs. Whenever text flows between two or more text blocks, those blocks are threaded.

Let your text flow

InDesign gives you several ways to flow text on your pages. They all begin with the loaded place cursor, which appears when you have imported text ready to be placed. As shown in Figure 5-5, the loaded place cursor takes on one of several different looks depending on the task at hand.

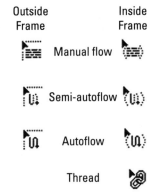

Figure 5-5:
The many
different
looks of the
loaded
place
cursor.

✔ Click in a column with the *manual flow* icon — which is the default mode for the loaded place cursor — to place (or pour) text into a single column. If the amount of text exceeds the size of the column, you need to reload the text icon by clicking on the text block's out port (labeled back in Figure 5-3) with the arrow tool. Then you can click in another column to continue placing the text. If the column already contains a text frame, the loaded place cursor changes to the *thread* icon (labeled in Figure 5-5), letting you know that you are about to link, or thread, two text blocks.

Repeat this process until the out port is an empty box, indicating that no more text is available to be placed. The triangles that appear in the in ports and the out ports of the frames indicate that the text blocks are threaded.

You don't have to place text in an existing text frame. If you click in a column that doesn't contain a frame, InDesign creates one for you as it places the text.

✔ To automatically reload the place icon after you place text, press Option or Alt to change the loaded place cursor to the *semi-autoflow* icon. Then click in a column or text frame and release the Option or Alt key. InDesign places the text in a single text block just as it does when you click with the manual flow icon, only it automatically reloads the place cursor so you can immediately click in another column or frame to continue flowing the text. It's simply a convenience feature.

✔ You can also place all the text in a story in a single click. Press Shift to display the *autoflow* icon. Then click at the spot where you want the text to begin. InDesign automatically flows all the text into your document, adding pages and text frames as necessary. If you want to automatically flow text onto only existing pages, press and hold Option+Shift on the Mac or Alt+Shift under Windows and then click in your document.

~ You can cancel a loaded place cursor at any time by clicking on any tool in the toolbox.

Changing the threading of blocks

After you flow a story through multiple text blocks, you may decide you need to make changes. For example, you might want to unthread a series of text blocks and reflow a story. Or you might want to add or remove a single text block in a series. You can do all these things. But before you start tearing your threads to shreds, you need to keep one important fact in mind: In InDesign, adding and removing threaded text blocks does not add or remove text in a story. In other words, the text doesn't change; it simply reflows to accommodate changes to the threading of blocks. You can change threaded text blocks as follows:

~ First, choose View⇨Show Text Threads so you can see the threads on screen, as shown in Figure 5-6. You can also press ⌘+Option+Y on the Mac or Ctrl+Alt+Y under Windows. The threads run between the in ports and the out ports of connected text blocks.

~ To unthread all the text blocks in a story, select the first block in the sequence with the arrow tool and click on its out port. The cursor changes to the *unthread* icon, as shown in Figure 5-6. Then click inside the first text block to unthread all subsequent blocks. All the text that was previously threaded through the series of text blocks becomes over-set text in the first block, as shown in Figure 5-7.

Threads

Figure 5-6:
Click on the
in port or
out port of a
threaded
text block to
display the
unthread
icon.

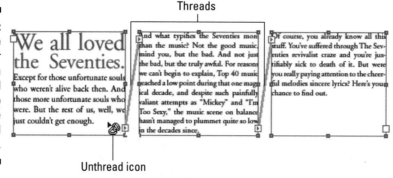

Unthread icon

Figure 5-7:
Clicking in a
text block
with the
unthread
icon
removes the
threads
between all
subsequent
blocks.

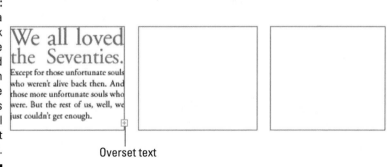

Overset text

✔ To add a new text block between two threaded blocks, select the first text block with the arrow tool and click on its out port. Then drag with the loaded place cursor to create a new text block between the two existing blocks. The new text block is automatically added to the threaded series and the text in all subsequent blocks reflows accordingly.

✔ Click on a text block with the arrow tool and press ⌘+X on the Mac or Ctrl+X under Windows to remove the block from a story. You can also press Delete or Backspace. Either way, the text block is deleted and the text within it reflows into subsequent blocks (if there are any) or becomes overset text in the previous block.

To remove a text frame *and* the text within it from a series of threaded text blocks, drag with the type tool to select the text and then press Delete or Backspace. Next, select the frame with the arrow tool and then press Delete or Backspace again.

Customizing a text block

If all this flowing, threading, and navigating doesn't already have you feelin' groovy about your text blocks, check out the controls in the Text Frame Options dialog box. This dialog box lets you create columns within a text block and add space between the frame and your text. Select a text block and choose Object➪Text Frame Options or press ⌘+B on the Mac or Ctrl+B under Windows to display the dialog box shown in Figure 5-8.

Here's how the options work:

✔ To change the number of columns in a text block, enter a new value in the Number option box. Then enter a value in the Gutter option box to set the amount of space between the columns. By default, InDesign changes the value in the Width option box to create evenly spaced columns within the current boundaries of the text block. If you resize the block later, InDesign automatically adjusts the width of the columns.

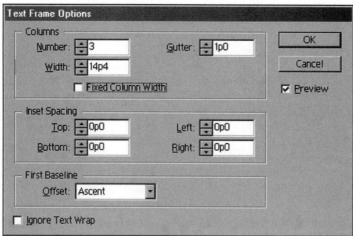

Figure 5-8:
The settings in this dialog box let you create columns in a text block and add space between the text and the frame.

✔ If you want the column widths to stay the same when you resize the text block, select the Fixed Column Width check box. When this option is turned on, changing the size of the text block can change the number of columns, but not their width. Similarly, changing the number of columns changes the size of the block, not the width of the columns.

✔ Select the Preview check box so you can see the effect of your changes before you apply them.

✔ You can also add space between a frame and the text inside it. This space is called an *inset*. Enter values in the Top, Bottom, Left, and Right option boxes to set the inset spacing for the text block.

Checking Your Spelling

After you have your stories all nicely arranged in columns with multiple text blocks, you might want to spell-check your text. If you want to check the spelling in only a particular story, click in the story with the type tool. Then follow these steps:

1. **Choose Edit⇨Check Spelling.**

   You can also press ⌘+I on the Mac or Ctrl+I under Windows. The dialog box in Figure 5-9 appears.

2. **In the Search pop-up menu, choose an option.**

   Choose Document to spell-check the entire document. To spell-check all the documents you have open, choose All Documents. If a story has a text insertion point, you can choose the Story option to spell-check the entire story or the End of Story option to check the spelling from the text insertion point to the end. If text is selected, you can choose Selection to spell-check only the selected text.

3. Click on the Start button.

This tells InDesign to begin looking for misspelled words. When InDesign finds a word it doesn't recognize, it displays the word in the Not in Dictionary option box and offers alternatives in the Suggested Corrections list, as shown in Figure 5-9.

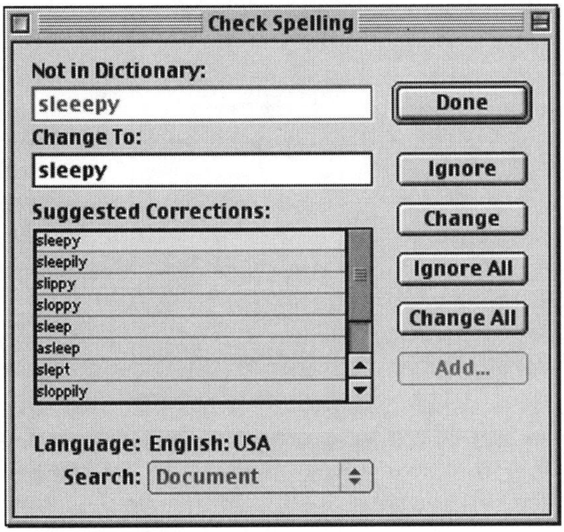

Figure 5-9:
The Check Spelling dialog box finds misspelled words and offers a list of alternatives.

At this point, you have several options:

- ✔ Click on the Ignore button to continue spell checking without changing the word.

- ✔ Click on the Ignore All button to continue spell checking ignoring all occurrences of the word.

- ✔ If the correct spelling is listed under Suggested Corrections, select it. Then click on the Change button to change only that occurrence of the word or click on the Change All button to change all occurrences of the word in your story or document.

- ✔ To add the word to the dictionary so that subsequent occurrences aren't considered misspellings, click on the Add button. This brings up the Dictionary dialog box, which is the subject of the next section.

Customizing the Dictionary

You can display the Dictionary dialog box not only by clicking on the Add button in the Check Spelling dialog box, but also by choosing Edit➪Edit Dictionary. Check out Figure 5-10.

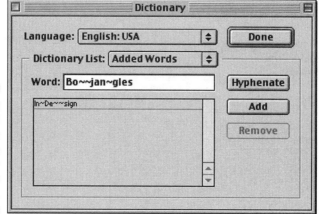

Figure 5-10: Add words to InDesign's dictionary using this dialog box.

If you clicked the Add button in the Check Spelling dialog box or selected a word in your document, the word appears in the Word option box. Otherwise, you need to enter the word you want to add and then do the following:

✔ Click on the Hyphenate button to see how InDesign would hyphenate the word. Tilde (~) symbols divide the word into syllables, indicating possible hyphen locations. The number of tildes indicates hyphenation preference. InDesign is more likely to break a word at a one-tilde point than at a two-tilde point.

✔ If you don't like InDesign's hyphenation preferences, feel free to change them. Type one tilde at the best point to break the word; type two tildes at the next best hyphenation point; type three tildes at the least desirable point. For example, if you prefer to hyphenate *Bojangles* as *Bo-jangles*, but *Bojan-gles* is still acceptable if necessary, remove one of the tildes between the *o* and *j* and add a tilde between the *n* and *g*, as in *Bo~jan~~gles*. You can type more than three tildes in a row, but it won't do you any good. InDesign only recognizes up to three tildes. If you don't ever, under any circumstances, want InDesign to hyphenate *Bojangles* as *Bojan-gles*, remove all tildes between the *n* and *g*.

✔ If you never want the word to be hyphenated, type a tilde before the first letter of the word.

✔ If you need to include a tilde in the spelling of the word, type a backslash before the tilde (\~).

✔ When you've finished setting hyphenation preferences, click on the Add button to add the word to the dictionary. The word is then displayed in the list box below the Word option box. If at some point you decide you want to remove the word from the dictionary, select the word in the list box and click on the Remove button.

Finding and Changing Stuff

Now that you're feeling confident that your text could grab the gold at cranky old Ms. Beetle's most challenging spelling bee, it's sure to impress your client. Suddenly, you remember all those placeholder references to your client's "Stupid Product." That could spell disaster, so you need to be sure you removed them all before the document leaves your desktop.

Never fear, the Find/Change dialog box is here to save the day. You can use it to find specific occurrences of characters or words and then change them on the fly. As with the Check Spelling dialog box, you need to click in a text block with the type tool if you want to restrict the find and change operation to a specific story. Then choose Edit⇨Find/Change or press ⌘+F on the Mac or Ctrl+F under Windows to display the dialog box shown in Figure 5-11.

Figure 5-11:
Use this
dialog box
to find and
change text.

> **Find/Change**
>
> **Find what:**
> | Stupid Product | ▾ | ▶ |
>
> **Change to:**
> | Glue-on Shoes | ▾ | ▶ |
>
> **Search:** | Document ▾ |
>
> ☐ **Whole Word**
> ☐ **Case Sensitive**
>
> Done
> Find Next
> Change
> Change All
> Change/Find
> More

Finding and replacing text

To search for one or more words, enter them in the Find What option box. Then enter the characters you want to replace them with in the Change To option box. Choose an option from the Search pop-up menu — which is identical to the one in the Check Spelling dialog box discussed previously in this chapter — to set the parameters of the search. The last two check boxes let you modify your search as follows:

✔ Select the Whole Word check box to disregard instances of the text within a larger word. For example, if you search for *sea* with the Whole Word option selected, InDesign won't find *sea*gull, nau*sea*, or un*sea*sonable.

✔ If you select the Case Sensitive check box, InDesign finds only those occurrences of a word that match the capitalization of the text in the Find What option box. So if you search for *Maneater*, InDesign ignores all references to sharks and the like and finds only the title of that unforgettable Hall and Oates song.

To begin your search, click on the Find Next button. When InDesign finds an occurrence of the text, you have several options:

✔ Click on the Find Next button again to continue searching without changing the text.

✔ To replace the found text with the text entered in the Change To option box, click on the Change button.

✔ Click on the Change All button to tell InDesign to go ahead and replace all instances of the text.

✔ If no text is entered in the Change To option box, clicking on the Change or Change All button will remove the found text.

✔ Click on the Change/Find button to change the currently found text and then continue searching.

✔ To stop searching and close the Find/Change dialog box, click on the Done button.

✔ If you change your mind and want to continue searching after you close the dialog box, you can resume your search by choosing Edit➪Find Next. You can also press ⌘+Option+F on the Mac or Ctrl+Alt+F under Windows.

If you're wondering what the More button is for, we tell you all about it in Chapter 9. Now that's something to look forward to, huh?

Searching for special characters

You can also use the Find/Change dialog box to search for special characters (such as em dashes, quotes, and discretionary hyphens) and invisible characters (such as paragraph returns, tabs, and line breaks) using the Find What and Change To pop-up menus or by entering special codes. Suppose that a couple hours before your big deadline, you learn that your client's house style calls for en dashes (–) instead of em dashes (—). Here's a quick fix. Press ⌘+F on the Mac or Ctrl+F under Windows to display the Find/Change dialog box, and then follow these steps:

1. **Click on the right-pointing arrow next to the Find What option box.**

   A pop-up menu of special characters appears, as shown in Figure 5-12.

2. **Choose the character you want to find.**

   In this example, we chose Em Dash.

   You can also enter the special character search code from the keyboard. All codes begin with the caret character (^), which you create by pressing Shift+6. For example, the code for em dash is ^_, so you would press Shift+6 to get the caret and then Shift+hyphen to get the underscore. Table 5-2 lists the codes for some of the most common characters.

3. **From the Change To pop-up menu, choose the character you want to replace the found character with.**

   In this example, we choose En Dash. Alternatively, you could enter ^=, which is the search code for en dash, in the Change To option box.

4. **Click on the Find Next button to search and replace as you normally would.**

   That's all there is to it.

Table 5-2	Special Character Search Codes
Character	*Search Code*
Bullet	^8
Caret	^^
Em dash	^_
En dash	^=
Left single quote	^[
Right single quote	^]
Left double quote	^{
Right double quote	^}
Forced line break	^n
Tab	^t
Paragraph return	^p

(continued)

Table 5-2 *(continued)*

Character	Search Code
Discretionary hyphen	^-
Nonbreaking hyphen	^~
Standard space	^w
Nonbreaking space	^s
Em space	^m
En space	^>
Thin space	^<

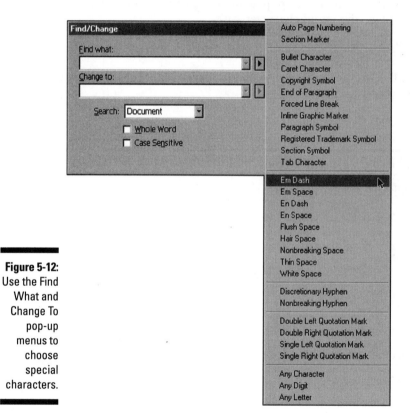

Figure 5-12:
Use the Find What and Change To pop-up menus to choose special characters.

The last three options in the Find What pop-up menu let you search for any character (^?), any digit (^9), or any letter (^$) using *wildcard characters*. For example, if you enter *r^$ck*, you'll find *rack*, *rick*, and *rock*. You can also use more than one wildcard character in a row. So if you enter r^$^$k, you'll also find *rank*, *rink*, *rook*, and so on.

To find out more about working with special characters, take a look-see at Chapter 6.

Correcting Mysterious Characters

When you import Mac text files into InDesign documents on a PC and vice versa, you're likely to find some wacky characters in your text. For example, you may discover that all of your em dashes (—) have turned into weird *ó* symbols or your apostrophes (') have changed to a strange *i* character. The reason for this is that some characters don't map correctly between Macs and Windows machines. Unfortunately, this problem isn't preventable, but it can be fixed. The easiest way is to find and change each incorrect character using the Find/Change dialog box, which you can display by pressing ⌘+F on the Mac or Ctrl+F under Windows. First, proofread your document, noting the characters that are incorrect. Then copy and paste them one at a time into the Find What option box. Enter the correct character in the Change To option box and do a search and replace for each one.

Chapter 6

Fonts in the 21st Century

● ●

In This Chapter

▶ A basic primer on typography

▶ Discovering the differences between PostScript and TrueType

▶ Delving into typefaces and type styles

▶ Understanding how type is measured

● ●

*I*f your experience with page design or laser printing is limited or next to nil, you might have difficulty understanding how it is that so many people devote so much attention to the appearance of a bunch of letters. If you've seen one typeface, you've seen them all, right? What's all the commotion? Why not just enter your text, print it, and have done with it?

This is the point at which another book on desktop publishing might offer a flowery discussion about the rich heritage of typesetting and letterforms and all that other twaddle that you so rightly don't care about. We lay it on the line as simply as possible: The purpose of good type design is to make people *want* to read your pages.

Many folks wrongly construe this to mean that you should sweat over your designs until you've rendered elaborate works of art that'll knock your readers' socks off. Some of our earliest designs, for example, look like something out of a turn-of-the-century Sears and Roebuck catalog as interpreted by Jackson Pollack. (Worse yet, many of them managed to find their way into publication.) Fortunately, we quickly learned a sobering fact: Elaborate is not the same thing as beautiful. A lot of nit picking and worrying can render some chaotic and downright ugly designs.

Good designs tend to be simple. Although stylish pages might elicit more oohs and ahs, a loose, straightforward, and unobtrusive use of type is more likely to be read by a wider variety of people.

So don't start thinking you need to expand your font library or purchase a $10,000 typesetter. The road from word processing to type design is paved with little more than a few basic terms and concepts.

If we had a Don't Freak Out icon, we'd use it here, but the Remember icon will have to do. Keep in mind that this is only an introduction to the terms and techniques of typesetting and desktop publishing. Everything that we talk about in this chapter is covered in more detail in later chapters. This is your chance to get your feet wet without getting in over your head.

Talking Type

In computer typesetting, the term *font* is frequently used as a synonym for *typeface*. But back in the days of hot metal type, a clear distinction existed between the two. Because characters had to be printed from physical hunks of lead, a separate container — or *font* — of characters was required to express a change in typeface, type style, or type size.

Nowadays, things have changed quite a bit. Computer users can access *scalable fonts*, which are mathematical definitions of character outlines. These outlines can be scaled to any size, independent of the resolution of your screen or printer. Assuming that you have the required typeface files installed on your computer, letters appear smoothly on-screen and when printed, as shown in Figure 6-1.

Figure 6-1:
Normally, type in InDesign is smooth as silk, regardless of size (top). If it appears jagged (bottom), you're missing an essential font file.

Smooth type
jagged type

Although a single font can satisfy any number of size requirements, it typically conveys just one *type style*. For example, in a standard PostScript font, the plain and bold styles are supplied as two separate files. Therefore, in computer typesetting, every font carries with it both unique typeface and type style information.

Publishers prefer PostScript

InDesign lets you work with any font that you can use with other Macintosh and Windows programs. But while InDesign is exceedingly flexible, the design industry isn't. Using the wrong kind of font can get you in trouble in the so-called "real world."

The two most popular font formats in use today are PostScript and TrueType. *PostScript* fonts were developed about 15 years ago by Adobe, the same company that created InDesign. PostScript fonts were immediately a big hit with service bureaus and print houses — you might say they made the industry what it is today. Naturally, such dominance could not go unchallenged, so five years later, Microsoft and Apple decided to develop their own format, TrueType.

TrueType fonts have the advantage of being integrated into the system software. This means they're compatible with every piece of software under the sun. But because service bureaus and commercial print houses rely almost exclusively on PostScript printers, TrueType fonts rarely find their way into professional documents. Some companies refuse to print documents formatted with TrueType fonts; others will tell you that you run the risk of having your pages print incorrectly, in which case they wash their hands of all responsibility.

Although some of the concerns are overstated, a danger does exist when using TrueType fonts with PostScript printers. Suppose you create a document using the TrueType font Arial. If you hand that document off to a service bureau, they'll probably convert it to the closest PostScript equivalent, Helvetica. As shown in Figure 6-2, the two fonts are similar, but not identical. The gray ovals highlight key differences. You can also see that the two typefaces are spaced differently. (Type aficionados say Arial and Helvetica have different *font metrics*.) As a result, letters converted from one font to the other may jam together, words can move between lines of type, and lines can shift from one page to the next. In other words, all heck can break loose. Your pages will most likely print differently than you formatted them.

Why run the risk when you can use PostScript fonts and be safe? To make PostScript fonts appear smooth on-screen, you need a program called Adobe Type Manager, or ATM for short. Apple recently decided it liked PostScript fonts and now includes ATM with its OS 8.5 and later. ATM for Windows is available from Adobe's Web site at www.adobe.com. By sticking with PostScript fonts, you ensure compatibility with the larger design industry.

TrueType Arial

abcG!&@123

PostScript Helvetica

abcG!&@123

Serif and sans serif

The earliest and most common PostScript typefaces are Helvetica and Times, shown in Figure 6-3. We chose these typefaces to illustrate their differences, as follows:

- Although Times was created in 1931 for the London *Times* newspaper, it derives much of its classic appeal from the *transitional* faces of the 1700's. The lines of each character change gradually in thickness, a phenomenon known as *variable stroke weight*, and terminate in tapering — or *bracketed* — wedges called *serifs*.

- Helvetica, by contrast, is a modern font. Influenced by the 20th-century Bauhaus school of design, which fostered a disdain for old-style ornamentation, the strokes of Helvetica characters are rigid and almost entirely uniform in weight. Helvetica also lacks serifs, making it a *sans serif* face. (*Sans* is latin for without, or minus.)

No one expects you to know any of that historic information — we just toss it out in case you're hurting for something to talk about at a dull party. Everyone, however, will expect you to know the difference between serif and sans serif.

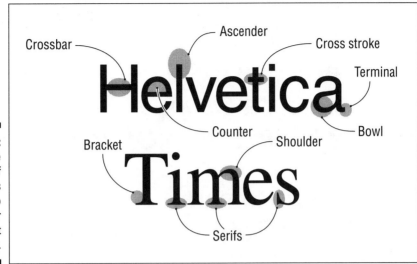

Figure 6-3:
The
anatomy of
type, as
applied to
two popular
PostScript
fonts.

Designer type styles and families

To enhance the visual interest of a page, you might be tempted to mix some Helvetica text with some Times. But the unpleasant fact is that Helvetica and Times don't look so hot together. Helvetica is heavy and large; Times is more fragile and tends to appear smaller at similar type sizes.

To help you spark up a page without mixing incompatible typefaces, designers create style variations. Because these type styles are designed to be used together, you run no risk of mucking up a page as you diversify its text. For example, you can mix different styles of Helvetica within a document to add variety to a page without worry that the styles might clash.

Helvetica and Times can each be displayed in four designer type styles, as shown in Figure 6-4. Each type style is a separate font. Together, each set of four type styles makes up a *type family*.

Helvetica
Helvetica Bold
Helvetica Oblique
Helvetica Bold Oblique

Times Roman
Times Bold
Times Italic
Times Bold Italic

Figure 6-4: Different fonts from the Helvetica family are designed to be used together. The same is true of members of the Times family.

Different type styles emphasize text in different ways, as follows:

- Plain or regular text — sometimes called *roman*, meaning upright with serifs — is by far the most common variety. It's used for *body copy*, which are the large blocks or columns of text that represent the heart and soul of information contained on a page.

- The *italic* (cursive) or *oblique* (slanted) style may be used within body copy to highlight a foreign or unfamiliar phrase or simply to stress a word.

- The *bold* style is relegated to special text, such as captions and headlines.

- You can likewise apply italic to special text; you may even italicize and bold text to create a *bold italic* style.

Plain, italic, and bold aren't the only styles. Some fonts have no style variations; others have tens or even hundreds. Figure 6-5 shows a few of the more than a hundred styles that have grown up around Helvetica. Fortunately, InDesign is specially suited to handling large and small typeface families alike. It doesn't let you assign a bold style to a font that doesn't include bold — as some programs quite stupidly do — and it offers immediate access to styles that do exist.

Helvetica Light
Light Oblique
Helvetica Black
Black Oblique
Helvetica Condensed
Condensed Bold Oblique
Helvetica Compressed
Helvetica Ultra Compressed
Helvetica Inserat
Helvetica Neue 25 Ultra Light
Neue 37 Thin Condensed Oblique
Neue 55 Roman
Neue 73 Bold Extended
Helvetica Rounded
Rounded Condensed Oblique
Ђєlvзтісл Cўяillic

Figure 6-5: Helvetica is one of the rare type families that contains more than a hundred styles.

Type size terminology

Once you've chosen a font to govern the fundamental appearance of your text, you may further enhance and distinguish elements of your page by changing the size of individual characters and words. Large type indicates headlines, logos, and the like; moderately small type serves as body copy;

and very small type indicates incidental information including copyrights and disclaimers. Combined with type style, the size of your text directs the attention of your readers and helps them quantify messages and isolate the information that is most important to them.

To understand how to size type, you must first understand how it is measured. The horizontal guidelines that serve as boundaries for characters are labeled in Figure 6-6.

Figure 6-6: Type is measured using a series of horizontal guidelines.

The following four basic kinds of characters are available:

- *Capital letters* extend from the *baseline* upward to the *cap height* line. Examples include *A*, *B*, and *C*. Numerals (*0123456789*) also qualify as capitals, since they violate neither baseline nor cap height line.

- *Medials* fit within the space between the *baseline* and the *x-height* line. Examples include *a*, *c*, and *e*.

- *Ascenders* are lowercase characters that extend above the cap height line. Examples include *b*, *d*, and *k*.

- *Descenders* are lowercase characters that extend below the baseline. Examples include *g*, *j*, and *p*.

Not every character fits snugly into one of these categories. For example, the lowercase characters *i* and *t* violate the x-height line, but are nonetheless considered medials; the dot of the *i* is not viewed as an integral part of the character and the *t* does not extend even so far as the cap height line. Other times, a letter will qualify as both an ascender and a descender, as is the case for the italic *f* in a serif font. Non-letters, such as %, #, and &, are generally capitals, but several violations exist — among them, *$*, *§*, and many forms of punctuation, including parentheses.

Hot stuff, huh? Well, to make a long story short, the size of a character —
known predictably as its *type size* — is measured from the topmost point of
the tallest ascender to the lowest point of the deepest descender. Type size is
calculated in a unit of measure called *points*, where one point equals ¹⁄₇₂ inch
(just over ⅓ millimeter), which is why you frequently see type size called
point size. Therefore, a character that measures 0.167 inch from tip to tail is
12-point type, the equivalent of pica-sized type on a conventional typewriter.

Getting into Character

If you look at your keyboard, you'll see represented a total of 94 characters —
lowercase and uppercase letters, numbers, punctuation, and a few symbols.
That might sound like a lot of characters, but it's less than half of the more
than 200 included in a typical PostScript font, and an even smaller fraction of
the 600 or more characters offered by some TrueType fonts.

Figure 6-7 shows the characters included in the PostScript font Times, a
common typeface. The characters against a gray background are the 94 commonly accessible from any keyboard, whether you use a Mac or a PC. These
are referred to as the common ASCII (pronounced *ask-ee*) set, and they
appear in PostScript and TrueType fonts alike. Only specialty symbol fonts,
such as Symbol, Zapf Dingbats, and Wingdings, lack these characters.

The characters against a white background are equally common; you'll find
them in virtually every alphanumeric font in use today. But they're a bit
harder to get to. The following sections explain three different methods for
accessing a font's more extraordinary characters.

Typing special characters

Just because your keyboard doesn't show a character on the key doesn't
mean it's not there. The 7 key, for example, also features an ampersand (&),
but it doesn't show a paragraph mark (¶). And yet, if you press Option+7
on the Mac or Alt+7 under Windows, InDesign adds a paragraph mark to
your text.

So many hidden keyboard characters are available that it's impossible to
keep track of them all. We've been at this for almost two decades, and we still
can't remember all the keyboard tricks. But we've managed to memorize a
few that you'll probably want to use as well.

!	"	#	$	%	&	'	(	)	*	+	,
-	.	/	0	1	2	3	4	5	6	7	8
9	:	;	<	=	>	?	@	A	B	C	D
E	F	G	H	I	J	K	L	M	N	O	P
Q	R	S	T	U	V	W	X	Y	Z	[	\
]	^	_	'	a	b	c	d	e	f	g	h
i	j	k	l	m	n	o	p	q	r	s	t
u	v	w	x	y	z	{	|	}	~	¡	¢
£	/	¥	*f*	§	¤	'	"	«	‹	›	fi
fl	–	†	‡	·	¶	•	,	„	"	»	...
‰	¿	`	´	^	~	–	˘	·	¨	°	˛
"	˛	ˇ	—	Æ	ª	Ł	Ø	Œ	º	æ	1
ł	ø	œ	ß	1	–	º	ó	Ö	ö	É	û
¼	¬	Ê	½	Õ	ú	é	í	È	î	µ	¡
þ	Å	ý	Ÿ	™	®	ô	À	Š	Ù	Ë	Ú
õ	ñ	ÿ	Á	ð	â	å	Ò	ç	×	÷	2
Ñ	ù	Û	Ã	ž	ï	Â	Î	Ý	Ó	Ä	Ž
à	3	ò	¾	Ð	±	ü	ë	á	ì	Ï	ä
Í	©	Ì	Ç	š	è	Ô	Þ	ã	Ü	ê	

Figure 6-7: The 227 characters included in a typical PostScript font. The gray characters are available from any keyboard, Mac or PC.

Table 6-1 lists the most common special characters and how you can get to them. To get a character on the Mac, press the key combination shown. On the PC, some characters require more work than others. It's easy to get to the bullet character — just press Alt+8. But to type the cent sign (¢), you have to press Alt+[0162]. By this crazy nomenclature, we mean you press and hold the Alt key, press 0-1-6-2 on the numeric keypad, and then release Alt.

This is so important that we're emphasizing it with an icon. When using an Alt+[0000] shortcut, be sure to: A) press and hold Alt the entire time you're typing the number keys and B) use the number keys on the keypad on the right side of your keyboard.

Table 6-1	Keys to Press for Special Characters	
Character	*Mac Keystroke*	*PC Keystroke*
Cent (¢)	Option+4	Alt+[0162]
Pound (£)	Option+3	Alt+[0163]
Yen (¥)	Option+Y	Alt+[0165]
Florin (*f*)	Option+F	Alt+[0131]
Bullet (•)	Option+8	Alt+8
Dagger (†)	Option+T	Alt+[0134]
Curly apostrophe (')	Shift+Option+]	Shift+Alt+]
Curly left quote (")	Option+[	Alt+[
Curly right quote (")	Shift+Option+[	Shift+Alt+[
Degree sign (°)	Shift+Option+8	Alt+[0176]
Per thousand (‰)	Shift+Option+R	Alt+[0137]
One quarter (¼)	*none*	Alt+[0188]
One half (½)	*none*	Alt+[0189]
Three quarters (¾)	*none*	Alt+[0190]
Fraction slash (/)	Shift+Option+1	*none*
Ellipsis (...)	Option+semicolon (;)	Alt+semicolon (;)
Em dash (—)	Shift+Option+hyphen (-)	Shift+Alt+hyphen (-)
En dash/minus (–)	Option+hyphen (-)	Alt+hyphen (-)
Plus or minus (±)	Shift+Option+equal (=)	Alt+[0177]
Multiply (x)	*none*	Alt+[0215]
Divide (÷)	Option+/	Alt+[0247]
Trademark (™)	Option+2	Alt+2
Registered trademark (®)	Option+R	Alt+[0174]

(continued)

Table 6-1 *(continued)*

Character	Mac Keystroke	PC Keystroke
Copyright (©)	Option+G	Alt+[0169]
Paragraph mark (¶)	Option+7	Alt+7
Legal section (§)	Option+6	Alt+6

Just so you know, this Alt-key weirdness is not InDesign's fault. It's a Windows thing. For some reason, Microsoft thinks it's easier to dial in characters numerically, so that's what we're stuck with. Those few characters that are easier to access, such as Alt+8 for the bullet, are special tricks that work only inside InDesign.

Two final notes about Table 6-1: First, if you're a Windows user, be aware that some keystrokes work in other programs, but others don't. So if one of these tricks doesn't work inside your favorite word processor, for example, don't be surprised. (Mac users need not worry — the keystrokes are consistent from one application to the next.) Second, when you see the word *none* in the table, it means you can't access that specific character from the keyboard. For example, you can type ¼ under Windows but not on the Mac. Fortunately, you can access these and other pesky characters another way, as explained in the next section.

Typing super special characters

Who would've thought typing a symbol could be so complicated? Makes you long for the days of typewriters and rub-on letters. But never fear, InDesign provides a more straightforward method that lets you enter a character as easily as selecting it from a list. It's not as seamless as entering a character from the keyboard, but it eliminates guesswork.

To find every single character offered by a font — bar none — choose Type⇨ Insert Character. This displays the list of characters shown in Figure 6-8. (If text is selected, the command becomes Replace Character.) Scroll to find the character you want to enter, click on it to select it, and click on the Insert button. You can insert as many characters as you like. When you're finished, click Done.

You can change fonts by selecting a different typeface from the pop-up menu at the bottom of the Insert Character dialog box. This command is particularly useful for locating characters in symbol fonts such as Zapf Dingbats and Wingdings, where the keyboard is no help.

Figure 6-8:
Choose the
Insert
Character
command
from the
Type menu
to access
one of the
many
hidden
characters
included in
every font.

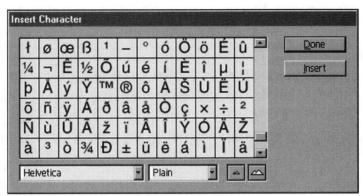

Figure 6-8:
Choose the Insert Character command from the Type menu to access one of the many hidden characters included in every font.

Thanks to the Insert Character command, InDesign lets you access some characters that virtually no other program can get to. For example, on the Mac, you can't type the common fraction characters ¼, ½, and ¾. Meanwhile, on the PC, it's often impossible to type the everyday curly apostrophe. Microsoft Word for Windows automatically turns *Rock 'n' Roll* into *Rock 'n' Roll*, with the first apostrophe curling in the wrong direction. But in InDesign, every character under the sun is right there at your fingertips any time you want it.

Typing super-duper special characters

By now you're probably thinking, "What's left? Hieroglyphics?" But the fact is, InDesign offers still another layer of characters *that aren't even part of the typeface*. That's right, InDesign makes these special characters available regardless of what font you're using.

These super-duper special characters are different kinds of hyphens and spaces. What do you need with extra hyphens and spaces? Well, suppose you enter a long, unreadable, frequently mispronounced name — such as McClelland or Buscaglia — and you want InDesign to hyphenate that name at a specific place, such as McClel-land or Bus-caglia. You would enter a *discretionary hyphen* between the two *l*'s or between the *s* and the *c*. If either word falls in the middle of a line of type, as in the first example of Figure 6-9, no hyphen is required and the word appears normally. But if InDesign needs to hyphenate the word to make it wrap to the next line, as in the second example in the figure, the hyphen pops up exactly where you specified.

It's no fun to hear your name mispronounced. The name **McClelland** is pronounced *mi-klehl-land*, with a short E, not *mi-klee-land* to rhyme with *spree* or *bee* or any other long E word. When you say **Buscaglia,** the U is long and the G is silent. The result is *boos-kal-ya*, not *buh-skag-lia*. Now if you see us in the

your name mispronounced. The name **McClelland** is pronounced *mi-klehl-land*, with a short E, not *mi-klee-land* to rhyme with *spree* or *bee* or any other long E word. When you say **Buscaglia,** the U is long and the G is silent. The result is *boos-kal-ya*, not *buh-skag-lia*. Now if you see us in the street, you'll know what to

Figure 6-9: A discretionary hyphen is normally invisible (bold words, top) but pops into action when needed (bold words, bottom).

Other kinds of characters are available as well:

- ✔ A *nonbreaking hyphen* always keeps two words together. Even if the words fall at the end of a line of type, they're glued together. The same goes for a *nonbreaking space*.

- ✔ An *em space* is a space as wide as the type size is tall. An *en space* is as wide as a capital N.

- ✔ InDesign also provides you with *thin space* and a *hair space* if you want to make the space incrementally thinner. Hair spaces are especially useful for offsetting punctuation, such as an em dash, that might otherwise squish neighboring characters.

- ✔ The *flush space* is the coolest space of all. The flush space grows to fill all extra space in the last line of a fully justified paragraph. For example, you might use the flush space to fill the gap between the period at the end of a paragraph and an ornamental character that indicates the end of a story. Chapter 20 explains how. For more information on justifying text, see Chapter 8.

Table 6-2 tells how to access InDesign's various hyphens and spaces from the keyboard.

Table 6-2	Hyphens and Spaces	
Character	*Mac Keystroke*	*PC Keystroke*
Discretionary hyphen	⌘+Shift+hyphen (-)	Ctrl+Shift+hyphen (-)
Nonbreaking hyphen	⌘+Option+hyphen (-)	Ctrl+Alt+hyphen (-)
Em space	⌘+Shift+M	Ctrl+Shift+M
En space	⌘+Shift+N	Ctrl+Shift+N
Thin space	⌘+Shift+Option+M	Ctrl+Shift+Alt+M
Hair space	⌘+Shift+Option+I	Ctrl+Shift+Alt+I
Flush space	⌘+Shift+Option+J	Ctrl+Shift+Alt+J
Nonbreaking space	⌘+Option+X	Ctrl+Alt+X

If you can't keep all the key combinations in Table 6-1 straight, just turn to the context-sensitive menu. When entering text on the PC, right-click with the type tool and choose the Insert Special Character command. On the Mac, Control-click and choose Insert Special Character. Either way, InDesign displays a submenu of common characters, including hyphens, spaces, and a few of the special characters we mentioned in the previous sections.

When Typical Type Won't Do

Having ten or so type styles and 200 characters per font are nice, but they might not be enough. Adobe has long believed that designers need more freedom than the typical PostScript typeface provides. That's why the company designed two specialty brands of fonts. The expert collection typefaces include a wealth of helpful characters; *multiple master* fonts harbor literally thousands of variations in styles. InDesign is the only program that takes special advantage of both of these specialty fonts and automatically integrates them into your pages.

Expert collections definitely fall outside the boundary of stuff you absolutely need to know to learn InDesign. Most expert users don't even know about expert collections and multiple masters (though they should). So feel free to skip to the next chapter if you want to stick to the essentials. On the other hand, these fonts are lots of fun, so you might want to keep reading.

Culling from the expert collections

A typeface doesn't have to end with one font. Adobe broadens the scope of many of its typeface families by offering expansion fonts. For example, the Helvetica Fractions font adds prebuilt fractions to Helvetica. Times Phonetic adds a phonetic alphabet to Times. But the most useful of these are the expert collections. As shown in Figure 6-10, these special expansion fonts add alternative numbers, fractions, letter combinations (known as *ligatures*), and reduced capital letters.

They're all nifty, of course, but the reduced capital letters have added significance in InDesign. Called *small caps*, reduced capitals are often used to introduce a story, as in the first words in Figure 6-11. The figure also illustrates the difference between fake small caps and real ones. Fake small caps are merely smaller versions of regular capital letters. The size and spacing of the letters doesn't look right. Worse, the letters look too thin. By contrast, the real small caps in an expert collection font are sized and spaced just right, plus they're just as fat and meaty as the letters around them.

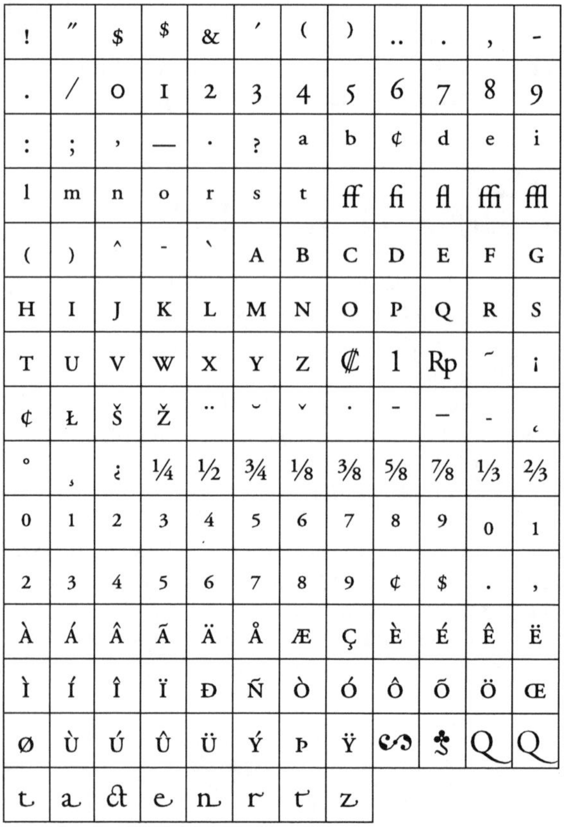

Figure 6-10: The Adobe Caslon Expert Collection provides hundreds of additional characters that fill out the standard Adobe Caslon family.

When you choose the Small Caps command from the Character palette menu, InDesign is smart enough to grab the real small caps from an expert collection font, assuming such a font is available. If no expert collection exists — as more often than not is the case — InDesign simply creates small capital letters, just like every other program.

By the way, don't fret if you're having problems finding the Small Caps command. We discuss it and the Character palette in explicit detail in Chapter 7.

Multiple master fonts

If you thought small caps seemed a bit obscure, they're nothing compared to multiple masters. But just like an expert collection, a multiple master font can make your text look a lot better. Plus, multiple masters give you a lot more freedom. On the down side, they're a bit harder to use, especially when you're just starting out.

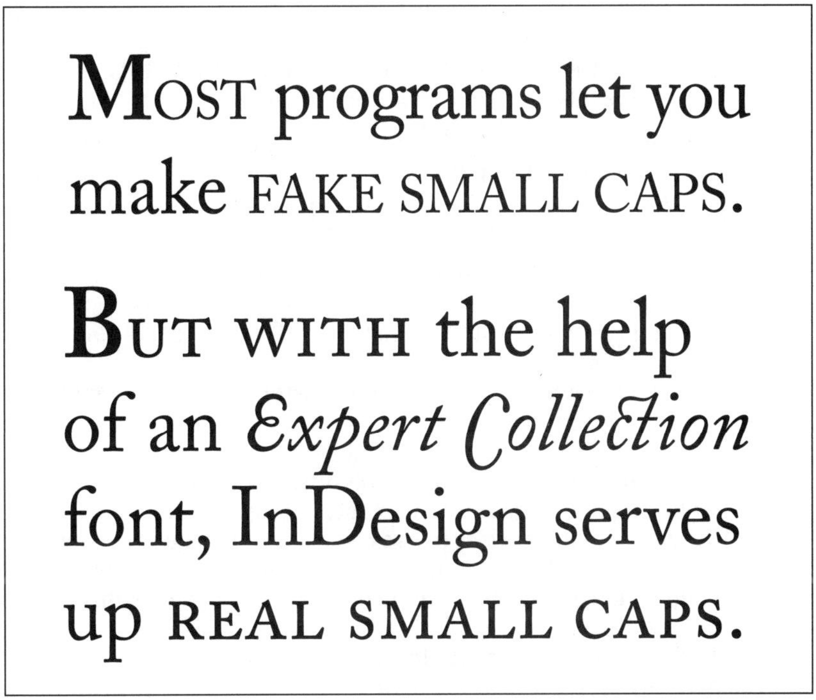

Figure 6-11:
Fake small caps (top) are just small capital letters. Real small caps are special characters designed to match the lowercase letters around them (bottom).

Most programs let you make FAKE SMALL CAPS.

But with the help of an *Expert Collection* font, InDesign serves up REAL SMALL CAPS.

The best way to understand the idea behind multiple master fonts is to take a look at Figure 6-12. At first glance, the figure appears complicated. It's the kind of illustration someone might look at and think, "What in the world is this doing in a *...For Dummies* book? You'd have to be a Rhodes Scholar to interpret the thing." All you need, however, is a kind friend to tell you what you're looking at, and that's where we come in. Just think of us as Deke and Amy, your multiple master chums.

For the record, the multiple master font pictured in Figure 6-12 is called Myriad. It's the first of many multiple master fonts in existence. Here's how Myriad and other multiple masters work:

- Several styles are built into one font. In the case of Myriad, one font includes a light condensed style, a black condensed style, a light extended style, and a black extended style. In type style parlance, *black* means bolder than bold; *condensed* and *extended* refer to the width of the character. In Figure 6-12, the black B's in gray boxes represents these four styles.

- Each style represents an extreme. You can then blend between those extremes to create a custom style. For example, you might blend between the light and black extremes to create your own bold style. The gray letters in the figure show possible blended styles. Hundreds of thousands of permutations are possible.

- Different varieties of extremes are called *axes*. The light and black extremes make up the Weight axis, the condensed and extended extremes make up the Width axis. Although Myriad contains just two axes, a multiple master font may contain as many as four.

- Each font ships with several predefined style variations, called *instances*. The dark gray *B*'s in Figure 6-12 are the instances included with Myriad. You can make your own instances using ATM (Adobe Type Manager).

Now you see why the first multiple master font was called Myriad. This one font contains myriad styles.

Where multiple master fonts are concerned, InDesign is dumber than some applications but smarter than most. On the dumb side, it can only see instances. So if you want to use a special style, you first have to create it in ATM. (Another Adobe program, the drawing program Illustrator, lets you blend styles on the fly. We hope one day InDesign gets this smart too.)

On the smart side, if a font includes an Optical Size axis, InDesign can automatically blend characters to optimize their legibility, even at very small type sizes. Not all multiple master fonts include an Optical Size axis — Myriad doesn't, for example — and how it works is pretty darn technical. To make a long story short, just make sure the check box called Automatically Use Correct Optical Size is turned on in the Preferences dialog box and everything will work fine. We explain the Automatically Use Correct Optical Size option in more detail in Chapter 7.

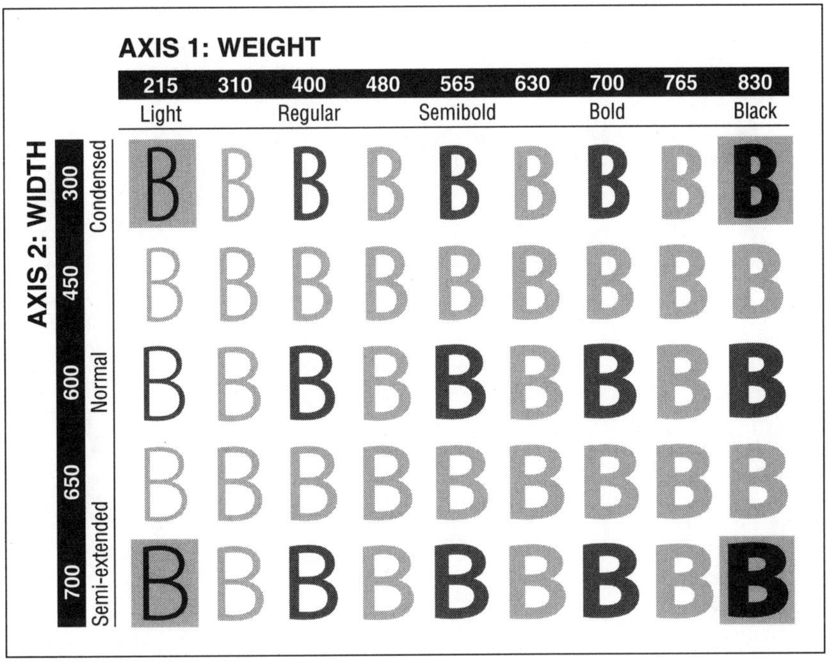

Figure 6-12:
A multiple
master font
lets you
create
thousands
of styles
by blending
a few
extremes,
shown here
in black.

AXIS 1: WEIGHT

215	310	400	480	565	630	700	765	830
Light		Regular		Semibold		Bold		Black

AXIS 2: WIDTH

300 Condensed
450
600 Normal
650
700 Semi-extended

For that matter, we discuss *everything* about working with type in more detail in the next two chapters. Now that you've read this chapter, everything you read in those chapters should make perfect sense.

Chapter 7

The Look of Type

*W*hether you're creating the biggest, fattest, mac-daddy annual report to ever hit the planet or just whipping up a simple letter home to mom, chances are your text will be judged as much on its appearance as on its content. (Just in case you're thinking Mom doesn't care about things like that, remember back in the third grade when she casually mentioned — several times — how neat it was that little Billy Biggins won the handwriting award for the second year in a row? Need we say more?) Type is a powerful thing. Just think, every day it coaxes people into buying magazines, ordering food, entering sweepstakes, and signing off on business proposals—sometimes even bad ones.

No matter how good the content of your document is, if your type is all scrunched up or too big or too small, no one will want to read it. On the other hand, good text formatting could almost make a VCR manual seem like an appealing read.

This chapter and the next explore all the different ways you can change the look (or formatting) of your type. In this chapter, you find out how to choose a typeface, a type size, and a type style, how to adjust the spacing between individual characters and lines of text, and how to give your text some color. You can also apply formatting attributes such as paragraph alignment, indents, and tabs, but we save those goodies for Chapter 8.

A First Look at Formatting Text

Fortunately, you don't have to be a professional designer to create good-looking type. You just need to be willing to experiment a little. To change the formatting of your text, you need to select it or click to insert a text insertion point with the type tool. Then you can apply formatting attributes to individual characters, called *character formatting,* or entire paragraphs, called *paragraph formatting.* For example, choosing a font, a type size, or a type style affects only the selected text characters, so that is considered character formatting. But changing the paragraph alignment or setting indents and tabs for a bulleted list affects the entire paragraph, so those operations fall under the domain of paragraph formatting.

Being the logical program that it is, InDesign gives you access to most of the character and paragraph formatting controls in the Character and Paragraph palettes, respectively. Both palettes share a window with the Transform palette — which provides controls for positioning, scaling, and otherwise manipulating text blocks and graphics — as shown in Figure 7-1. (If for some reason the palettes aren't visible on-screen, choose Type⇨Character or press ⌘+T on the Mac or Ctrl+T under Windows to display all three palettes with the Character palette selected.) These three palettes work dynamically with each other. When the arrow tool is selected, the Transform palette is active. When the type tool is selected, either the Character or Paragraph palette is active, depending on which you used last.

By default, the palettes appear horizontally near the bottom-left corner of the document window. But you can make them vertical, like other palettes, so they fit nicely along the edge of the screen. Just choose Vertical Palette from the palette menu in each palette.

To access a palette menu, click on the right-pointing arrow in the upper-right corner of the palette.

Figure 7-1:
The Character palette shares a window with the Transform and Paragraph palettes.

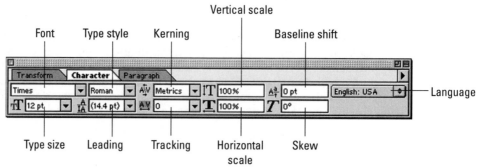

Vertical scale

Font   Type style   Kerning   Baseline shift

Language

Type size   Leading   Tracking   Horizontal scale   Skew

Paragraph formatting is discussed in Chapter 8, and we tackle the Transform palette in Chapter 10. This chapter is all about character formatting, most of which takes place in the Character palette.

The controls in the Character palette (labeled in Figure 7-1) are explained throughout the chapter, but here are a few factoids to keep in mind. If you choose an option from a pop-up menu, the change is automatically applied to the selected text. If you type a value in an option box, you need to press Tab, Return, or Enter to put your change into effect. If no text is selected, any changes you make will be applied to the next characters you type.

Choosing a Font and Type Style

Most likely, the first formatting attributes you'll want to apply to your text are a font and a type style. As in most word processing and page layout programs, the process is straightforward: You simply select the text you want to change, choose a font from the Font pop-up menu, and choose a style from the Type Style pop-up menu, as shown in Figure 7-2. But unlike in most other programs, the process doesn't involve any goofy buttons — you know, the boldface **B**, the italic *I*, the underlined U, and so on. That's because InDesign is smarter than your average page layout program and recognizes that some styles don't apply to some typefaces.

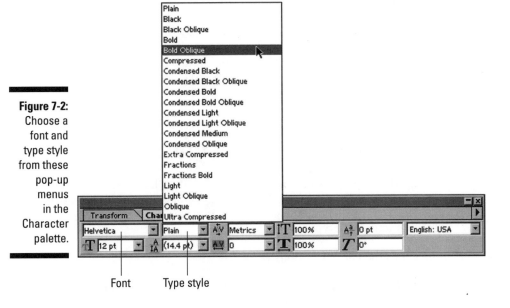

Figure 7-2:
Choose a font and type style from these pop-up menus in the Character palette.

Font   Type style

As explained in Chapter 6, every type family includes its own set of stylized fonts. Some, like Helvetica, include loads of different type styles — Plain, Black, Black Oblique, Bold, Bold Oblique, Compressed, and so on — as shown in Figure 7-2. Others have very few. Charlemagne, for example, is an upper-case roman typeface designed for use in headlines and subheads, so it includes only two styles: Regular and Bold. If InDesign let you apply an italic style to a typeface like Charlemagne, which doesn't include an italic style, it might look okay on-screen but chances are it would look ugly or even appear nonitalic when printed.

You can also specify a font and type style using the keyboard. Just click before the current font or type style name in the Font or Type Style option box and enter the first few letters of the name you want. InDesign scans all active fonts or type styles in nanoseconds and displays the one that matches the letters you've typed so far. For example, if you type the letter *t* in the Font option box, InDesign displays the first font (alphabetically) on your system that begins with the letter *t* — let's say that's Tekton. If you then type the letter *i*, Tekton changes to Times.

InDesign also provides a few keyboard shortcuts you can use to quickly apply bold and italic to typefaces that include those styles. On the Mac, press ⌘+Shift+B to make selected text bold or press ⌘+Shift+I to make it italic. Under Windows, press Ctrl+Shift+B or Ctrl+Shift+I to apply bold or italic styles, respectively. Remember, if the typeface of the selected text doesn't include a bold or italic type style, pressing these keyboard shortcuts won't apply any changes. To return to the normal (or regular) type style, press ⌘+Shift+Y on the Mac or Ctrl+Shift+Y under Windows.

If you have an aversion to doing things the easy way — maybe Grandpa taught you that life has to be hard — you can also choose Type⇨Font and choose a font and type style from the Font menu. But why not take it easy? Just gently explain to Grandpa that things are different now that we're at the dawn of a new millennium.

Applying Special Type Styles

You can also apply several special styles from the Character palette menu, as shown in Figure 7-3. To apply these styles, you must first select some text with the type tool. If no text is selected, the style you choose is applied to the next characters you type.

Here's how the various options work:

  ✔ **All Caps:** Choose this option from the palette menu to change all selected text to capital letters. You can also press ⌘+Shift+K on the Mac or Ctrl+Shift+K under Windows. As you might expect, this option does not affect numbers and other symbols.

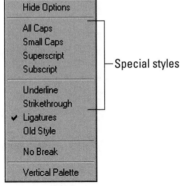

Special styles

✔ **Small Caps**: This option changes selected text to small capital letters that are about the size of a lowercase *x*. Small caps are generally used for acronyms in body text or to tastefully call attention to elements such as bylines. In addition to choosing the Small Caps option in the palette menu, you can press ⌘+Shift+H on the Mac or Ctrl+Shift+H under Windows. If the typeface for the selected text includes a small caps style, InDesign automatically applies the built-in style just as if you had selected it from the Type Style pop-up menu.

To change the size of your small caps, choose File⇨Preferences⇨Text to display the dialog box shown in Figure 7-4. Then enter a new value in the Small Caps option box. The value represents the size of the small caps relative to the regular font size. For example, the default value of 70 means small caps will be 70 percent of the size of the regular font.

✔ **Superscript:** Choose this option to slightly raise selected text and make it a little smaller. The most common uses of superscripts are in equations, fractions, and footnotes. To apply a superscript from the keyboard, press ⌘+Shift+equal (=) on the Mac or Ctrl+Shift+equal under Windows. As with small caps, you can adjust how your superscript text appears by changing the values in the Superscript option boxes in the Text panel of the Preferences dialog box. But unlike small caps, both the size and position of the superscript can be changed relative to the regular text.

✔ **Subscript:** The opposite of superscript, the subscript option slightly lowers text and makes it smaller. Subscripts are mostly used in equations. To apply a subscript from the keyboard, press ⌘+Shift+Option+equal (=) on the Mac or Ctrl+Shift+Alt+equal under Windows. As with superscripts, you can change the size and position of subscripts in the Text panel of the Preferences dialog box.

Figure 7-4:
Use the
Character
Settings
options in
the Text
panel of the
Preferences
dialog box
to specify
settings for
superscript,
subscript,
and small
caps.

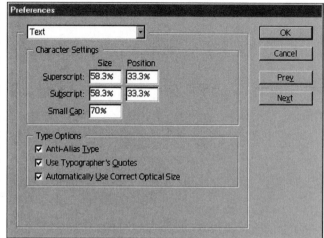

You can also create subscripts and superscripts manually using the baseline shift option in the Character palette, as explained later in this chapter.

✔ **Underline:** This option doesn't really require any explanation. You probably won't need to use it much, but if you do, just choose Underline from the palette menu or press ⌘+Shift+U on the Mac or Ctrl+Shift+U under Windows.

✔ **Strikethrough:** The strikethrough style can be handy as an editing tool when more than one person is reviewing a document. Simply strikethrough text to mark it for deletion. In addition to choosing this option from the palette menu, you can apply a strikethrough also by pressing ⌘+Shift+slash (/) on the Mac or Ctrl+Shift+slash (/) under Windows.

To remove any of these styles from selected text, simply choose the option from the palette menu or press the keyboard shortcut again. A check mark next to an option in the palette menu means the option is turned on. If no check mark appears, the option is off.

Squishing, Stretching, and Slanting Type

If neither the type family's built-in type styles nor the special styles in the palette menu seem to fit the bill, you can take matters into your own hands. Using the controls in the Character palette, you can distort the shapes of characters to create fake styles. For example, you can squish or stretch letters horizontally, which can be a handy trick when you need to fit some body copy into a particular space. You c an also slant type to simulate the look of italics. The following two sections tell all.

Scaling up, down, and sideways

The Character palette provides vertical and horizontal scaling controls (labeled back in Figure 7-1) that let you change the height and width of the selected type, respectively, to create condensed and expanded effects. Enter a value larger than 100 percent in the Horizontal Scale option box to expand the width of selected characters; enter a value lower than 100 percent to condense them. The Vertical Scale option box works the same way, but it affects the height of your type. Enter a value larger than 100 percent to make selected characters taller or a value lower than 100 percent to make them shorter. If you're so inclined, you can enter any value from 1 to 1000 percent.

Entering the same value into both the Horizontal Scale and Vertical Scale option boxes is the same as changing the size in the Type Size option box (a process we explain shortly). So if you type 50 percent into both option boxes, the result is the same as if you had changed the value in the Type Size option box to half its original value.

To restore scaled type to its original size, enter 100 in both the Horizontal Scale and Vertical Scale option boxes. You can also press ⌘+Shift+X on the Mac or Ctrl+Shift+X under Windows to restore horizontally scaled type to its normal scale. Press ⌘+Shift+Option+X on the Mac or Ctrl+Shift+Alt+X under Windows to return vertically scaled type to normal.

Figure 7-5 shows examples of 36-point New Century Schoolbook Roman type with different scaling values applied. Notice how changing the scaling value changes the length of a line of type. For this reason, scaling can be useful when you need to squish or stretch some copy to fit into a particular space.

Scaling also affects the thickness of characters, which can result in some ugly and hard to read type, as shown in the last two examples of Figure 7-5. Unless you're trying to achieve some wacky effects, you should keep scaling to a minimum — generally between 90 and 110 percent, depending on the typeface.

Many designers wince at the thought of scaling type. This is because each typeface has been carefully designed to be displayed at a certain size and weight. So when you scale a font, you're messing with something some type designer spent tens or hundreds of hours to create and perfect. This shouldn't dissuade you, however. Careful and moderate scaling of type can be effective and appropriate. Besides, it's your document, so you're the boss.

It's not disco (Normal scaling — 100%)

It's not disco (Vertical scaling — 90%)

It's not disco (Horizontal scaling — 110%)

Figure 7-5:
Scaling type
squishes or
stretches
individual
characters.

It's not disco (Horizontal scaling — 50%)

It's not di (Horizontal scaling — 200%)

Slanting type your own way

The Skew option box in the Character palette lets you slant selected text by a specific value, from –85 to 85 degrees. Why would you want to do that? For one, you can slant type to create a false italic effect for a typeface that doesn't include an italic style. Or you may want to slant some type to create a snazzy effect in a headline for an advertisement or a brochure.

Check your scales

You can scale entire text blocks using the scale controls in the Transform palette and the scale tool in the toolbox (both discussed in Chapter 10). But be careful! Scaling a text block with the Transform palette controls or the scale tool scales the text frame and all the text in it, but the scaling applied to the text is not reflected anywhere in the Character palette.

So what's the big deal? Just imagine this little scenario. Suppose you use the scale tool to scale the width of a text block to 110 percent. Later, you scale the same text to 110 percent using the Horizontal Scale option in the Character palette. The Character palette now says your text has a horizontal scale of 110 percent, but in fact it's scaled to 110 percent of 110 percent of its original horizontal size, which is 121 percent. It sounds confusing because it is confusing. So scale with care.

Enter a negative value in the Skew option box to slant type up and to the right, like italics. Enter a positive value to slant type up and to the left. A value of 0 means no skew is applied to the selected text.

Applying a skew to a nonitalic font does not create true italic characters. Figure 7-6, for example, shows some type skewed to –20 degrees in Times Roman (top) and then set in Times Italic with no skew applied (bottom). Notice that the individual letters are different in each version. That's because Times Roman and Times Italic are two different sets of characters. When you apply a skew, you are simply slanting the characters in the font and style of the selected text.

Figure 7-6:
Skewed type (top) creates an italic effect, but it isn't the same as true italics (bottom).

I am not alive
I am not alive

Sizing Up Your Type

So now you know how to give your type some style, but what if you just want to change its size? Simply select the text you want to resize and choose a new size from the Type Size pop-up menu (labeled back in Figure 7-1). Alternatively, you can choose Type⇨Size and click on a size in the resulting menu. If neither of these choices satisfies you, Control-click or right-click on the selected text and choose a size from the Size menu.

But the options in the Character palette and Size menu aren't the only sizes you can use. To specify a custom size, double-click on the value in the Type Size option box (or choose Type⇨Size⇨Other to select the value), enter any size between 1 and 1296, and press Return or Enter. You can even enter decimal values in .1 to .001 point increments, such as 30.2, 14.78, and 12.006.

You can change the size of selected type from the keyboard, too. Press ⌘+Shift+< on the Mac or Ctrl+Shift+< under Windows to reduce the type in 2-point increments. Press ⌘+Shift+> on the Mac or Ctrl+Shift+> under Windows to enlarge the type in 2-point increments. To enlarge the type by five times that amount (which would be 10 points, by default) press ⌘+Shift+Option+> on the Mac or Ctrl+Shift+Alt+> under Windows. Similarly, press ⌘+Shift+Option+< or Ctrl+Shift+Alt+< to reduce the type by five times.

To change the default increment from 2 points to something else, choose File⊏>Preferences⊏>Units & Increments, enter a new value in the Size/Leading option box, and press Return or Enter. If you change the Size/Leading value to 4, for example, pressing ⌘+Shift+< or Ctrl+Shift+< will reduce selected type in 4-point increments, and pressing ⌘+Shift+Option+< will reduce it by five times that amount (20 points).

If you use multiple master typefaces, as explained in Chapter 6, choose File⊏>Preferences⊏>Text and make sure the Automatically Use Correct Optical Size check box is selected. When this option is turned on, InDesign automatically uses a multiple master font's optical size when you change its type size.

To find out how to create a drop cap at the beginning of an article or story, see Chapter 8.

Raising and Lowering Text

The Baseline Shift option in the right half of the Character palette lets you move selected type above or below its baseline. A positive value raises characters, and a negative value lowers them. The default value of 0 means the characters are resting on their baseline.

You can change the baseline shift to create manual superscripts and subscripts. Select some text, enter any value between −5000 and 5000 points in the Baseline Shift option box, and press Return or Enter.

You can quickly raise or lower the baseline shift of selected text in 2-point increments by pressing Shift+Option+up arrow or Shift+Option+down arrow, respectively, on the Mac. Under Windows, press Shift+Alt+up arrow or Shift+Alt+down arrow, respectively. To raise or lower the baseline shift value by five times that amount, press ⌘+Shift+Option+up arrow or ⌘+Shift+Option+down arrow, respectively, on the Mac. Press Ctrl+Shift+Alt+up arrow or Ctrl+Shift+Alt+down arrow, respectively, under Windows.

Giving Your Text Some Space

Relationships between characters of text are a lot like relationships between people. Give them too much space and they run wild and free, making them difficult to predict and even harder to follow. Don't give them enough space and they're all cramped and stifled, yearning for a little room to breathe. But with just the right amount of space, your text is comfortable, confident, predictable — okay, you get the idea.

The amount of space between individual characters and entire lines of type is as important to the appearance of your text as your choice of font, size, and type style. You've probably encountered poorly spaced text before. Maybe it looked something like the left-hand example in Figure 7-7. Yikes! The good news is, you'd have to work pretty hard to make your text look this bad in InDesign. The even better news is, the next few sections explain how you can use the various spacing controls in the Character palette to give your text just the space it needs to really shine, like in the right-hand example in Figure 7-7.

Adjusting the space between lines

Word processors call the distance between lines of type *line spacing*, and let you adjust line spacing by applying options such as single space and double space. Well, that approach to line spacing is old news. Just shake the idea right out of your head because that's not how it works in InDesign. In InDesign, the space between lines of type is called *leading* (pronounced "ledding"), and it's measured in points, just like type size.

Figure 7-7: Don't let this happen to you (left). Give your text just the right amount of space (right).

In the following quiz, Shenbop—our deceased but genial amphibious moderator—asks you to match each of several Top 40 song titles with the lyrics that immediately follow the utterance of the title in the song's chorus.

This initial test—the first in a giddy series—is so obscenely easy that we fully expect you to get every answer right. If you fail to match so much as one song title with its lyrics, you're either hopelessly out of touch with popular culture or you've successfully managed to expunge an entire decade from your memory.

Either way, congratulations!

In the following quiz, Shenbop—our deceased but genial amphibious moderator—asks you to match each of several Top 40 song titles with the lyrics that immediately follow the utterance of the title in the song's chorus.

This initial test—the first in a giddy series—is so obscenely easy that we fully expect you to get every answer right. If you fail to match so much as one song title with its lyrics, you're either hopelessly out of touch with popular culture or you've successfully managed to expunge an entire decade from your memory.

Either way, congratulations!

Just in case you're curious, the term *leading* has been around for hundreds of years. Back in the way old days, printers spaced out lines of type by inserting thin strips of lead between them, so the distance between the lines came to be called leading.

Former QuarkXPress users should note that leading is a character level attribute in InDesign, so you can have more than one leading value applied to lines in a paragraph.

The value in the Leading option box (below the Type Style control in the Character palette) specifies the amount of space between a selected line of type and the line above it, measured from baseline to baseline. So 12-point leading leaves a space of 2 points between two lines of 10-point type. You can adjust leading as follows:

✔ To change the leading between selected lines of type, choose a new value from the Leading pop-up menu. Or you can enter any value from 0 to 5000 points in .001 increments in the Leading option box.

✔ To speed things up, select some text and press Option+up arrow or Option+down arrow on the Mac or Alt+up arrow or Alt+down arrow under Windows to increase or decrease, respectively, the leading in 2-point increments (or whatever value you may have entered in the Size/Leading option box in the Units & Increments panel of the Preferences dialog box). Press ⌘+Option+up arrow on the Mac or Ctrl+Alt+up arrow under Windows to increase the leading by five times that amount. As you might expect, pressing ⌘+Option+down arrow on the Mac or Ctrl+Alt+down arrow under Windows decreases the leading by five times that amount.

✔ Choose Auto from the Leading pop-up menu to set the leading to 120 percent of the type size, which is generally appropriate for body text. When the Auto setting is applied, the value in the Leading option box appears in parentheses.

✔ To quickly apply auto leading to selected text, press ⌘+Shift+Option+A on the Mac or Ctrl+Shift+Alt+A under Windows.

✔ You can change the value of the Auto leading setting if you like. Just click on the Paragraph palette tab, or press ⌘+M on the Mac or Ctrl+M under Windows, and choose Justification from the Paragraph palette menu to display the Justification dialog box. Then enter a new value in the Auto Leading option box and press Return or Enter.

If you think it's strange that you have to choose an option from the Paragraph palette menu to change a setting for a character formatting attribute, you're not alone. Go figure.

✔ When a line of text contains characters with two different leading values, the larger value determines the leading for the entire line. This can be problematic when a line of text contains differently sized characters — such as a drop cap and regular body text — and the Auto setting is applied to both. In such a case, InDesign would apply the leading value for the drop cap, which would result in a big space between lines of text. The solution? Turn Auto leading off by choosing a different option in the Leading pop-up menu or entering a value in the Leading option box.

✔ For headlines and other large type treatments, you might want to set the leading to match the type size, which is known as *solid leading*.

You can also adjust leading at the paragraph level by aligning text to the baseline grid, as explained in Chapter 8.

Changing the space between pairs of characters

The process of adjusting the amount of space between two characters is called *kerning*. Like most page-layout programs, InDesign lets you kern characters automatically or manually. But unlike other programs, InDesign offers two methods of automatic kerning: metrics and optical.

Metrics kerning

Most typefaces are designed so that certain pairs of letters, called *kerning pairs*, are positioned more closely together than the normal letter spacing. For example, the letters *A* and *v* are a kerning pair. Why? Because when they appear next to each other in normal letter spacing (without kerning), they look weird and uneven, as shown in the top example in Figure 7-8. But if you choose Metrics from the Kerning pop-up menu (the third control in the top row of the Character palette), InDesign automatically recognizes all kerning pairs so that they fit together more closely, as shown in the bottom example in Figure 7-8. In fact, the Metrics option is the default kerning setting, so unless you've been applying other kerning options, you don't even have to choose it.

When you apply metrics kerning to selected text, the word *Metrics* appears in the Kerning option box. If you then click with the type tool between two characters, the Kerning option box displays the kerning value in parentheses, such as (–92).

Figure 7-8:
The *A* and *v*
kerning pair
look odd
with no
kerning
applied
(top), but
more nat-
ural when
the Metrics
option is
selected
(bottom).

Aversion

Aversion

Optical kerning

InDesign's other automatic kerning option — Optical — is something you won't find in any other page-layout program, and it's simply awesome. When you choose Optical from the Kerning pop-up menu, InDesign analyzes the letterforms of any two adjacent characters (whether or not they are kerning pairs) and determines the ideal amount of space to put between them based on their appearance. Pretty smart, huh?

Optical kerning offers a couple of big advantages over metrics kerning. For one, as we just mentioned, it adjusts the space between every two characters, not just kerning pairs. Consider Figure 7-9. The top example shows the word *Toasty* with the Metrics kerning option applied; the bottom example uses optical kerning. Now take a closer look at the spacing between the following letter pairs in both examples: *o* and *a*, *a* and *s*, and *s* and *t*. Notice how they fit together more comfortably in the bottom example? That's because these characters aren't kerning pairs, so the Metrics option (top example) doesn't adjust the spacing at all. But the Optical option (bottom example) considers the space between each letter pair and kerns accordingly.

Another advantage of optical kerning is that it's visually-based whereas metrics kerning is font-based. Now take a look at the *T* and *o* in both examples in Figure 7-9. Again, the optical kerning in the bottom example looks better because rather than using specified kerning pair values, it adjusts the spacing based on appearance.

As with metrics kerning, when you apply optical kerning to selected text, the word *Optical* appears in the Kerning option box. If you click between two characters, the kerning value appears in parentheses.

Figure 7-9:
The Metrics option kerns only kerning pairs (top), but the Optical option kerns all letter pairs based on appearance (bottom).

Toasty

Toasty

Manual kerning

If neither the Metrics nor Optical option satisfies you, you can adjust the kerning manually. Click with the type tool between two characters and then choose a value from the Kerning pop-up menu or enter a value between –1,000 and 10,000 in the option box. You can also use the following keyboard shortcuts:

- ✔ Press Option+left arrow on the Mac or Alt+left arrow under Windows to kern characters together by .02 ($^{20}/_{1000}$) of an em space. An *em space* is a space as wide as the type size is tall. So if the type size is 12 points, an em space is 12 points wide. Press Option+right arrow on the Mac or Alt+right arrow under Windows to kern characters apart by $^{20}/_{1000}$ of an em space.

- ✔ You can change the default increment of $^{20}/_{1000}$ em space by choosing File⇨Preferences⇨Units & Increments and entering a new value in the Kerning option box.

- ✔ To decrease or increase kerning by five times the value in the Units & Increments panel of the Preferences dialog box, press ⌘+Option+left arrow or ⌘+Option+right arrow, respectively, on the Mac. Under Windows, press Ctrl+Alt+left arrow or Ctrl+Alt+right arrow.

- ✔ If you change your mind after you've manually kerned characters, you can press ⌘+Shift+Q on the Mac or Ctrl+Shift+Q under Windows to quickly apply metrics kerning.

You can't apply manual kerning to selected text. When text is selected, only the Metrics, Optical, and 0 options are available.

Tracking type

Tracking is the process of adjusting the spacing across a range of characters. But unlike kerning, the Tracking option in the Character palette applies uniform spacing between all selected characters. Tracking can be helpful when you're copyfitting long stretches of type, but when applied in excess it can result in some unattractive text. It's best to use tracking sparingly.

You can apply tracking to selected text by choosing an option from the Tracking pop-up menu or entering a value between –1000 and 10000 in the Tracking option box. Like kerning, tracking is measured in $\frac{1}{1000}$ of an em space, and you can use the same keyboard shortcuts to increase or decrease the tracking value. Press Option+left arrow on the Mac or Alt+left arrow under Windows to decrease the space between characters; press Option+right arrow or Alt+right arrow to increase the space.

Tracking works cumulatively with kerning, so you can adjust the space between letter pairs and then tighten or loosen a range of text. For example, if you kern a letter pair –20 units, and then apply tracking of –20 to those characters, the space between them is –40.

Automatically Replacing Special Characters

The Character palette menu and the Text panel of the Preferences dialog box offer options that enable you to automatically replace certain characters with special typographic characters: typographer's quotes, ligatures, and old style figures. Here's how the options work:

✔ **Typographer's Quotes:** Chances are you'll want to use typographer's quotes (" and ") — also known as smart quotes or curly quotes — rather than straight quotes in most instances in your documents. But sometimes you'll want to use straight quotes to denote feet (') or inches (") or for some other purpose. That's why InDesign lets you turn typographer's quotes on and off through Preferences. Just choose File⇨Preferences⇨Text and select the Use Typographer's Quotes check box. A check mark indicates that the option is on and an empty check box means it's off.

You can quickly turn the typographer's quotes preference on and off (called *toggling*) by pressing ⌘+Shift+Option+apostrophe (') on the Mac or Ctrl+Shift+Alt+apostrophe (') under Windows.

To automatically convert straight quotes to typographer's quotes when importing text, select the Convert Quotes check box in the Place dialog box.

✔ **Ligatures:** Some typefaces, such as those that include an Expert Collection from Adobe, contain *ligatures*, which are two characters joined into one. Choose the Ligatures option from the Character palette menu to automatically replace the character combinations *ff, fi, fl, ffi,* and *ffl* with their respective ligatures, as shown in Figure 7-10. Although ligatures appear as one character, you can still edit them by clicking between the letters.

✔ **Old Style:** As with ligatures, some typefaces include *old style figures,* which are Arabic numerals (such as 1, 2, 3) characterized by ascenders and descenders, as shown in the bottom example in Figure 7-11. To automatically replace regular modern numbers with old style figures, choose Old Style from the Character palette menu.

Figure 7-10:
Characters with the Ligature option turned off (top) and on (bottom).

ff fi fl ffi ffl
ff fi fl ffi ffl

Figure 7-11:
The Old Style option in the Character palette menu replaces regular numbers (top) with old style figures (bottom).

Top 40 songs from the 1970s

Top 40 songs from the 1970s

Watching your language

Sometimes a document might contain words or passages in more than one language — such as a travel article. In such a case, you might want to use the Language pop-up menu, located on the far right side of the Character palette. This option lets you apply more than a dozen languages to a selected range of characters. The language you specify determines how words are spell-checked and hyphenated.

Giving Your Text Some Color

One way to give your text a little zing is to give it some color using the Color palette. The Color palette is explained in detail in Chapter 11. For now, just follow these steps:

1. **Select the characters you want to color.**

   Don't select an entire text block with the arrow tool. Just drag to select characters with the type tool.

2. **Choose Window⇨Color to display the Color palette.**

   You can also just press F6. Either way, the Color palette (shown in Figure 7-12) appears on the screen.

3. **Choose an option from the Color palette menu.**

   The palette menu lists three *color models*: LAB, CMYK, and RGB. Selecting a color model determines what the primary colors are, as explained in Chapter 11. For this exercise, choose CMYK because that's the option you'll use the most. The Color palette changes to display four color sliders, as shown in Figure 7-12.

4. **Make sure the Fill icon in the Color palette is selected.**

   The Fill icon is labeled in Figure 7-12. This tells InDesign that you want to apply a color to the entirety of selected characters (rather than creating a colored *stroke* around their perimeters).

5. **Click on the spectrum bar at the bottom of the Color palette to approximate the color you want.**

   Then you can modify the color by dragging the triangles on the color sliders or entering new values in the option boxes next them. As you modify the color, the Fill icon shows the effects of your changes.

Fill icon

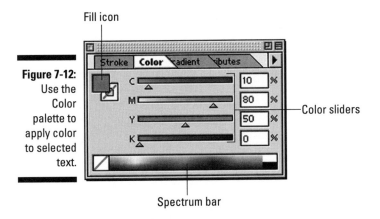

Figure 7-12:
Use the
Color
palette to
apply color
to selected
text.

Color sliders

Spectrum bar

6. **When you're satisfied with your color, click inside the document
   window.**

   This deselects your text, which now appears in its new color.

If this little exercise whets your appetite for more color, feel free to jump
ahead to Chapter 11 for the full deal. But if you prefer to do things in sequen-
tial order, proceed to Chapter 8 to find out about the other half of InDesign's
text formatting controls.

Chapter 8

All the Justification You Need

*F*ormatting text is a hefty job, and although the Character palette can help you make your words look wonderful, it can't go it alone. It's just one half of a dynamic duo, like Batman and Robin or the Wonder Twins.

In this chapter, you find out how to harness the powers of the Character palette's superhero partner — the Paragraph palette — which provides controls for applying paragraph formatting attributes such as justification, indents, and spacing between paragraphs. Just in case this superhero analogy strikes you as a bit thin, consider this: No page-layout program justifies text like InDesign. And if you think about it, that's really all the justification you need. So as one boy wonder might put it, *bam, zowie, zap* — "Holy hyphenation Batman, let's go!"

Meeting the Paragraph Palette

As explained in Chapter 7, the Paragraph palette shares a window with the Transform and Character palettes. If one of those two palettes is displayed on-screen, you can simply click on the Paragraph tab to display the Paragraph palette, as shown in Figure 8-1. Otherwise, choose Type⇨Paragraph or press ⌘+M on the Mac or Ctrl+M under Windows.

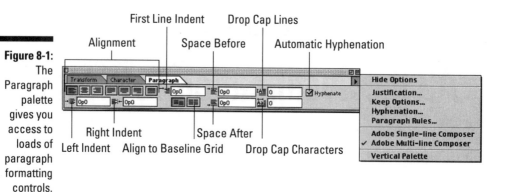

Figure 8-1:
The Paragraph palette gives you access to loads of paragraph formatting controls.

By default, the Paragraph palette appears horizontally near the bottom-left corner of the document window. To make it fit vertically along the edge of the screen, choose Vertical Palette from the palette menu.

Figure 8-1 shows all paragraph formatting attributes you can apply using the Paragraph palette. (If your screen doesn't have all the options shown in the figure, choose Show Options from the palette menu.) Here are a few things you should know about how these controls work:

✔ You don't need to select an entire paragraph to apply a formatting attribute to it. Just click in the paragraph with the type tool to place a text insertion point.

✔ If you click on a button in the palette, the change is automatically applied. If you type a value in an option box, you need to press Tab, Return, or Enter to apply your change. Press Shift+Return or Shift+Enter to apply the change while keeping the option box selected.

✔ If there's no insertion point in a paragraph, any changes you make will be applied only if you create a new text frame and start typing.

✔ The second group of options in the palette menu leads to dialog boxes with more controls; the third group applies changes immediately.

Aligning and Justifying Your Type

So far as we know, every computer program that lets you create type lets you specify how the rows of type in a paragraph line up respective to the left and right edges of a margin or column — a process known around the world as *alignment*. InDesign gives you seven alignment choices, which you can select by clicking on the alignment icons in the Paragraph palette (labeled in Figure 8-2) or by using keyboard shortcuts.

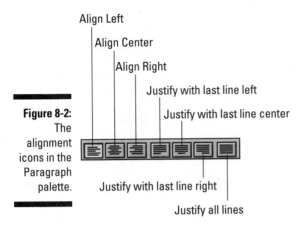

Align Left

Align Center

Align Right

Justify with last line left

Justify with last line center

Justify with last line right

Justify all lines

Figure 8-2:
The alignment icons in the Paragraph palette.

Here's how the first three alignment options work:

✔ To align a paragraph so that each line begins at the same left edge (*flush left, ragged right*), click on the Align Left icon in the Paragraph palette. Or press ⌘+Shift+L on the Mac or Ctrl+Shift+L under Windows.

✔ To *center* all lines in a paragraph, click on the Align Center icon or press ⌘+Shift+C on the Mac or Ctrl+Shift+C under Windows.

✔ If you want the right edges of a paragraph to line up (*flush right, ragged left*), click on the Align Right icon. Alternatively, press ⌘+Shift+R on the Mac or Ctrl+Shift+R under Windows.

The last four alignment options let you *justify* paragraphs (so they fill the entire width of the text block) while specifying the behavior of the last line. In other words, you can tell InDesign to position the last line of type flush left, centered, flush right, or force justified. For the record, no other page layout program gives you this kind of control over the alignment of the last line in a justified paragraph. The options work as follows:

✔ To justify a paragraph with the last line set flush left, click on the first Justify icon in the Paragraph palette. You can also press ⌘+Shift+J on the Mac or Ctrl+Shift+J under Windows.

✔ To justify a paragraph with the last line centered, click on the second Justify icon.

✔ Click on the third Justify icon to justify a paragraph with the last line flush right.

By the way, the last line centered and last line flush right justification options have no keyboard shortcuts. You'll just have to buck up and use your trusty old mouse.

✔ If you want to *force justify* the last line in a paragraph, click on the last Justify icon in the Paragraph palette. You can also press ⌘+Shift+F on the Mac or Ctrl+Shift+F under Windows.

Figure 8-3 shows examples of all seven alignment options. When in doubt about which alignment to use, align left (or flush left) is generally a safe bet. Justification (usually with the last line flush left) is also commonly used for body copy in long documents. But hey, feel free to experiment with other alignment options as well.

Modifying the way text justifies

When you justify text, InDesign needs to make decisions about how much it can shrink or expand the standard word and letter spacing to make each line of type stretch from the left to right edge of the text block. You can change the parameters InDesign uses to make these decisions by choosing Justification from the Paragraph palette menu to display the dialog box shown in Figure 8-4.

Flush left (ragged right)

Except for those unfortunate souls who weren't alive back then. And those more unfortunate souls who were. But the rest of us, well, we just couldn't get enough.

Centered

Except for those unfortunate souls who weren't alive back then. And those more unfortunate souls who were. But the rest of us, well, we just couldn't get enough.

Flush right (ragged left)

Except for those unfortunate souls who weren't alive back then. And those more unfortunate souls who were. But the rest of us, well, we just couldn't get enough.

Justified (last line left)

Except for those unfortunate souls who weren't alive back then. And those more unfortunate souls who were. But the rest of us, well, we just couldn't get enough.

Justified (last line centered)

Except for those unfortunate souls who weren't alive back then. And those more unfortunate souls who were. But the rest of us, well, we just couldn't get enough.

Justified (last line right)

Except for those unfortunate souls who weren't alive back then. And those more unfortunate souls who were. But the rest of us, well, we just couldn't get enough.

Figure 8-3: The seven alignment options in InDesign.

Force Justified

Except for those unfortunate souls who weren't alive back then. And those more unfortunate souls who were. But the rest of us, well, we just couldn't get enough.

Figure 8-4:
Use this
dialog box
to change
the settings
InDesign
uses to
justify text.

Justification				
	Minimum	Desired	Maximum	OK
Word Spacing:	80%	100%	133%	Cancel
Letter Spacing:	0%	0%	0%	☑ Preview
Glyph Scaling:	100%	100%	100%	
Auto Leading:	120%			

The Justification dialog box contains three rows of options — Word Spacing, Letter Spacing, and Glyph Scaling. Each option offers Minimum, Desired, and Maximum settings. The values in these option boxes represent the percentage of normal word spacing, letter spacing, or glyph scaling InDesign uses to justify lines of type. (*Glyph scaling* is the process of changing the width of characters, just like horizontal scaling in the Character palette.) For example, the default Minimum, Desired, and Maximum values for the Word Spacing option are 80 percent, 100 percent, and 133 percent, respectively. That means InDesign will try to use the font's full word spacing, but will shrink it to 80 percent or expand it to 133 percent if necessary. InDesign always attempts to adjust word spacing first, then letter spacing and glyph scaling, respectively, if required.

You can change any value in the Minimum, Desired, and Maximum option boxes, but the minimum value must always be lower than the desired value, and the maximum value must always be higher than the desired value. You can enter values from 0 to 500 percent in the Word Spacing option boxes, from –200 to 200 percent in the Letter Spacing option boxes, and from 50 to 200 percent in the Glyph Scaling option boxes. Select the Preview check box to see the effects of your changes before you apply them.

You may be wondering how letter spacing differs from kerning. After all, both affect the amount of space between letters, right? Well, that's true, but kerning applies to selected characters whereas letter spacing affects entire paragraphs. Also, the two are measured differently — kerning is measured as a fraction of an em space but letter spacing is measured as a percentage of a standard space character. Most importantly, kerning is fixed and letter spacing is flexible, which is why the letter spacing settings appear in the Justification dialog box.

The glyph scaling values are all set to 100 percent by default. Setting the minimum and maximum values to about 98 percent and 102 percent, respectively, can help solve minor justification problems without creating a discernable difference in the width of characters. But don't go hog-wild with the glyph scaling options because changing the values by more than a few percent can result in some odd looking text.

Using a feature called the Adobe Multi-line Composer, InDesign can justify text more intelligently than the average page layout program. We'll tell you all about the Multi-line Composer later in this chapter.

Indenting Paragraphs

InDesign gives you several ways to indent a selected paragraph using the indent controls in the Paragraph palette (labeled in Figure 8-1). Here's a rundown on how they work:

- ✔ Enter a value in the Left Indent option box and press Return or Enter to indent the entire left side of a paragraph from the edge of the text block. For example, if you type 1p, the entire paragraph is indented by 1 pica.

- ✔ To indent the entire right side of a paragraph, enter a value in the Right Indent option box.

  You can enter values in both the Left Indent and Right Indent option boxes to reduce the width of a paragraph. This can come in handy when you need to set off a long quote from surrounding text.

- ✔ The indent setting you'll use most often is the First Line Indent option. Enter a value in this option box to indent only the first line in a paragraph. The First Line Indent is relative to the Left Indent setting. So if you set the left indent to 1 pica and the first line indent to 1 pica, the first line will be indented 2 picas from the left edge of the text block.

- ✔ A *hanging indent*, in which all lines except the first line are indented, is useful for formatting bulleted or numbered lists. To create a hanging indent, enter a positive value in the Left Indent option box and the same value, only negative, in the First Line Indent option box. In Figure 8-5, for example, we set the Left Indent value to 1p6 and the First Line Indent value to –1p6.

  You also have to set a tab so that the first line of text lines up with the left indent. In Figure 8-5, we pressed the Tab key after the numbers in the left column and the letters in the right column to insert tab characters. Then we chose Type⇨Tabs to display the Tabs palette and created a left tab at the 1p6 mark so it lined up with the left indent. For a complete rundown on how to work with tabs, read the next section.

- ✔ If you create numbered lists that use drop caps, you don't need to insert a tab at the left indent marker. InDesign automatically aligns the first line of text to the left indent for you. We explain how to create drop caps later in this chapter.

> ## Match the song title on the left... ... with the lyrics on the right.
>
> | | |
> |---|---|
> | 1. » Kung Fu Fighting¶ | A. » Don't be a fool with your life¶ |
> | 2. » Ride Captain Ride¶ | B. » 'Cuz dreamin' can make you mine.¶ |
> | 3. » Dance with Me¶ | C. » The honesty's too much.¶ |
> | 4. » Sometimes When We Touch¶ | D. » Baby, we're still worth one more try.¶ |
> | 5. » Torn Between Two Lovers¶ | E. » Those cats were fast as lightning.¶ |
> | 6. » I Like Dreamin'¶ | F. » Whoa oh whoa.¶ |
> | 7. » Midnight at the Oasis¶ | G. » Upon your mystery ship.¶ |
> | 8. » Don't Give Up on Us¶ | H. » Feelin' like a fool.¶ |
> | 9. » Billy, Don't Be a Hero¶ | I. » Send your camel to bed.¶ |
> | 10. » Feelings | J. » I want to be a partner. |
>
> Answers (if you really need the help): 1.E, 2.G, 3.J, 4.C, 5.H, 6.B, 7.I, 8.D, 9.A, 10.F

Figure 8-5: Use hanging indents to create bulleted or numbered lists.

You can enter any value between 0 and 720 picas in the Left Indent and Right Indent option boxes and any value between –720 and 720 picas in the First Line Indent option box.

InDesign won't let you extend text beyond the left edge of a text block. So if your left indent — or the combination of your first line indent and your left indent — is a negative number, you get an error message.

You can also set indents by dragging the Indent markers in the Tabs palette, as explained in the next section. You might find this approach easier because it's more visual.

Keeping Tabs on the Tabs Palette

Tabs are one of the most useful and underused paragraph formatting attributes. They make it easy to align columns of data and create bulleted and numbered lists, like the ones shown in Figure 8-5. When working with tabs, it's often helpful to choose Type⇨Show Hidden Characters (that's ⌘+Option+I on the Mac or Ctrl+Alt+I under Windows) so you can see the tab characters in your text.

To set tabs for a paragraph, click in the paragraph and choose Type⇨Tabs to display the Tabs palette, shown in Figure 8-6. You can also call forth the Tabs palette — known in some circles as the *tab ruler* — by pressing ⌘+Shift+T on the Mac or Ctrl+Shift+T under Windows.

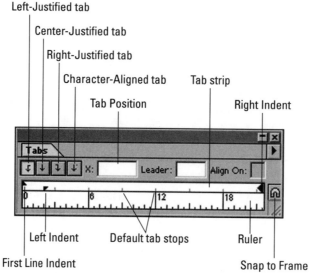

Left-Justified tab
Center-Justified tab
Right-Justified tab
Character-Aligned tab   Tab strip
                        Tab Position   Right Indent

Figure 8-6:
Use the
Tabs palette
to position
tab stops
and align
tabbed text
in a
paragraph.

Left Indent   Default tab stops   Ruler

First Line Indent   Snap to Frame

To set tabs for an entire story, click inside a text block with the type tool, press ⌘+A on the Mac or Ctrl+A under Windows to select all the text, and choose the Tabs command. When you first display the Tabs palette, InDesign automatically aligns it to the selected paragraph, provided the top-left corner of the text block is visible. To align the palette to a different paragraph, select the paragraph and click on the Snap to Frame button. You can then set tabs as follows:

✔ To create a new tab stop, click in the tab strip above the ruler or enter a location in the Tab Position option box (it's the one with the X before it).

✔ By default, InDesign places tab stops every 3 picas (or ½ inch) along the ruler. When you add a new tab stop, all default tab stops to the left of the new tab stop disappear. If you add another tab, any default tabs between that tab and the first one you created are deleted.

✔ If you drag the tab stop along the tab strip, a vertical line appears in every text block in which the selected paragraph resides. The line moves with the tab stop so you can easily see how changing the tab position will affect the alignment of text. When you release the mouse button, the line disappears. You can also reposition a tab by selecting the tab and entering a new location in the Tab Position option box.

✔ To change the identity of a tab stop, select the tab stop and click on a different tab icon in the upper-left corner of the palette. In a left-justified tab, text after the tab character begins at the tab location and continues to the right. In a center-justified tab, the tab becomes the center point for text entered after the tab. In a right-justified tab, text entered after the tab begins to the left and ends at the tab. In a character-aligned tab, text aligns according to a character you specify in the Align On option box. Character-aligned tabs are ideal for aligning numbers by decimal points or fraction bars.

✔ A fast way to change the identity of a tab stop is to Option-click (Mac) or Alt-click (Windows) on it. Each time you Option-click or Alt-click, the tab stop changes to the next kind, from left to center to right to character back to left, and so on.

✔ If you want to create a series of evenly spaced tab stops, you don't have to add them all manually. You can just use the Repeat Tab command from the palette menu. Here's how it works: Suppose you have an 18-pica column. If you create a tab stop at the 3-pica mark and choose Repeat Tab from the palette menu, InDesign places a tab every 3 picas across the column.

✔ To delete a tab stop, simply drag it up or down off the tab strip. To delete all tab stops, choose Clear All from the palette menu.

✔ A *tab leader* is a repeated pattern of characters — usually periods or dashes — that fills the space between the text before the tab and the text after the tab. The most common example of a tab leader is in a book's table of contents, where a repeating period (. . . . .) fills the space between a chapter name and the corresponding page number. (Flip back to the table of contents in this book to see an example.) InDesign lets you create tab leaders containing up to eight characters. Just select a tab stop, type the characters you want in the Leader option box, and press Return or Enter.

Don't use tab stops to indent the first line of a paragraph. Instead, use the First Line Indent option in the Paragraph palette, as explained earlier, or drag the First Line Indent marker in the Tabs palette (labeled in Figure 8-6). You can also drag the Indent markers in the Tabs palette to set the left and right indents for a paragraph.

By default, dragging the Left Indent marker moves the First Line Indent marker as well. But you can press the Shift key while you drag the Left Indent marker to move it independently of the First Line Indent marker.

Adjusting Paragraph Spacing

You can add space between paragraphs by entering values in the Space Before and Space After option boxes in the Paragraph palette. If you insert space after one paragraph, that automatically adds space before the paragraph that follows it. So why does InDesign give you two separate controls? Suppose you're creating paragraph styles to apply formatting attributes to different kinds of paragraphs (as explained in Chapter 9). You might want a heading style to include Before and After spacing so that a larger spacing is used between headings and the text that appears above and below them (like the headings in this book, for example).

Here are a few tips about using Before and After spacing:

✔ Don't just use *carriage returns* (by pressing Return or Enter) to add space between paragraphs. That can really mess up your layout if a carriage return ends up at the top of a column. So use the Space Before and Space After controls to put space between paragraphs. After all, that's what they're for.

✔ The Space Before and Space After controls add space only *between* paragraphs. That means you can't add space before a paragraph at the top of column or text block using the Space Before option. If you want to add space before a paragraph at the top of a column or text block, increase the leading of the first line of the paragraph, as explained in Chapter 7.

✔ Like first line indents, Before and After spacing are commonly used to distinguish the beginning and ends of paragraphs. Each is an acceptable method, but don't use first line indents and Before or After spacing at the same time. Using both is overkill, so choose one or the other.

✔ If you want to separate text onto two lines without creating a paragraph break, press Shift+Return on the Mac or Shift+Enter under Windows.

Controlling paragraph breaks

In addition to adding space between paragraphs, you can control how paragraphs break across columns, pages, and text frames using the options in the Keep Options dialog box, shown in Figure 8-7. To display the dialog box, choose Keep Options from the Paragraph palette menu.

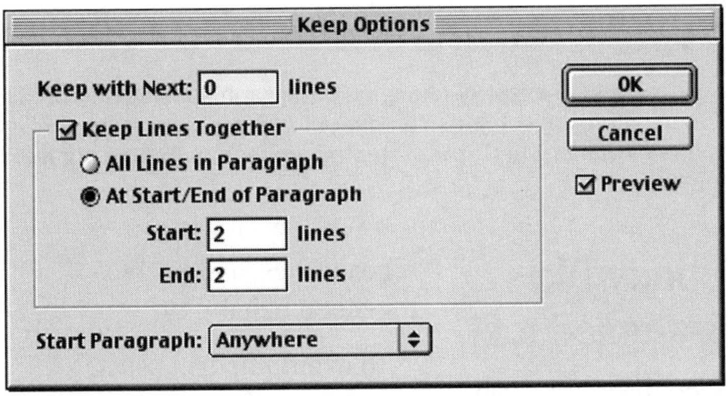

Figure 8-7:
Use the
settings in
this dialog
box to con-
trol how
paragraphs
break.

Keep Options

Keep with Next: 0 lines

☑ Keep Lines Together
  ○ All Lines in Paragraph
  ● At Start/End of Paragraph
    Start: 2 lines
    End: 2 lines

Start Paragraph: Anywhere ▲▼

OK

Cancel

☑ Preview

In publishing, letting the first or last line of a paragraph go solo at the bottom or top (respectively) of a column or page is a big no-no. When the offending line is the last line of a paragraph, it's called a *widow*; when it's the first line, it's an *orphan*. It's equally horrible to let a heading end up all alone at the bottom of a page. Fortunately, you can avoid these kinds of earth-shattering disasters using the Keep Options settings:

✔ To ensure that the last line of a paragraph stays with one or more lines above it, enter a number of lines (up to 5) in the Keep with Next option box. You can also use this option to keep a heading with the paragraph that follows it.

✔ If you want to prevent a paragraph from breaking at all, click on the Keep Lines Together check box and select the All Lines in Paragraph radio button.

✔ To set the minimum number of lines that can appear at the beginning or end of a paragraph, select the At Start/End of Paragraph option and enter a number of lines in the Start option box, or End option box, or both. For example, if you enter a Start value of 2 and the selected paragraph falls at the end of a page, InDesign keeps at least the first two lines of the paragraph at the bottom of the page before it breaks. If it can't fit at least two lines at the bottom of the page, InDesign pushes the entire paragraph over to the next page.

✔ From the Start Paragraph pop-up menu, choose the In Next Column option to force a paragraph to the next text frame or column within a text frame. Choose On Next Page to force the paragraph to the first column or text frame on the next page. If you choose Anywhere, which is selected by default, InDesign starts the paragraph where it naturally would appear.

To preview the effects of any changes you make in the Keep Options dialog box, select the Preview check box.

Aligning text in neighboring columns

One possible side-effect of changing paragraph spacing and breaks is that text in neighboring columns can get out of whack, as shown in Figure 8-8. In fact, lots of things can throw off text alignment, including big headlines and graphics.

Figure 8-8:
Use the
Align to
Baseline
Grid option
to correct
misaligned
text across
columns.

Nobody likes misaligned text.

In fact, many folks have reported that reading documents in which the baselines of text in neighboring columns don't line up can cause eye strain,

headaches, and lead to general irritability.

To avoid imposing such maladies on innocent readers, you'd best learn to use the Align to Baseline Grid feature in the Paragraph palette.

Fortunately, you can bring text back into alignment by aligning it to the baseline grid. Just follow these steps:

1. **Jot down the leading value used for the text.**

   Remember, the leading value is displayed in the Character palette.

2. **Note the location of the first baseline of your body copy.**

   The easiest way to do this is to ⌘-drag (Mac) or Ctrl-drag (Windows) a guide from the horizontal ruler and align it with the baseline of the first line of text in your body copy. Then note the Y value in the Transform palette.

   You can display the Transform palette by choosing Window⇨Transform or by pressing F9.

3. **Choose File⇨Preferences⇨Grids.**

   The Grids panel of the Preferences dialog box appears, as shown in Figure 8-9. The top part of the dialog box includes settings for the Baseline Grid.

4. **In the Increment Every option box, enter the leading value from Step 1.**

   For example, if the leading value is 14 points, type **p14** in the option box. This tells InDesign how far apart to place the grid lines.

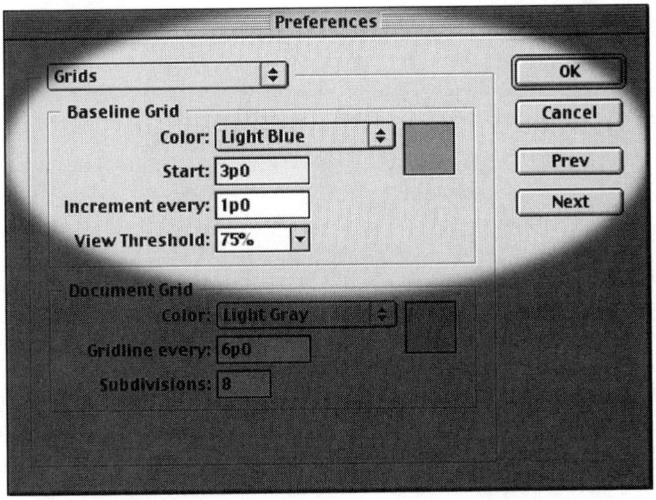

Figure 8-9:
Set up your
baseline
grid in this
dialog box.

5. **In the Start option box, enter the value from Step 2 and then press Return or Enter.**

   By default, InDesign starts the baseline grid 3 picas (or ½ inch) from the top of the page. But you want the baseline grid to begin at the first baseline of your body copy so that text will align properly.

6. **Select each paragraph that contains misaligned text and click on the Align to Baseline Grid option in the Paragraph palette.**

   Now your paragraphs are all nicely balanced.

To display the baseline grid on-screen, choose View⇨Show Baseline Grid. Alternatively, you can press ⌘+Option+apostrophe (') on the Mac or Ctrl+Alt+apostrophe (') under Windows. If the baseline grid doesn't appear, choose a lower value from the View Threshold pop-up menu in the Text panel of the Preferences dialog box. While you're there, you can also change the color of the grid lines by choosing a new color from the Color pop-up menu. Or double-click on the color swatch next to the pop-up menu and choose a color from the system color picker.

Giving Paragraphs Rules

One way to make a paragraph, or a group of paragraphs, stand out from surrounding text is to add a line (called a *rule*) above or below it. To do so, select one or more paragraphs and choose Paragraph Rules from the Paragraph palette menu to display the dialog box shown in Figure 8-10.

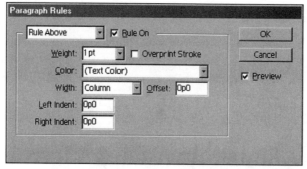

Figure 8-10:
Use the
settings in
this dialog
box to add
rules above
or below
paragraphs.

First, select the Preview check box so you can see how your changes look before you apply them. Then click on the Rule On check box. Choose Rule Above or Rule Below from the pop-up menu at the top of the dialog box to specify whether you want to create a rule above or below the selected paragraph. The rest of the options work as follows:

- ✔ **Weight:** This option specifies the thickness of the rule, measured in points. Choose a preset value from the pop-up menu or enter a value in the option box.

- ✔ **Overprint Stroke:** We discuss overprinting in Chapter 11, but here's what you need to know for now: Select this check box if the rule will be printed over another color and you want the two colors to mix. If you don't want the rule color to mix with the background color, leave this option turned off.

- ✔ **Color:** This option lets you apply a color to the rule. The only colors available in the pop-up menu are those listed in the Swatches palette. To learn how to add colors to the Swatches palette, see Chapter 11.

- ✔ **Width:** Choose Column or Text from this pop-up menu to set the rule to span the entire column width or the width of the paragraph, respectively.

- ✔ **Offset:** The value in this option box determines the vertical position of the rule. Higher values move the rule farther away from the paragraph; smaller values move it closer.

- ✔ **Left Indent:** Enter a value in this option box to set a left indent for the rule.

- ✔ **Right Indent:** This option box lets you set a right indent for the rule — like you needed us to tell you that.

When you're happy with your paragraph rules, press Return or Enter to make them permanent. Well, semipermanent really. You can always go back and modify them later.

Dropping Down Caps

An easy way to add a little extra visual appeal to your document is to begin each story with a *drop cap*, which is the first letter of a story lowered into the following one or more lines of text. Creating a drop cap is simple work using the controls in the Paragraph palette. Just click in a paragraph, and in the Drop Cap Lines option box, enter the number of lines you want the drop cap to fill. If you enter 3, for example, InDesign adjusts the size of the first letter in the selected paragraph, aligns its baseline to the baseline of the third line, and adjusts the space between the drop cap and all adjacent characters. Figure 8-11 shows a drop cap of three lines.

Figure 8-11:
Creating
drop caps is
a breeze
using the
controls
in the
Paragraph
palette.

W|e all loved the Seventies. Except for those unfortunate souls who weren't alive back then. And those more unfortunate souls who were. But the rest of us, well, we just couldn't get enough.

You can also create drop caps with more than one character. In the Drop Cap Characters option box, simply enter the number of characters you want to drop. To further add to the effect, you can resize, skew, or change the font of drop cap characters using the controls in the Character palette, as explained in Chapter 7.

One character formatting attribute you're likely to want to apply is kerning. Suppose you have optical or metrics kerning turned on and you apply a drop cap to a paragraph in which the first word is *We* — like we did in Figure 8-11. When the letters *W* and *e* are aligned along their baselines, as they are normally, a fair amount of kerning is applied (–34, for example) to bring them closer together. When you apply the drop cap, the letters *W* and *e* are no longer aligned along their baselines but the kerning value remains the same, which might cause them to look too scrunched. The solution? Manually kern the letters apart.

When you kern between a drop cap and a subsequent character, InDesign kerns all the lines affected by the drop cap. This is convenient because it means you can kern without disrupting the vertical alignment of the drop cap lines.

The Joys of Hyphenation

Together with justification, hyphenation is one of the most important factors in determining how your text looks. You see, hyphenation gives InDesign more opportunities to create even spacing across lines of type. By hyphenating words at the ends of lines, InDesign can achieve more consistency between the number of characters on each line in a paragraph.

As you'll soon see, InDesign sports the smartest hyphenation controls of any page-layout program around. But before you can put them to work, you need to make sure automatic hyphenation is turned on, as it is by default. If there's a check mark in the Hyphenate check box in the Paragraph palette, you're good to go. If not, click on the check box to enable it.

The battle of the composers

So what's so great about the way InDesign hyphenates words? The answer is the Adobe Multi-line Composer, which is located in the Paragraph palette menu and turned on by default. Other page-layout programs, including QuarkXPress and PageMaker, can consider only one line of type at a time when determining how to adjust spacing (justification) and hyphenate words to create a line break. But the Multi-line Composer lets InDesign look ahead several lines in a paragraph when determining the best possible line breaks. This allows InDesign to make more optimal spacing and hyphenation choices. In other words, you get more evenly spaced text with fewer hyphens.

InDesign doesn't completely discard the old ways, however. If you choose Adobe Single-line Composer from the Paragraph palette menu, InDesign uses the traditional one-line-at-a-time approach to determining line breaks. When applied to large chunks of text, the Single-line Composer usually produces inferior results, as demonstrated in Figure 8-12. But for small bits of text, such as headlines and captions, it's perfectly acceptable.

You can customize how the Multi-line Composer works by choosing File⇨Preferences⇨Composition to display the Composition panel of the Preferences dialog box, as shown in Figure 8-13. The following options are at your fingertips:

  ✔ To specify the number of lines you want the Multi-line Composer to consider when determining line breaks, enter a value between 3 and 30 in the Look Ahead option box.

  ✔ You can also specify the maximum number of possible break points the Multi-line Composer can consider for each line by entering a value between 3 and 30 in the Consider up To option box.

✔ If you want InDesign to alert you to less-than-ideal hyphenation and justification situations in your text, select the H&J Violations check box. When this option is selected, any text with compositional problems is highlighted on-screen in yellow.

Figure 8-12:
The Single-line Composer can result in uneven spacing and frequent hyphenation (left), whereas the Multi-line Composer produces more evenly spaced paragraphs with fewer hyphens (right).

So you passed the first test and you're feeling pretty proud of yourself. Possibly, you forgot that David Soul—famous from TV's *Starsky and Hutch*—sang "Don't Give Up on Us." And very likely, no one ever brought it to your attention that the song writing team of Murray & Callander who gave us "Billy, Don't Be a Hero" also penned "The Night Chicago Died." (Wow, lightning really does strike twice!) But you knew what you needed to know to get through the quiz. And now, thanks to us, you can't get those ghastly tunes out of your head.

So you passed the first test and you're feeling pretty proud of yourself. Possibly, you forgot that David Soul—famous from TV's *Starsky and Hutch*—sang "Don't Give Up on Us." And very likely, no one ever brought it to your attention that the song writing team of Murray & Callander who gave us "Billy, Don't Be a Hero" also penned "The Night Chicago Died." (Wow, lightning really does strike twice!) But you knew what you needed to know to get through the quiz. And now, thanks to us, you can't get those ghastly tunes out of your head.

Figure 8-13:
Specify settings for the Multi-line Composer here.

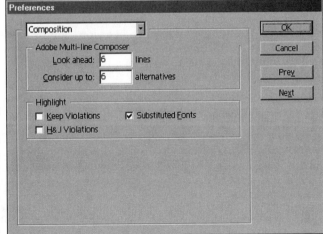

Preferences

Composition

Adobe Multi-line Composer
Look ahead: 6 lines
Consider up to: 6 alternatives

Highlight
☐ Keep Violations   ☑ Substituted Fonts
☐ H&J Violations

OK
Cancel
Prev
Next

Controlling hyphenation

To tell InDesign how you want it to hyphenate your text (whether it's using the Multi-line Composer or the Single-line Composer), select a paragraph and choose Hyphenation from the Paragraph palette menu. The Hyphenation dialog box appears, as shown in Figure 8-14.

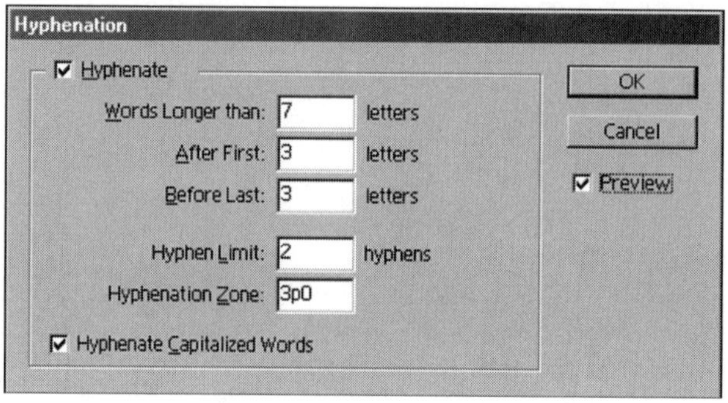

Figure 8-14:
Choose your hyphenation settings in this dialog box.

Here's how the options work:

- First, select the Preview option so you can check out how different settings look on-screen.

- Small words aren't good candidates for hyphenation. For example, you probably wouldn't want to hyphenate the word *un-do* because it would look weird. To specify the minimum number of letters a word must have to be eligible for hyphenation, enter a value in the Words Longer Than option box.

- The After First and Before Last options let you specify how many letters must appear before and after a hyphen in a word. For example, using the default values of 3 and 3, InDesign can hyphenate the word *cha-grin* because both the first and last syllables are at least three letters long.

- Enter the maximum number of consecutive lines that can end with a hyphen in the Hyphen Limit option box. The default setting of 2 is a safe bet, but some typographer types say 3 is acceptable as well.

- The Hyphenation Zone setting applies to only the Single-line Composer. The value you enter in this option box creates an invisible zone along the right margin of each text block beyond which a word cannot break. The general gist is this: Larger zones equal fewer hyphens and smaller zones equal more.

- If you don't want capitalized words to be hyphenated, click on the Hyphenate Capitalized Words check box to disable it.

You can also prohibit InDesign from hyphenating certain words, such as proper names. Just select the word and choose No Break from the Character palette menu or enter a discretionary hyphen at the beginning of the word. The No Break command also applies to groups of words. For example, if you want to keep first initials together with a last name (as in *B.B. King*), just select all the text and choose the No Break command.

You can quickly switch to the Character palette by pressing ⌘+T on the Mac or Ctrl+T under Windows. And you can enter a discretionary hyphen by pressing ⌘+Shift+hyphen (-) on the Mac or Ctrl+Shift+hyphen (-) under Windows.

Hanging Punctuation and Characters

Making hyphens, other punctuation, and even edges of characters hang slightly outside column edges can give your text a cleaner look. Some page-layout programs call this *hanging punctuation*. But because InDesign lets you hang characters too, it had to come up with a new name — *optical margin alignment*. To apply optical margin alignment to an entire story (you can't apply it to a single paragraph), select a text block or click in a paragraph and choose Type⇨Story to display the Story palette, as shown in Figure 8-15.

Figure 8-15:
Use the
Story palette
to turn on
optical
margin
alignment.

See the option that looks a heck of a lot like the drop cap controls in the Paragraph palette? Well, enter the point size of your body text there. Then select the Optical Margin Alignment check box and watch your punctuation and edges of characters such as *W* and *A* hang. Figure 8-16 shows a text block before and after enabling optical margin alignment.

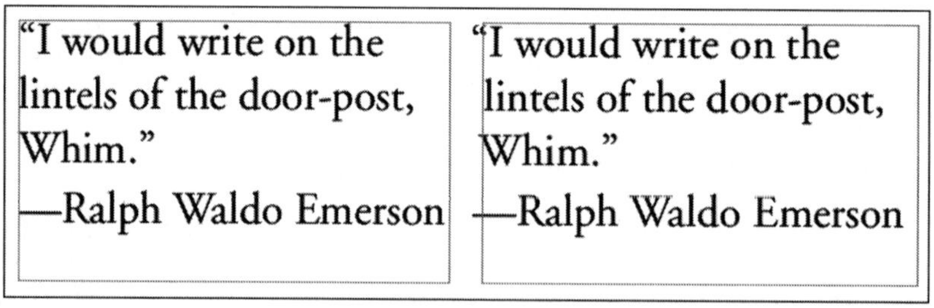

Figure 8-16:
Normal text
(left) and
with optical
margin
alignment
turned on
(right).

> "I would write on the lintels of the door-post, Whim."
>
> —Ralph Waldo Emerson

> "I would write on the lintels of the door-post, Whim."
>
> —Ralph Waldo Emerson

To really see how this gives your column a cleaner appearance, try turning off guides and text frame edges by pressing ⌘+semicolon (;) and ⌘+H, respectively, on the Mac or Ctrl+semicolon and Ctrl+H, respectively, under Windows.

Chapter 9

Making Files with Style

*W*e're no soothsayers, but we do know what you're doing right now — reading this page in this book. There's a pretty good chance you're also sitting in front of your computer, maybe even working on an InDesign document. Now, imagine yourself taking your dog for a walk in the park, meeting some friends for cocktails after work, or just vegging out in front of the TV watching *Seinfeld* reruns. Sounds good, doesn't it? Okay, now picture yourself formatting all the headings and captions in a 100-page document, one at a time, one after another. Hmm.

Here's the deal: Formatting text can be fun, but it can also be time-consuming and mind-numbingly repetitive. The bottom line is that we'd rather do loads of other things — and the faster we can finish our formatting, the sooner we can do them.

In this chapter, we explore InDesign's number one timesaving formatting feature — *styles*. You find out what they are and how to use them to make your job faster and easier, so you can get back to more important stuff, such as napping.

What Are Styles and Why Should I Care?

A *style* is simply a bunch of text formatting attributes — such as font, type size, type style, indents, and leading — grouped together and given a name. The big benefit of styles (also called *style sheets*) is that you can apply multiple formatting attributes with just a single mouse-click or keystroke.

For example, suppose you decide you want all your headlines to be 18-point Bodoni, centered, with 3 pica spacing before the headline. You can create a style called Headlines with all those attributes. Then instead of choosing the font, type size, type style, alignment, and before spacing for each headline in your document one by one, you can just apply the Headlines style to all the heads and let InDesign do the formatting for you.

You can create one style for headlines, one for captions, one for body text, and one for each level of subhead. And there's no reason to stop there — you can create a different style for every kind of text element in your document. In fact, you might want to follow this general rule: If you use an element more than once in a document, create a style for it.

Not only do styles save you time, they ensure consistency and prevent mistakes. When you use styles, you don't have to worry about forgetting to change the type size in a caption or the alignment of a headline. You simply apply the appropriate style and you're all set. Suddenly, your whole world gets much simpler.

Paragraph versus character styles

InDesign offers two kinds of styles: paragraph styles and characters styles. *Paragraph styles* are those that apply to an entire paragraph, such as the styles we just described. They include both paragraph and character formatting attributes and they affect all the lines in a selected paragraph. So, for example, you can create a paragraph style that specifies alignment, before and after spacing, and drop caps (paragraph formatting attributes), as well as font, type size, and leading (character formatting attributes) for an entire paragraph.

Character styles can contain only character formatting attributes and can be applied to a single character, a word, a sentence, or a selected range of text. They're useful for creating run-in heads and numbered lists where the number is set in a different font or style than the text, or for emphasizing certain words using italics or some other type style.

Paragraph styles and character styles work together. So after you apply a paragraph style to a paragraph, you can apply one or more character styles to individual words or characters within that paragraph. The left example in Figure 9-1, for instance, shows a numbered list formatted using a paragraph style that specifies the font, type size, type style, indents, tabs, and so on. In the right example, we applied a character style to the numbers to change their font.

Figure 9-1:
You can
apply a
paragraph
style to a
paragraph
(left) and
then apply a
character
style to
individual
characters
(right).

1 This is the first item in this numbered list. More items are sure to follow because one item does not a numbered list make.

2 Well, here we are at number two. We're guessing that there will be at least one more item.

3 Now it's a crap shoot. Will there be another number? Doesn't look like it.

1 This is the first item in this numbered list. More items are sure to follow because one item does not a numbered list make.

2 Well, here we are at number two. We're guessing that there will be at least one more item.

3 Now it's a crap shoot. Will there be another number? Doesn't look like it.

Meeting the Styles palettes

In InDesign, paragraph styles and character styles live in two separate palettes sensibly called Paragraph Styles and Character Styles. These palettes serve as command central for working with styles. They share a common palette window and are nearly identical in appearance and function. To display the Paragraph Styles palette, choose Type⇨Paragraph Styles or press F11. To bring up the Character Styles palette, choose Type⇨ Character Styles or press Shift+F11. Figure 9-2 shows both palettes with a few styles displayed.

Figure 9-2:
The
Paragraph
Styles and
Character
Styles
palettes.

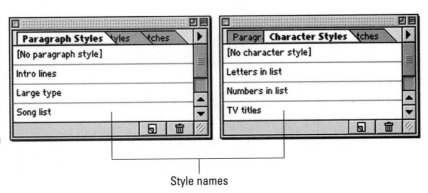

Style names

Making Styles

InDesign gives you several ways to get styles into your document. You can import them with text from your word processor, create them based on existing text or styles in your document, or define them from scratch. The following sections explain all.

Importing styles from word processors

When you import text from a word processor such as Microsoft Word or WordPerfect and select the Retain Format option in the Place dialog box, InDesign automatically loads any styles defined in the word processor document in the Paragraph Styles and Characters Styles palettes. Little disk icons to the right of the style names flag imported styles. You can then edit the styles if you like, as explained later in this chapter.

If an imported style has the same name as an existing style in your InDesign document, the imported style is overridden and the existing InDesign style prevails.

Defining styles

The process of creating new styles is pretty much the same for paragraph and character styles. We'll show you the ropes by walking you through the creation of a new paragraph style. Press F11 to display the Paragraph Styles palette, and follow these steps:

1. **From the Paragraph Styles palette menu, choose New Style.**

   The dialog box shown in Figure 9-3 appears. If an existing style was selected in the Paragraph Styles palette, its name appears in the Based On pop-up menu. If you selected text before choosing the New Style command, all formatting attributes for the selected paragraph appear in the Style Settings box, which means InDesign will base the new style's characteristics on it. If no existing style or text was selected, the Based On pop-up menu displays [No paragraph style] and no formatting attributes appear in the Style Settings box.

   By the way, although you can create a style from scratch, it's much easier to base it on an existing style or selected text. If you're creating the very first style in a document, for example, you're better off formatting some text with the attributes you want the style to have. Then select the text and choose New Style from the palette menu.

2. In the Style Name option box, enter a name for the new style.

If you want to base the new style on an existing style, choose that style from the Based On pop-up menu. Basing one style on another has several advantages. First, it gives you a head start on specifying the formatting attributes of the new style. More importantly, the two styles become linked. The existing style becomes a *parent* style and the new style becomes a *child* style. If you need to make changes to those styles later, you can simply update the parent style and the matching attributes in the child change as well.

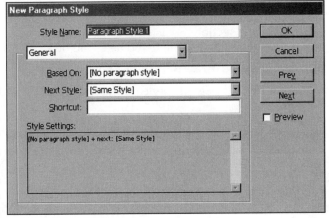

Figure 9-3:
Create new paragraph styles using the options in this dialog box.

3. Choose the Next Style.

To specify that your new style is always followed by another existing style, choose that style from the Next Style pop-up menu.

Using the Next Style option can be a real time-saver. For example, you can specify that a headline is always followed by normal body copy or that a sidebar head is always followed by the style used for sidebar text. This means you don't have to manually select these styles.

4. In the Shortcut option box, enter a keyboard shortcut if you like.

On the Mac, press ⌘, Option, or Shift (or any combination of them except ⌘+Shift) plus a number on the numeric keypad. Under Windows, press Ctrl, Shift, or both plus a number on the numeric keypad. You can also use the Alt key in combination with the Ctrl and Shift keys, but you can't simply press Alt plus a number. Why? As Chapter 6 explains, under Windows, pressing the Alt key plus a number is reserved for inserting special characters, such as bullets and curly quotes.

For these keyboard shortcuts to work, you need to use the numbers on the numeric keypad and numbers lock must be turned on.

5. From the pop-up menu below the Style Name option box, choose the kinds of formatting attributes you want to specify for your new style.

The options in this pop-up menu lead to panels containing the various paragraph and character formatting options described in Chapters 7 and 8. You can navigate between the panels using the Prev and Next buttons.

If your new style is based on an existing style or selected text, the settings in the dialog boxes will reflect the characteristics of the Based On style or selected text. Otherwise, they will display InDesign's default character and paragraph formatting settings.

Read the upcoming section "Stylish style tips" for some advice on setting attributes for headlines, numbered lists, and other styles.

6. When you're finished, press Return or Enter.

Well done! Your new paragraph style now appears in the Paragraph Styles palette.

You can create a character style in much the same way. Just press Shift+F11 to display the Character Styles palette and choose New Style from the palette menu to bring up the New Character Style dialog box, shown in Figure 9-4. This dialog box and the New Paragraph Style dialog box have only a couple differences. First, no Next Style option appears because character styles don't follow each other in your documents the way that paragraph styles do. Second, only character formatting options are accessible from the pop-up menu below the Style Name option box. The reason for this is pretty obvious: Paragraph formatting attributes don't apply to character styles.

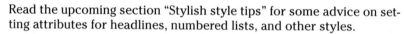

Figure 9-4:
Use this
dialog box
to create
new
character
styles.

Stylish style tips

Now we don't mean to beat a dead donkey, but this point bears repeating: The more formatting you can apply using styles, the less time the whole process will take. No, we're not covertly selling time management seminars and we're not advocates of some secret society of styles. Our only motive is to get you home from work in time to catch all those *Seinfeld* reruns. To that end, the following list contains a few pointers for getting the most out of your styles:

✔ When you define paragraph styles for headlines, always assign a Keep with Next value in the Keep Options panel of the New Paragraph Style dialog box (shown in Figure 9-5) to make sure they appear with the first two or three lines of text that follow them. You should also use the Keep with Next option when defining figure and caption styles to make sure those elements never get separated at the top or bottom of a column or page. (You can also specify before and after spacing for headlines, figures, and captions, as described next.)

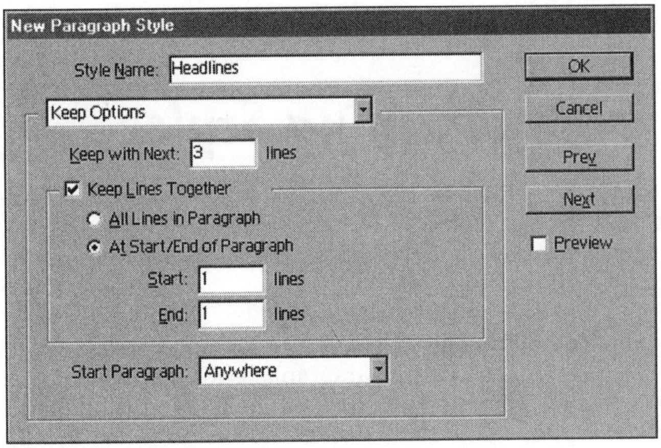

Figure 9-5:
Specify
Keep with
Next values
for headlines
and other
styles in the
Keep
Options
panel of the
New
Paragraph
Style dialog
box.

New Paragraph Style	
Style Name: Headlines	OK
Keep Options ▼	Cancel
Keep with Next: 3 lines	Prev
☑ Keep Lines Together	Next
○ All Lines in Paragraph	
◉ At Start/End of Paragraph	☐ Preview
Start: 1 lines	
End: 1 lines	
Start Paragraph: Anywhere ▼	

✔ If your document includes bulleted and numbered lists, create separate styles for the first, last, and in-between bulleted or numbered items. Then set before and after spacing for the styles in the Indents and Spacing panel of the New Paragraph Style dialog box (shown in Figure 9-6) to set the lists apart from surrounding text.

For example, for numbered lists, you might create styles called *Num List First, Num List Last,* and plain old *Num List.* Now let's say you use 9-point after spacing for your body text paragraphs. To set off the first numbered item from the preceding text, you could assign before spacing of 3 points to the Num List First style to increase the total spacing to 12 points. Then you could assign after spacing of 9 points to separate the first and second numbered items by the usual amount of space. For the regular Num List style, just specify after spacing of 9 points. Finally, for the Num List Last style, assign 12 points of after spacing to set it off from the text that follows.

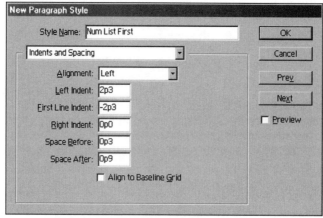

Figure 9-6:
Use before and after spacing for numbered and bulleted list styles here.

Applying and Modifying Styles

Okay, you've gone to the trouble to create oodles of styles — so now what? Well, lots. This section and the next take you on a whistle-stop tour of all the amazing things you can do with your new arsenal of styles. Our first stop is the scenic town of Apply:

✔ To apply a paragraph style, select a paragraph with the type tool and click on a style name in the Paragraph Styles palette. If you assigned a keyboard shortcut when you defined the style, you can just press the shortcut keys to apply it. All formatting attributes of the selected paragraph are changed to those defined in the style.

Well, almost all. Neither paragraph nor character styles override less common formatting attributes such as superscript, subscript, underline, strikethrough, and baseline shift. And by default, applying a paragraph style does not override any character styles applied within the selected paragraph. If you *want* to override character styles when applying a paragraph style, press Option on the Mac or Alt under Windows while you click on the paragraph style name.

Let's say you italicized some text for emphasis and now you want to apply a paragraph style to the paragraph containing that text. You don't want to lose your italics, so what do you do? Press and hold Option+Shift on the Mac or Alt+Shift under Windows and click on the name of the style you want to apply in the Paragraph Styles palette. InDesign applies the style but preserves your existing formatting.

Applying paragraph styles is a lot like applying formatting from the Paragraph palette. You don't need to actually select an entire paragraph to select it. Just click somewhere in the paragraph with the type tool.

✔ To apply a character style, select one or more characters with the type tool and click on the style name in the Character Styles palette. If the style has a keyboard shortcut, you can press that instead.

For keyboard shortcuts for styles to work, numbers lock must be turned on.

✔ You can change the paragraph or character style applied to selected text by clicking on a different style name in the Paragraph Styles or Character Styles palette.

Another big benefit of using styles in your documents is that you can edit and otherwise modify them. When you change the characteristics of a style, all the text with that style applied is automatically updated to match the new properties of the style. This can save you loads of time when you need to make formatting changes to long documents. The following list explains a bunch of ways you can work with existing styles:

✔ To edit an existing style, make sure no text is selected and then double-click on a style name in the Paragraph Styles palette to display the Modify Paragraph Style Options dialog box. Double-click on a style name in the Character Styles palette to display the Modify Character Style Options dialog box. You can also display these dialog boxes by selecting a style name and choosing Style Options from the palette menus. Either way, these dialog boxes offer the same options as the New Style dialog boxes discussed previously in this chapter. Just change the settings for the style as desired and press Return or Enter.

✔ To make a copy of an existing style, choose Duplicate Style from the Paragraph Styles or Character Styles palette menu. You'll be greeted by the Duplicate Paragraph Style or Duplicate Character Style dialog box, respectively, which offer the same options as the New Style dialog boxes.

✔ To update a style based on the formatting of selected text, choose Redefine Style from the Paragraph Styles or Character Styles palette menu.

✔ If you see a plus sign (+) after a style name, the selected paragraph or text has been modified from the style's settings. For example, perhaps you italicized some text or applied a baseline shift to create a fraction. The plus sign is nothing to worry about; it's there to let you know that you applied extra formatting.

✔ If you see a little disk icon after a style name, you imported the style from a word processor, as we mentioned previously.

✔ If you want to delete a style, select it and click on the trash can icon in the bottom-right corner of the palette. When you're asked to confirm your choice to delete it, click on the Yes button. You can also drag a selected style to the trash can icon or choose Delete Styles from the palette menu. If the deleted style was applied to text, the formatting of that text doesn't change; it's just no longer associated with a style.

✔ To delete styles you aren't using in your document, choose Select All Unused Styles from the Paragraph Styles or Character Styles palette menu and then choose Delete Styles.

✔ You can also remove a style from selected text by choosing [No Paragraph Style] or [No Character Style] from the Paragraph Styles or Character Styles palettes. As with deleted styles, the text's formatting doesn't change, but it's no longer associated with the style.

✔ If you want to use styles you've created in another InDesign document, choose Load Paragraph Styles or Load Character Styles from the Paragraph Styles or Character Styles palette menu, respectively. Or choose Load All Styles from either palette menu. This displays the Open a File dialog box. Double-click on the file whose styles you want to import. InDesign chugs away for a few seconds, and then the imported styles appear in the palettes.

Finding and Changing Styles

Suppose you format a 50-page report and send it to your boss for review. She says it looks great except for that funky font you used for notes. Gotta change 'em to the regular body text font. Fortunately, you used styles, so it's no big deal. You simply press ⌘+F on the Mac or Ctrl+F under Windows to display to the Find/Change dialog box, and then click on the More button in the lower-right corner. The dialog box expands to reveal additional options, as shown in Figure 9-7.

Now all you need to do is find all instances of the offending style and replace them with the body text style. Here's how:

1. **Under Find Style Settings, Click on the Format button.**

   The Find Format Settings dialog box appears, as shown in Figure 9-8.

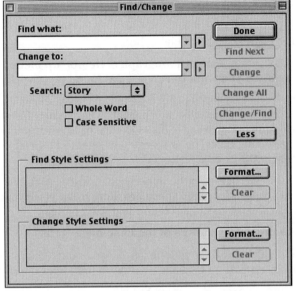

Figure 9-7:
The
expanded
version
of the
Find/Change
dialog box.

Figure 9-8:
Choose the
style you
want to find
and replace
in this
dialog box.

2. From the Character Style or Paragraph Style pop-up menu, choose the name of the style you want to find.

The pop-up menus contain all the styles in your document. After you select a style, click OK or press Return or Enter to return to the Find/Change dialog box. The style you just selected now appears in the Find Style Settings box.

3. Under Change Style Settings, click on the Format button.

This displays the Change Format Settings dialog box, which looks just like the Find Format Settings dialog box.

4. From the Character Style or Paragraph Style pop-up menu, choose the name of the style you want to replace the found style with.

If you want, you can even replace a paragraph style with a character style or vice versa, although that's probably not something you'll do too often. After you choose a style, press Return or Enter to return to the Find/Change dialog box. The style you just selected now appears in the Change Style Settings box.

You'll also see two icons on the upper-right corners of the Find What and Change To option boxes. These are there to let you know you've specified that the formatting of found text will change.

5. Find and change all instances of the lame duck style.

Use the Find Next and Change buttons as explained back in Chapter 5. Or click on Change All to find and change all instances in one fell swoop.

6. Click on Done or press Return or Enter.

That was a breeze, huh?

Part III
Pictures on the Paper Trail

The 5th Wave   By Rich Tennant

"Of course graphics are important to your project, Eddy, but I think it would've been better to scan a _picture_ of your worm collection."

In this part . . .

After the Part II intro, we really shouldn't be making any more analogies. But this time, we think we've come up with a winner: Graphics are a publication's signposts. Makes sense, right? After all, when you see a picture on a page, you know what's coming. A picture conveys the basic sense of an article. It points you toward salient text. It provides you with a quick insight into something that might otherwise take several paragraphs to explain. And it tells you how many tons your rig can weigh and still pass over a bridge.

The following chapters go into detail on these and other kinds of graphics. You'll discover how to import photographs and line art, create simple shapes and page ornaments directly inside InDesign, make portions of an image transparent, and wrap words around a piece of artwork so that the text and graphics merge to form a cohesive whole. We bandy about terms such as *miter limit* and *clipping paths*, but we also include graphics to show you what the heck we mean. This is the kind of give and take between images and text that InDesign is famous for.

What about that old saw about a picture being worth a thousand words? Well, we ran a few pages of picture-only content in front of our focus group, and it didn't play well, particularly one sequence: man, tree, squirrel, tall building, slippery banana peel, very small rock. Obviously, it's a discussion of cropping, but several panelists thought they were supposed to press the Ctrl key when we — quite plainly — meant Shift. Go figure. That's when we came up with this signpost idea. Stop. Ped Xing. Fines Doubled for Speeding. McDonald's, Exit 3 Miles. Loosest Slots in Reno. Black Puppy Lost, Responds to Winky. Suddenly, everything started making sense again. Which is why — for our own sakes — we make no further mention of this in the chapters ahead.

Chapter 10

Graphic Language about Graphic Imagery

· ·

In This Chapter

▶ Importing graphics into your layout

▶ Scaling, cropping, and other adjustments

▶ Creating inline graphics

▶ Drawing lines and shapes

▶ Rotating, skewing, and flipping graphics

▶ Duplicating and positioning graphics

▶ Working with the Layers palette

· ·

*I*n this chapter, we get graphic about graphics. But you don't need to round up the kids and scoot them out of the room. This is, after all, a family book. And if books were rated like movies, we're confident that this little tome would be rated G. Well, then there's the introduction to Part II — okay, definitely nothing more than a soft PG.

Sure, we occasionally throw around terms such as *shear* and *stroke*, but our subject matter is really quite innocent. In fact, the only thing you're likely to find shocking about this chapter is how much you discover about importing, creating, positioning, and manipulating graphics in your InDesign documents.

Getting outside Graphics inside InDesign

Just as you create most of your text in a word processor and then import it into InDesign, you'll create most of your graphics in other programs and then import them into your documents. If you haven't spent much time pushing pixels and vying with vectors, the next few sections will bring you up to speed on the two basic kinds of graphics and their most common file formats. Oh, and in case that last sentence threw you for a loop, we explain what the heck pixels and vectors are in the very next paragraph.

All graphics live in one of two camps: bitmap or vector. *Bitmap graphics* (also simply called *bitmaps* or *images*) are composed of tiny square dots called *pixels. Vector graphics* (also called *drawings* or *illustrations*) are made up of independent lines. When printed small, a bitmap appears smooth. But when enlarged, you can see the individual pixels, as shown in Figure 10-1. A vector graphic, however, appears smooth when printed small or large, as demonstrated in Figure 10-2.

Figure 10-1:
Bitmap
images
appear
smooth
when
printed
small (left),
but look
jagged
when
enlarged
(right).

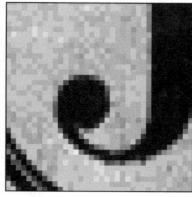

Figure 10-2:
Vector
graphics
look smooth
at any size.

You might be thinking, "If vector graphics look smooth at any size, why should I ever use bitmaps?" The reason is bitmap images are better for representing continuous color transitions, in which one color gradually changes into another. Because such color transitions are the norm in the real world, bitmaps are ideal for photographs. To create a bitmap image, you need to use an *image-editing program,* such as Adobe Photoshop or Corel Photo-Paint, or a *painting program,* such as Painter from MetaCreations.

Vector graphics are great for high-contrast artwork, which can range from schematic drawings (such as charts, maps, and logos) to cartoons (such as Shenbop). The lines and shapes that make up a vector drawing are known collectively as *objects*. For this reason, the programs used to create vector artwork such as Adobe Illustrator, Macromedia FreeHand, and CorelDraw — are often said to be *object oriented,* but we prefer the more down-to-earth term *drawing programs*.

To avoid driving you batty with too many technical terms, from here on out we generally call bitmap graphics *images* and vector graphics *drawings*. We reserve the term *graphic* to refer to both.

Yeah, but what format should I use?

After you create an image or drawing for use in a document, you need to save it in a file format that InDesign can import. Fortunately, InDesign can import just about any major graphics format. Here's the lowdown on some of the most common ones:

- ✔ **TIFF**, or Tagged Image File Format, is the most widely supported image format across both Macs and PCs, and it offers compression options to reduce the size of images on disk. If you were to use only one format for images in your documents, TIFF should be it.

- ✔ **JPEG** is named after the group of folks who created it, the Joint Photographic Experts Group. Like TIFF, JPEG is widely supported across platforms and applications. JPEG uses a lossy compression scheme, which means it sacrifices image quality to produce smaller file sizes. It's a good format for large photographs and other images that include gradual color transitions. It's also a common format for images posted on the World Wide Web.

- ✔ **GIF**, or Graphics Interchange Format, was developed specifically for trading images online through CompuServe. GIF images use the same type of compression as TIFF, but they are limited to 256 colors. Unless your document's images are destined for the Web, you can pretty much ignore the GIF format.

- ✔ **PCX,** originally designed for PC Paintbrush, is one of the oldest and most widely supported image formats on the PC, but in recent years its popularity has waned. If you need to use PCX images, go ahead. But if you have a choice, use TIFF instead.

- ✔ **BMP**, or Windows Bitmap, is the native format for the little paint program that comes with Windows. Like PCX, you can use BMP images if you need to. But if possible, use TIFF instead.

✔ **EPS**, or Encapsulated PostScript, is far and away the best format for saving drawings to import into InDesign. Any quality drawing program can create EPS files, and they're simply the most reliable format for printing. The only potential drawback is that non-PostScript printers can't print EPS files. But chances are, your document will ultimately be printed on a PostScript device, so this shouldn't cause any problems.

✔ **DCS**, or Desktop Color Separation, is a variant of EPS in which each of the four colors used in high-end printing — cyan, magenta, yellow, and black — has its own file. A fifth file that coordinates the other four is what gets imported into InDesign. DCS is the format of choice for full-color professional graphics.

✔ **PICT**, which stands for Macintosh Picture, was designed by Apple more than ten years ago. You can save both drawings and images in PICT format, but it's not the best format for either. You're much better off using TIFF for images and EPS for drawings.

Here's a feature that's sure to warm the hearts of Photoshop and Illustrator users everywhere. You can also import native Photoshop and Illustrator files, which carry the extensions PSD and AI, respectively. Doing so offers two big advantages. First, you save time and disk space by not having to save a TIFF or EPS version of a graphic. Second, if you need to go back and edit the graphic after importing it, which you can do using InDesign's Edit Original command (discussed in Chapter 16), any layers in your graphic remain intact.

Importing graphics into your layout

Importing graphics into InDesign documents is a lot like importing text from a word processor. You use the File⇨Place command. Make sure nothing in your document is selected by pressing ⌘+Shift+A on the Mac or Ctrl+Shift+A under Windows. Then follow these steps:

1. **Choose File⇨Place.**

   You can also press ⌘+D on the Mac or Ctrl+D under Windows. This displays the Place dialog box, shown in Figure 10-3. Locate the file you want and click on it. If you don't see the file you're looking for, try going back to the application you used to create it and resaving the file in one of the formats mentioned in the preceding section.

2. **Select the Show Import Options check box, if desired.**

   If you select the Show Import Options check box, you'll see a dialog box with import options specific to the type of graphic you are placing when you press Return or Enter. We discuss when and why you might want to specify import options later in this chapter and in Chapter 12.

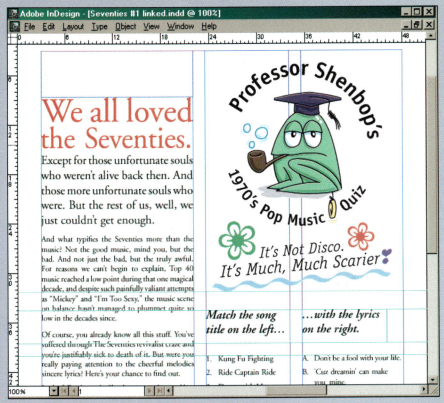

Color Plate 4-1: Professor Shenbop's first Seventies music quiz shows items snapped to margin, column, and ruler guides. The two text frame edges in the left and right columns that don't align to guides are not within the snap zone we defined in the Preferences dialog box.

Color Plate 11-1: The color sliders and option boxes in the New Color Swatch dialog box reflect the color values in the Color palette.

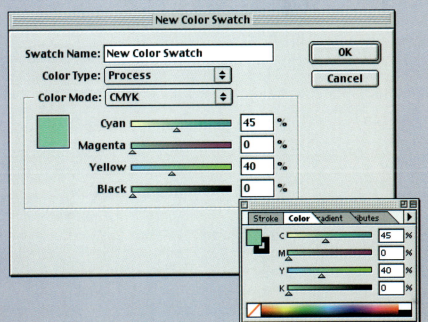

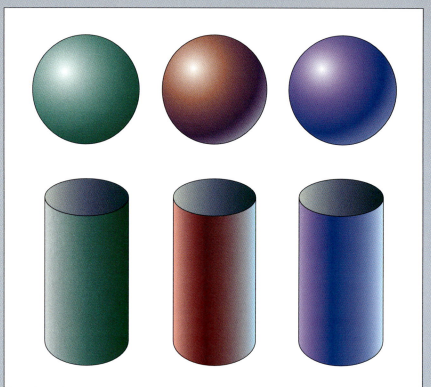

Color Plate 11-2: We used gradient fills to give these balls and cylinders an air of three-dimensionality. All of the balls sport radial gradients, and the cylinders are filled with linear gradients. We achieved slightly different effects using two-color (left), four-color (middle), and five-color (right) gradient fills.

Color Plate 11-3: The results of applying different color stop and midpoint marker positions on the gradient fade bar.

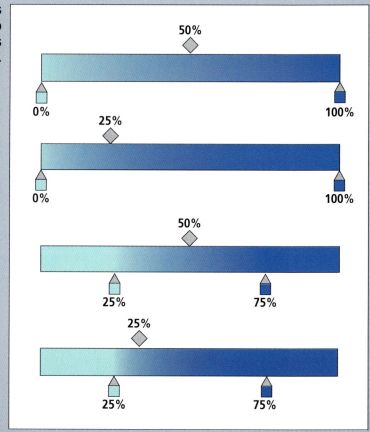

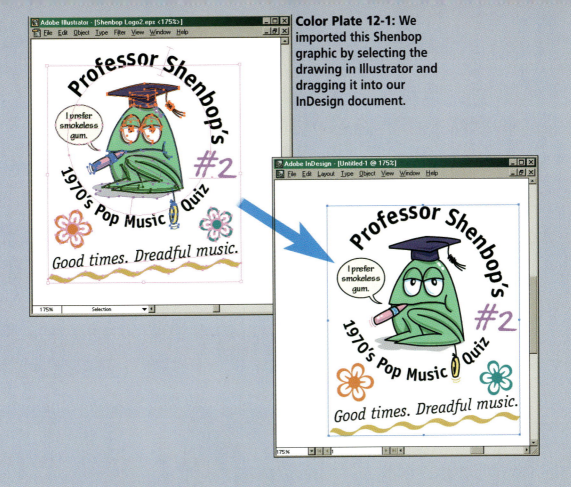

Color Plate 12-1: We imported this Shenbop graphic by selecting the drawing in Illustrator and dragging it into our InDesign document.

Color Plate 12-2: Because we dragged and dropped Shenbop from Illustrator, as illustrated in Color Plate 12-1, we can edit the paths that compose our friend by dragging points and control handles, as shown here.

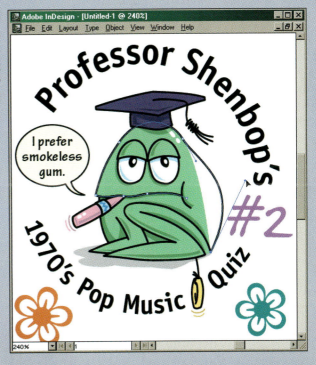

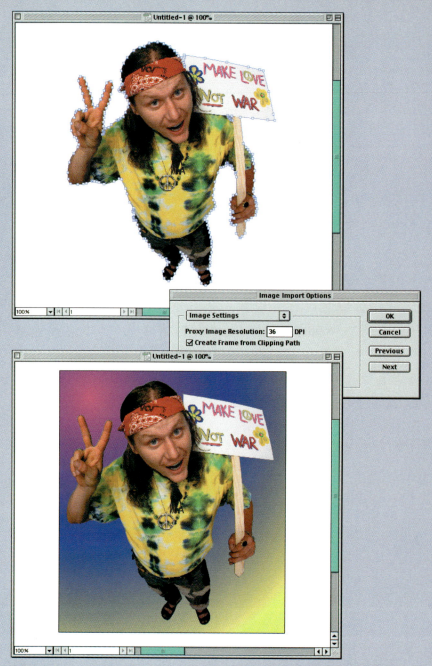

Color Plate 12-3: InDesign lets you preserve clipping paths saved with TIFF, EPS, or native Photoshop files when you import them. Just select the Create Frame from Clipping Path option in the Import Options dialog box. In this example, we imported the hippie guy with a clipping path (top) and placed him on a gradient background that seems to suit him (bottom).

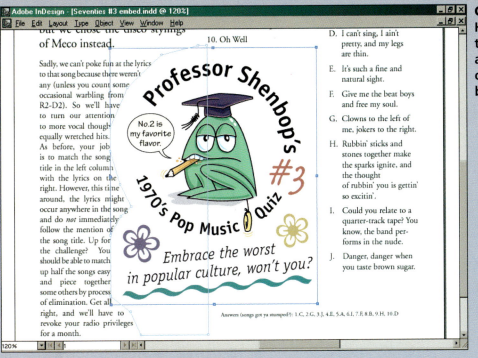

Color Plate 17-1: The cyan, magenta, and yellow separations (top row) take on greater detail when mixed with black (middle row). During the commercial printing process, the cyan ink is combined first with magenta, then with yellow, and finally with black (bottom row).

Color Plate 18-1: This shows an InDesign document (top) exported to HTML and viewed in Netscape Navigator (middle), and then exported to PDF and viewed in Acrobat Reader (bottom). Although InDesign does a nice job of preserving the positioning of page elements in the HTML file, colors shift and text and image quality are lost. The PDF document, however, preserves the layout, formatting, and colors of the original exactly.

Color Plate 20-1: InDesign lets you easily create some nifty type effects, such as fading text (top), type as an image (middle), and translucent type (bottom).

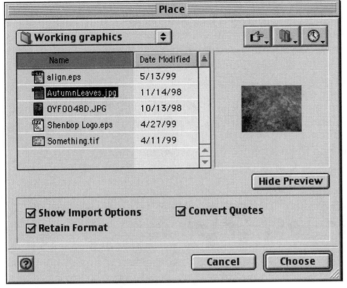

Figure 10-3:
Import
graphics
into your
document
using the
Place dialog
box.

3. **Press Return or Enter.**

   InDesign chugs away for a few seconds, and then you see a place cursor that looks like a paintbrush with an arrow in the upper-left corner.

4. **Click on the spot where you want to place the graphic.**

   InDesign places the upper-left corner of the graphic at the very spot you clicked on the page. Notice that the graphic is automatically surrounded by a *frame,* complete with handles — just like when you import and place text.

In addition to using the standard Place command, you can also drag and drop native Photoshop and Illustrator files directly into your document. Just drag the icon of a Photoshop or Illustrator file onto a page and release the mouse button.

Don't be alarmed if the graphic looks all choppy and blurry. That's simply because InDesign displays a low-resolution preview version, or *proxy,* of the graphic on-screen by default to help keep the file size of your document from getting too huge. The original graphic file has not been changed, so it will still print at full resolution.

But you don't have to accept InDesign's default graphics display settings. If you select Show Import Options in the Place dialog box when you import an image file (as just described), you can specify the resolution for the proxy image in the Image Import Options dialog box. You can also adjust how *all* graphics in your document are displayed by choosing File⇨Preferences⇨ General (or pressing ⌘+K on the Mac or Ctrl+K under Windows) to display the General panel of the Preferences dialog box. Then choose an option from the Display pop-up menu. Choose Full Resolution Images to display all graphics (including EPS files) at their full resolution. Choose Gray Out Images to prevent images from displaying at all.

For large documents with lots of graphics, you'll probably want to avoid full resolution display because it slows down the speed of your computer dramatically. In fact, you might want to gray out graphics when you're not working on them so you can move around your document and work with text faster.

Adjusting Your Graphics

Whatever size your graphic was in your drawing or painting program, that's the size at which it appears when placed in your layout. But the graphic doesn't have to stay that way. You can *scale* a graphic to make it bigger, smaller, thinner, fatter, taller, or shorter in a bunch of ways. You can also crop an image, move it around, and control the way it fits within its frame. If you're wondering how to do all these things, read on.

Making 'em bigger or smaller

To scale a graphic, click on it with the arrow tool to select it. Then use the graphic's frame handles, the scale tool, or the controls in the Transform palette — all of which are pictured in Figure 10-4.

Here's how they all work:

✔ To enlarge or reduce a graphic, ⌘-drag or Ctrl-drag a corner handle of the graphic's frame. Drag away from the graphic to make it bigger; drag toward it to make it smaller.

When you resize a bitmap image in InDesign, you are actually changing its resolution (the number of pixels per inch), which can result in a loss of image quality. Because InDesign isn't specifically equipped to monitor the effects of resizing on an image's resolution, you're better off not doing any significant scaling of images in InDesign. Instead, resize them in an image-editing program such as Photoshop.

✔ To scale a graphic horizontally, ⌘-drag or Ctrl-drag the handle on the left or right side of the graphic. Drag away from the graphic to make it fatter; drag toward the graphic to make it skinnier.

Scale tool   Origin Point

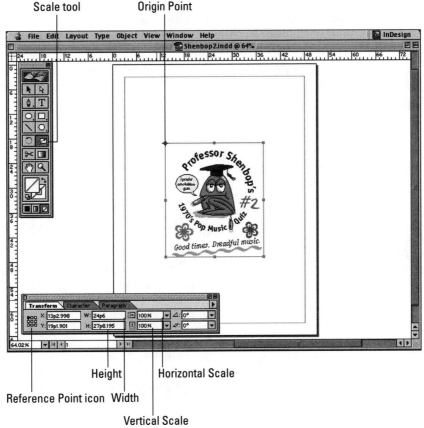

Figure 10-4:
Use the
frame
handles,
scale
tool, or
Transform
palette
controls to
resize a
graphic.

Height   Horizontal Scale

Reference Point icon   Width

Vertical Scale

> ✔ To scale a graphic vertically, ⌘-drag or Ctrl-drag a top or bottom handle. Drag in to make it shorter; drag away to make it taller.

> ✔ If you want to scale the graphic proportionally so that the horizontal and vertical proportions remain equal, press ⌘+Shift or Ctrl+Shift while you drag a handle.

> ✔ You can also scale a graphic using the scale tool, labeled in Figure 10-4. Click on the scale tool in the toolbox or press S to select it. An *origin point* appears on the upper-left corner handle of the graphic's frame, as shown in Figure 10-4, to establish a fixed point from which the graphic will be scaled. To position the origin point on another handle or in the center of the graphic, click on one of the nine little squares in the Reference Point icon on the left side of the Transform palette. You can also drag the origin point off the graphic to a new location anywhere in the document window.

After you set up your origin point, drag anywhere in the document window with the scale tool. InDesign resizes the graphic with respect to the point of origin. If you drag away from the origin, you enlarge the graphic. If you drag toward it, the graphic gets smaller.

Press F9 to display the Transform palette. And if you want the palette to appear vertically on-screen, choose Vertical Palette from the palette menu.

✔ You can scale a graphic by a specific percentage using the controls in the Transform palette. To change the horizontal scale, choose a preset percentage from the Horizontal Scale pop-up menu or enter a new value in the Horizontal Scale option box, labeled in Figure 10-4, and press Return or Enter. You can change the vertical scale in the same way: Choose a percentage from the Vertical Scale pop-up menu or enter a new value in the option box.

✔ Double-click the scale tool icon in the toolbox to quickly highlight the Horizontal Scale value.

✔ To change the horizontal and vertical scale proportionally, enter a value in the Horizontal Scale or Vertical Scale option box and press ⌘+Return or Ctrl+Enter. Alternatively, you can press ⌘ or Ctrl and choose a value from the horizontal or vertical scale pop-up menu.

If none of these options satisfy your craving to scale, try choosing Scale Content from the Transform palette menu. Then enter a value (in picas and points) in the Width or Height option box and press ⌘+Return or Ctrl+Enter. InDesign resizes the graphic proportionally based on the width or height value you entered.

Crop 'til you drop

Suppose that you import a graphic and then decide you want only a portion of it to be visible in your document. What do you do? Well, you crop it. In InDesign, cropping doesn't cut away parts of an image; it just hides the portions of the image you don't want to use.

To crop a graphic, simply select it with the arrow tool and drag one of the graphic's frame handles. Drag in toward the center of the graphic to crop it; drag away from the center to uncrop a previously cropped area.

Just like when you scale a graphic, the handle you drag determines whether the crop is horizontal, vertical, or diagonal. And pressing the Shift key while you drag makes the crop proportional.

If you're happy with the size of your cropped frame, but you want to show a different portion of the graphic, press A to select the hollow arrow tool. (It's next to the regular old arrow tool in the toolbox.) Then click on the graphic. A blue box appears around the cropped image, showing the outline of the entire graphic, hidden portion and all. Simply drag inside the image to reveal different areas of the graphic within the cropped frame.

By the way, InDesign calls the hollow arrow tool the direct selection tool. Call us simpletons, but we figure if it looks like a hollow arrow, call it a hollow arrow. So hollow arrow tool it is.

Cropping a graphic does not reduce its file size because, as mentioned, cropping only hides portions of an image. For this reason, if you need to do a lot of cropping, you should do it in your image-editing or drawing program and then re-import the graphics into your layout.

Making graphics and frames match

Suppose you crop a bunch of graphics, but then you change your mind and want to restore them all to full display. You could ⌘+Z or Ctrl+Z your way back through all your cropping operations or manually uncrop each image. But there's a faster way. Simply click on a graphic with the arrow tool to select it (or Shift-click to select multiple graphics) and choose Object⇨Fitting⇨Fit Frame to Content. You can also press ⌘+Shift+Option+V on the Mac or Ctrl+Shift+Alt+V under Windows. Either way, the graphic returns to its uncropped state.

Here are several other ways you can change how a graphic is displayed inside a frame:

✔ To resize a graphic so that it fits within a frame, choose Object⇨Fitting⇨Fit Content to Frame. Alternatively, you can press ⌘+Option+E on the Mac or Ctrl+Alt+E under Windows.

   If the graphic and frame have different proportions, choosing this command distorts the graphic, which is probably not what you want to do. To fit the graphic within the frame while maintaining its proportions, choose Object⇨Fitting⇨Fit Content Proportionally. You can also press ⌘+Shift+Option+E on the Mac or Ctrl+Shift+Alt+E under Windows.

✔ To center a graphic within a frame, choose Object⇨Fitting⇨Center Content or press ⌘+Shift+E on the Mac or Ctrl+Shift+E under Windows.

Giving a graphic a border

You can further adorn your graphics by giving them borders, which is kind of like framing a picture. Simply select a graphic with the arrow tool and choose Window⇨Stroke or press F10 to display the Stroke palette, shown in Figure 10-5. Then choose a value from the Weight pop-up menu in the Stroke palette to specify the size (in points) of the border. That's all there is to it.

Figure 10-5:
Use the
Stroke
palette to
add a
border
around a
graphic.

If you can't see the border after you apply it, try clicking outside the graphic to deselect it and then pressing ⌘+H on the Mac or Ctrl+H under Windows to hide frame edges. By default, the border appears black, but you can change it to just about any color you like, as explained in Chapter 11.

In general, it's a good idea to keep borders to 2 points or less. If you go much thicker, they may start to overwhelm your graphic and look clunky.

To find out more about working with the Stroke palette, read Chapter 11.

Putting Graphics Inline with Text

Sometimes you may want to insert a graphic, such as an icon or a symbol, within a text block so that it flows along with your text as you type. This type of graphic is called an *inline graphic* because it's positioned in line with characters of text, like the little microphone in the left column in Figure 10-6. Think of inline graphics as special characters that just happen to be pictures.

You can create an inline graphic in a couple of different ways. If you want to import a graphic directly into a text block, simply click with the type tool at the spot where you want the graphic to appear. Then import the graphic using the File⇨Place command as you normally would. InDesign places the graphic at the spot you clicked in the text block.

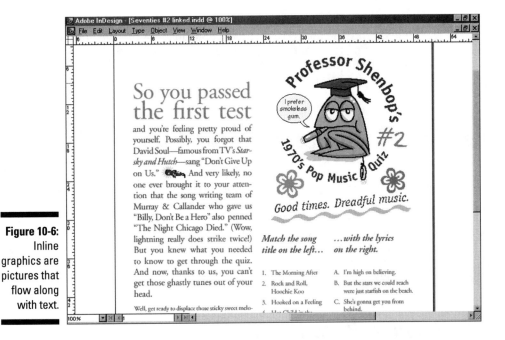

Figure 10-6:
Inline
graphics are
pictures that
flow along
with text.

To make an existing image or drawing an inline graphic, select it with the arrow tool and press ⌘+X on the Mac or Ctrl+X under Windows to cut it or press ⌘+C or Ctrl+C to copy it. Then click in a text block with the type tool and press ⌘+V on the Mac or Ctrl+V under Windows to paste the graphic.

After you create an inline graphic, you need to do some fine-tuning to make it fit nicely within your text.

✔ To change the size of an inline graphic, select it with the arrow tool and ⌘-drag or Ctrl-drag a handle to scale it as you would any graphic. ⌘+Shift-drag or Ctrl+Shift-drag to resize the graphic proportionally.

✔ You can crop an inline graphic just like any other graphic. Select the graphic with the arrow tool and drag a handle.

✔ To adjust the vertical position of the graphic in a line of type, select it with the arrow tool and drag or press the up and down arrow keys to nudge it up and down in 1-point increments. You can also drag with the type tool to select the graphic and then enter a value in the Baseline Shift option box in the Character palette.

If you're using the Auto leading option in the Character palette, adjusting the vertical position of an inline graphic can change the leading between the line above and below the line of type that includes the graphic. But the leading value in the Character palette won't reflect the change. So when working with inline graphics, it's best not to use Auto leading.

✔ To change the horizontal position of an inline graphic, you need to insert space using the spacebar or adjust spacing between the graphic and a neighboring text character by kerning. You can't select and drag the graphic with the arrow tool to change the graphic's horizontal position as you can to adjust its vertical position.

Drawing Graphics of Your Own

In addition to importing graphics created in other programs, you can create simple graphics using the drawing tools in InDesign. In this section, we explain how you can draw lines, boxes, circles, and other shapes.

Keep in mind that InDesign is a page-layout program and not a dedicated drawing application. So, if you need to create more complex, detailed illustrations — road maps, cartoons, and that sort of thing — use a drawing program such as Illustrator, FreeHand, or CorelDraw.

Laying down the line

One of the most useful graphic elements you'll create in InDesign is also the simplest: the straight line. Lines are handy as separators between stories in a document or rows in a table, as lead-ins for running heads, and for otherwise separating elements and enhancing the symmetry of a page.

To draw a straight line, click on the line tool in the toolbox (labeled in Figure 10-7) or press E to select it. Then click on the spot where you want the line to begin, press the Shift key, and drag to draw the line vertically, horizontally, or diagonally at a 45-degree angle.

Here are a few other things you need to know about working with lines:

✔ By default, InDesign gives your line a thickness of 1 point, but you can make it thicker or thinner by choosing a new option from the Weight pop-up menu in the Stroke palette, as described earlier in this chapter.

✔ When a line is selected with the arrow tool, the Width and Height options in the Transform palette change to a Length option, as shown in Figure 10-7. To change the length of a selected line, you can either drag one of its endpoints with the arrow tool or enter a new value in the Length option box.

✔ To move a line, select it with the arrow tool. Then click on the line segment (not the endpoints) and drag it to a new position. You can also enter new values in the X and Y option boxes in the Transform palette to position the line more precisely.

Line tool

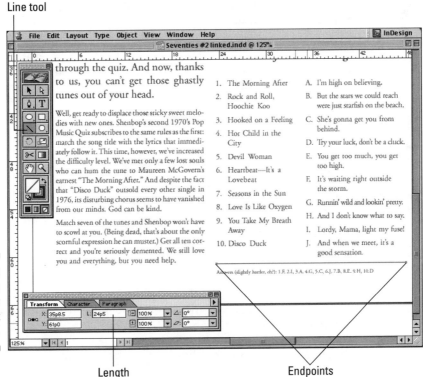

Figure 10-7:
Use the line
tool to draw
straight
lines.

Length

Endpoints

Drawing simple shapes

InDesign offers up three tools for creating basic shapes: the rectangle tool, the ellipse tool, and the polygon tool. In addition to combining them to create simple drawings, you can also use shapes to create attractive frames for other graphics, as discussed in Chapter 12. But we're getting ahead of ourselves. First, let's take a look at how to make some shapes:

- ✔ To draw a rectangle, select the rectangle tool (it's the one that looks like a rectangle, imagine that), click, and drag. The spot where you clicked becomes one corner of the rectangle and the point where you release the mouse button becomes the opposite corner. If you want to create a square, press Shift while you drag.

- ✔ You can draw an oval in the same way using the ellipse tool. Simply select the tool that looks like an ellipse, click, and drag. To create a circle, Shift-drag with the tool.

You can quickly select the rectangle tool by pressing the M key or the ellipse tool by pressing L.

✔ To create a multisided shape, use the polygon tool (that's N for you keyboard wizards). By default, dragging with the tool will create a six-sided shape, but you can change that by double-clicking on the tool's icon in the toolbox. The Polygon Settings dialog box appears, as shown in Figure 10-8. Enter a value between 3 and 100 in the Number of Sides option box.

Figure 10-8:
Change the settings for the polygon tool in this dialog box.

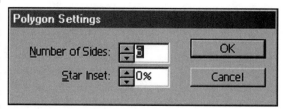

✔ If you want to create a star, enter a Star Inset value to specify the length and thickness of the star's spikes. Higher values create longer skinnier spikes; lower values make shorter fatter ones. The Number of Sides value determines the number of points on the star. Figure 10-9, for example, shows three stars with the same number of points but different Star Inset values.

Figure 10-9:
A six-pointed star with Star Inset values of 25 percent (left), 50 percent (middle), and 75 percent (right).

✔ To draw a polygon or a star with sides of equal length, press Shift while you drag.

✔ If you draw a polygon or a star and then decide you want to change the number of sides or points, you're out of luck. Unfortunately, you can't apply the settings in the Polygon Settings dialog box to existing shapes.

Just as with an imported graphic, you can scale a selected shape using its frame handles, the scale tool, or the controls in the Transform palette. If you need a refresher, flip back to the "Making 'em bigger or smaller" section earlier in this chapter.

Transforming Graphics

If circles and squares aren't exactly your idea of happenin' graphics, you might want to spend some time with InDesign's transformation features. With nothing more than a couple tools in the toolbox and a few controls in the Transform palette, you can rotate, skew, and flip any graphic into, well, something a whole lot more interesting than a plain old circle or square.

Just in case you care, scaling is a transformation as well. But we describe scaling near the beginning of this chapter, instead of here, because resizing is likely to be one of the first things you do to a graphic.

You may not know it yet, but you already have a pretty good idea about how to rotate and skew your graphics. You see, both these transformations work just like scaling. Your first order of business? Select a graphic with the arrow tool and follow along:

- ✔ You can rotate a graphic using the rotate tool, labeled in Figure 10-10. The rotate tool works just like the scale tool but it rotates rather than resizes the selected graphic. Click on the rotate tool (or press R), click on the Reference Point icon to establish an origin point, and drag in the direction you want to rotate the graphic. To constrain the angle of rotation to 45-degree increments, press Shift while you drag.

- ✔ To skew a graphic, select the shear tool by clicking and holding on the scale tool to display a flyout menu. Then move your cursor over the shear tool (it's the one on the right) and release your mouse. Or skip all that and just press the S key. Either way, click on the Reference Point icon to establish an origin point, and drag. To constrain the skew to 45-degree increments, press Shift while you drag.

  By the way, *shear* is the word InDesign uses to mean skew or slant. But since the word shear is more likely to make you think of a giant pair of scissors than skewing or slanting a graphic, we generally avoid it.

- ✔ To rotate or skew a graphic from the Transform palette, enter the angle of rotation or skew in the Rotation option box or Shear option box, respectively (both are labeled in Figure 10-10). You can also choose a value from the Rotation or Shear pop-up menus.

TIP

✔ Press and hold the Option or Alt key while you drag with the rotate or shear tool to duplicate a graphic while you rotate or skew it. This little trick is especially useful when you're creating patterns or special effects. Read the next section to find out more about duplicating.

✔ Double-click the rotate tool icon in the toolbox to quickly highlight the Rotation value. Double-click the shear tool icon to highlight the Shear value.

✔ You can rotate a selected graphic by 180 degrees, 90 degrees clockwise, or 90 degrees counterclockwise by choosing the appropriate Rotate command from the Transform palette menu.

To flip an object is to create a mirror image of it. InDesign lets you flip a selected graphic horizontally, vertically, or both by choosing Flip Horizontal, Flip Vertical, of Flip Both from the Transform palette menu.

Rotate tool

Shear tool

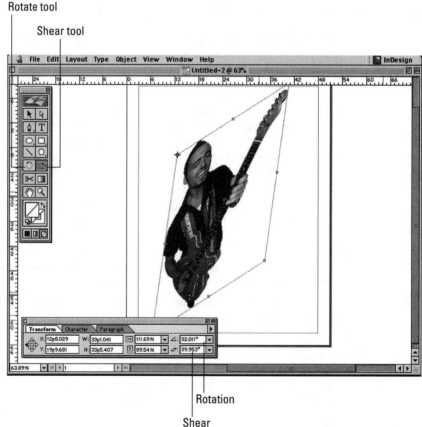

Figure 10-10: We rotated and skewed this rock star to the brink of discomfort.

Rotation

Shear

Because seeing is believing, Figure 10-10 shows a graphic that has been rotated and skewed. We thought about flipping it as well, but the poor guy looks uncomfortable enough as it is.

We have a sneaking suspicion the guy in Figure 10-10 doesn't really play guitar at all. That aside, this image, and several others that appear throughout the book, come from a company called Corbis, which offers a great variety of images you can purchase from their Web site at *www.corbis.com.*

Duplicating and Positioning Graphics

You can move, copy, and delete a graphic in the same way you do a text block. Select the graphic with the arrow tool and drag or enter new X and Y coordinates in the Transform palette to move it, press ⌘+C or Ctrl+C to copy it, or press Backspace or Delete to delete it. But you have other options for duplicating and positioning graphics. (Actually, the techniques described in this section apply to text blocks as well, but they're more likely to come in handy when you're working with graphics.)

Makin' copies

In addition to copying and pasting, you can duplicate a selected graphic in any of the following ways:

- Press and hold the Option key on the Mac or the Alt key under Windows while you drag a graphic with the arrow tool. Each time you release the mouse button, the graphic is duplicated. Shift+Option-drag or Shift+Alt-drag to constrain your duplicates to 45-degree angles.

- Select a graphic and choose Edit⇨Duplicate to create a duplicate that is slightly offset from the original. You can also press Shift+Option+D on the Mac or Shift+Alt+D under Windows.

- Enter a new X or Y value in the Transform palette and press Option+Return on the Mac or Alt+Enter under Windows to create a duplicate of a selected graphic at the specified location.

- To create many duplicates of a selected graphic across rows or columns on a page, choose Edit⇨Step and Repeat to display the dialog box shown in Figure 10-11. (You can also press ⌘+Shift+V on the Mac or Ctrl+Shift+V under Windows.) Enter the number of duplicates you want to make in the Repeat Count option box. Then specify how much horizontal and vertical space you want between each duplicate in the Horizontal Offset and Vertical Offset option boxes, respectively, and press Return or Enter. Figure 10-11 shows the result of duplicating a polygon 20 times using the default offset values in the Step and Repeat dialog box.

Aligning and distributing objects

So now you know how to duplicate graphics, but what if you just want to line up (*align*) and evenly space (*distribute*) a bunch of graphics (which are *objects,* after all) on a page? You choose Window⇔Align or press F8 to display the Align palette, as shown in Figure 10-12. Then select the objects that you want to align or distribute and click on an icon in the palette. InDesign adjusts the objects immediately.

The first three icons in the top and bottom rows let you align or distribute horizontally; the second three icons let you align or distribute vertically. For example, click on the first icon in the top row to align selected objects along their left edges, click on the second icon to center align them, and click on the third icon to align their right edges. Click on the fourth icon in the top row to top align objects, click on the fifth to center align them, and click on the sixth to bottom align them.

InDesign aligns to the most extreme of the selected objects. For example, if you right align objects, they all line up with the rightmost object.

Use the Distribute Objects options to evenly space three or more selected objects. These icons offer the same horizontal and vertical options as the Align Objects icons.

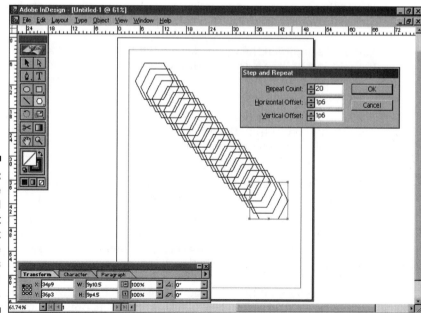

Figure 10-11:
Use the Step and Repeat dialog box to duplicate graphics across a page.

Figure 10-12:
Use this
palette to
line up and
evenly
space
selected
objects.

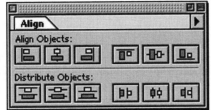

Graphic protection: grouping and locking

Imagine that you've whipped together a bunch of ovals and rectangles and
other shapes into the spitting image of your Great Aunt Edith. And now you
want to move the image off the pasteboard of that brochure you're working
on and place it in a letter to your brother Joe — it'll definitely get a few
laughs.

Of course, you want to be sure that Aunt Edith's nose doesn't get shifted out
of whack when you cut and paste her into your letter. And God forbid you
accidentally leave behind an ear. Fortunately, you can alleviate such concerns
by grouping all of the shapes together into a single object. Simply drag over
the shapes that comprise Aunt Edith with the arrow tool to select them and
press ⌘+G on the Mac or Ctrl+G under Windows. You can also choose
Object⇨Group. Now you can select Aunt Edith with a single click and then
move, cut, copy, and paste her with ease. If you need to go back and make
changes to individual shapes within the group, simply click on them with the
hollow arrow tool. To break up the group, select it with the arrow tool and
choose Object⇨Ungroup. You can also press ⌘+Shift+G on the Mac or
Ctrl+Shift+G under Windows.

After you have Aunt Edith positioned right where you want her, you can lock
her in place so she can't be moved accidentally. To lock a graphic, select it
and press ⌘+L or Ctrl+L or choose Object⇨Lock Position. You can still select
the object and make certain modifications, such as applying a stroke or a fill
as discussed in Chapter 11, but you can't move it, resize it, or perform most
other alterations. To unlock a locked object, choose Object⇨Unlock Position
or press ⌘+Option+L on the Mac or Ctrl+Alt+L under Windows.

Abiding by federal law, InDesign does not discriminate based on content. In
other words, you can group and lock text blocks, too.

Changing the stacking order

When you create a drawing composed of many objects, such as Aunt Edith, those objects are stacked on top of each other. The first shape you draw is at the back, the next one is on top of it, and so on. This hierarchy of objects is called the *stacking order,* and it determines which object is on top when two items overlap. You can change the position of any object in the stacking order by selecting it and choosing one of the following commands in the Object⇨Arrange submenu:

✔ Bring to Front moves the object to the top of the stack. Press ⌘+Shift+right bracket (]) on the Mac or Ctrl+Shift+right bracket under Windows.

✔ Bring Forward brings the object up one layer in the stacking order. Press ⌘+right bracket (]) on the Mac or Ctrl+right bracket under Windows.

✔ Send Backward moves the object one layer back in the stacking order. Press ⌘+left bracket ([)on the Mac or Ctrl+left bracket under Windows.

✔ Send to Back sends the object to the back of the stack. Press ⌘+Shift+left bracket ([) on the Mac or Ctrl+Shift+left bracket under Windows.

You can select through a stack by ⌘-clicking or Ctrl-clicking with the arrow tool. Each ⌘-click or Ctrl-click selects the next object down in the stack.

Sorting Graphics on Layers

If your document contains a lot of graphics, you might want to separate them onto *layers*. Layers are like those transparencies your teachers used to show you stuff on overhead projectors. Who could say what was on them? With the lights off and all, you were sound asleep. Anyway, you can create objects on any layer and see through all the layers in front of it and in back of it, like transparencies. You can create, edit, move, lock, and delete layers using the Layers palette, shown in Figure 10-13, which you can display by choosing Window⇨Layers or pressing F7.

Here's a quick overview of how the palette works:

✔ By default, a document contains only one layer. To create a new layer at the top of the Layers palette, click on the New Layer button or choose New Layer from the palette menu. If you do the latter, the Layer Options dialog box greets you. Enter a name and choose a color for the layer, if desired, and then press Return or Enter.

✔ When you select an object, the layer on which it's contained is high-lighted in the Layers palette. You'll also see a small selection marker on the right side of the layer name, indicating that objects on that layer are selected. To move selected objects from one layer to another, drag the selection marker to a new layer. If you want to copy selected objects from one layer onto another layer, press and hold the Option or Alt key while you drag the selection marker.

✔ The highlighted name in the Layers palette represents the active layer on which newly created objects will reside. To change the active layer, click on a different layer name.

✔ Option-click or Alt-click on a layer name to select all objects on that layer.

✔ To change the order of layers, drag a layer name up or down in the Layers palette. The top layer is in front and the bottom layer is in back.

✔ To hide a layer so that its contents aren't displayed on the screen, click on the eyeball in the View icon box. To redisplay it, click on the View icon box again.

✔ If you want to protect the contents of a layer from being changed, click on the Lock box next to the layer name. Click on the Lock box again to unlock the layer.

✔ To delete a layer, click on it and drag it to the trash can icon.

You might want to put your drawings on one layer and your images on another. That way, if you want to see an EPS or AI file at full resolution, you can turn off the image layer first so you don't have to wait for all the images to load at full resolution.

Figure 10-13:
Use the
Layers
palette to
keep
graphics
organized.

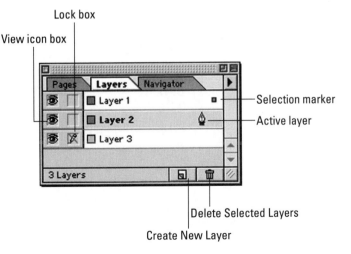

Lock box

View icon box

Selection marker

Active layer

Delete Selected Layers

Create New Layer

Chapter 11

The Fill, the Stroke, the Color, the Drama

*P*icture yourself lying on a beach in Tahiti. Your stomach is *filled* with sweet pineapple and the waiter who delivered your last daiquiri just *stroked* your ego by complimenting you on the golden brown *color* of your tan. Go ahead, close your eyes if it helps.

Not being trained psychiatrists, that's about as far as we can take you on that little visualization exercise, without putting ourselves in danger of being sued. However, we can help you treat your documents to similar pleasures. In this chapter, you discover how to fill and stroke elements to give them texture and depth and generally make them look good. You also find out how to create and apply colors that can turn a pale, sun-starved document into a multicolored masterpiece.

Fill 'Em Up, Stroke 'Em Down

Remember all those shapes you created back in Chapter 10? A square here, a circle there, maybe the occasional starburst. Each of those objects is made up of an outline and an interior, which appear black and white, respectively, by default. The thickness of an outline is called the *stroke*. In addition to changing the thickness (or weight) of the stroke, you can change its color. You can also apply a color to the interior of a shape by assigning it a *fill*.

When filling and stroking, you aren't limited to just shapes. You can fill and stroke text blocks and type, too. The top example in Figure 11-1, for instance, shows a selected text block containing one word. The bottom example shows the same text block with a stroke and fill applied. It's a whole new word.

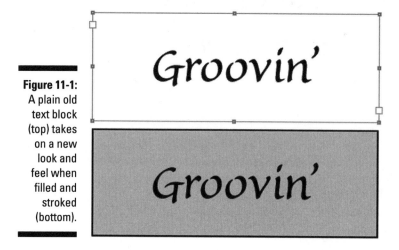

Figure 11-1:
A plain old text block (top) takes on a new look and feel when filled and stroked (bottom).

The primary fill and stroke controls reside in the toolbox. To apply a fill or a stroke to a shape, a text block, or type using the toolbox controls, follow these steps:

1. **Select the element that you want to fill or stroke.**

   You can use the arrow tool or hollow arrow tool to select shapes and text blocks. Use the type tool to select text.

2. **Specify whether you want to apply a fill or a stroke.**

   If you want to apply a fill, click on the Fill icon in the toolbox, labeled in Figure 11-2. To apply a stroke, click on the Stroke icon, also labeled in the figure. You can press the X key to toggle between the two icons.

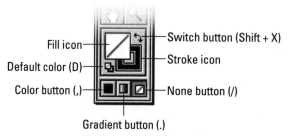

Figure 11-2:
The fill and stroke controls in the toolbox.

Fill icon

Default color (D)

Color button (,)

Switch button (Shift + X)

Stroke icon

None button (/)

Gradient button (.)

3. **Click on the Color or Gradient button in the toolbox.**

   To apply the last used color (which is black, by default), click on the Color button or press the comma (,) key. To apply the last used gradient, click on the Gradient button or press the period (.) key. A *gradient* is a fill pattern that fades from one color into another, as explained later in this chapter.

   If you change your mind after applying the color or gradient, click on the None button or press the slash (/) key to remove the fill or stroke. To swap the fill and stroke colors, click on the Switch button in the toolbox or press Shift+X.

4. **Edit the color of the fill or stroke as desired.**

   You can specify a color using the Color palette, as explained in the next section.

Creating Cool Colors

Unless you read and remembered our quick Color palette drill in Chapter 7, you were likely unimpressed with that last little exercise. After all, filling and stroking an object with black isn't all that exciting. You need color. Well, as luck would have it, the next few sections show you how to use the Color palette to whip up colors that would make an art professor drool.

Choosing a color model

Before you can get down and dirty with the Color palette, you need to know a thing or two about how colors work. Remember learning how to mix colors back in grade school? Start with the three primaries — red, blue, and yellow — and mix them together to make any other color.

Commercial printers also create colors by mixing primaries, only the primary colors are different. They use a light greenish-blue color called *cyan*, a hot pink color called *magenta*, a yellowish color called, well, *yellow*, and one of our Halloween favorites, *black*. Cyan, magenta, yellow, and black are called *process colors* and are known collectively as the CMYK color model. (Why *K* for black? Printers call black the *key* color.) The CMYK color model is designed for representing colors on paper, so if your document is bound for print, it's the color model of choice.

Computer monitors, television screens, and other viewing devices display colors on-screen by transmitting mixtures of red, green, and blue light. For this reason, RGB (red, green, and blue) is the best color model to use for documents that will be distributed on the Web, CD-ROM, or any other type of on-screen viewing.

InDesign offers a third color model called Lab. Whereas RGB is the color model of light and CMYK is the color model of the printed page, Lab is device independent. In other words, the Lab color model is designed to accurately represent colors regardless of whether they're displayed on-screen or in print. The downside to Lab is that it's more difficult to work with than RGB and CMYK. The primary reason InDesign includes Lab color is to support Photo CD images edited in Lab mode in Photoshop. Unless you're working with Photo CD images and you're a real color maven, just ignore the Lab color model.

Mixing colors in the Color palette

Now that you've suffered through that basic bit of color theory, you're ready to start mixing up some colors for your strokes and fills. First, you need to display the Color palette, shown in Figure 11-3, by choosing Window➪Color or pressing F6.

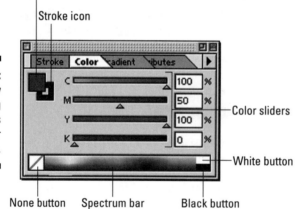

Figure 11-3: Create new colors using the controls in the Color palette.

Fill icon

Stroke icon

Color sliders

White button

None button   Spectrum bar   Black button

If you're familiar with Illustrator, you'll be able to define and apply colors in InDesign with your eyes closed. But the process bears little resemblance to the way things work in PageMaker or QuarkXPress. So if you've logged many hours, months, or years with either of those programs, you might want to stretch your legs, grab a cup coffee, and pay extra close attention to our jaunt down color lane.

The options in the Color palette work as follows:

✔ Like the toolbox, the Color palette contains a Fill icon and a Stroke icon. Click on the Fill icon if you want to apply your new color to the fill of a selected object. Click on the Stroke icon to apply the color to a selected object's outline. The active icon (Fill or Stroke) is the one that appears in the foreground, overlapping the other. In Figure 11-3, for example, the Fill icon is active.

✔ To create a color, choose a color model from the Color palette menu. (Remember, use CMYK if your document is destined for print; use RGB if it will be viewed on-screen.) Click on the spectrum bar along the bottom of the palette to choose an approximate color. To modify the color, drag the little triangles on the slider bars or change the values in the option boxes to the right of the slider bars, and then press Tab, Return, or Enter. InDesign automatically updates the fill or stroke of a selected object with the new color.

✔ You can also ⌘-drag or Ctrl-drag across the spectrum bar to adjust all the slider bars at once.

✔ With CMYK, the higher the values, the darker the color. For example, 100 percent cyan plus 50 percent magenta plus 100 percent yellow makes a dark green. If you bump up the magenta to 100 percent, you get black. With RGB, it's just the opposite — the higher the values, the lighter the color. Experiment a little to get a feel for how it works.

✔ If the Fill icon is active, you can quickly change the color of the Stroke icon by Option-clicking or Alt-clicking on a color in the spectrum bar. If the Stroke icon is active, Option-clicking or Alt-clicking on the spectrum bar changes the icon to the Fill icon.

✔ You can change color models while you're editing a color. Just choose the color model from the palette menu. InDesign automatically adjusts the values in the new color model to best represent the current color.

✔ If you're working in RGB or Lab mode and you want InDesign to warn you if you create a color that won't translate to CMYK, choose File⇨Color Settings⇨Document Color Settings, select the Enable Color Management check box, and press Return or Enter. Then if an exclamation point inside a yellow triangle appears below the Fill and Stroke icons in the Color palette, it means the color you've created can't be printed using CMYK inks. If you're not planning to print your document, you can simply ignore the warning. But if you are, click on the color swatch just to the right of the warning symbol to change your color to a closely matching color that falls within the CMYK spectrum.

✔ To clear a color from the Color palette, click on the None button. To reinstate the last color you were working on, click on the small color swatch that appears just above the spectrum bar.

✔ To use white, you could enter values of 0 in all four CMYK option boxes or values of 255 in the three RGB option boxes. But it's a heck of a lot easier to just click on the White button at the right end of the spectrum bar.

✔ You can also simply click on the Black button at the right end of the spectrum bar to color a selected object black.

Saving colors as swatches

After you've gone to all the work of creating the perfect color, you might want to save it in the Swatches palette for later use. Choose Window⇨Swatches or press F5 to display the Swatches palette, shown in Figure 11-4.

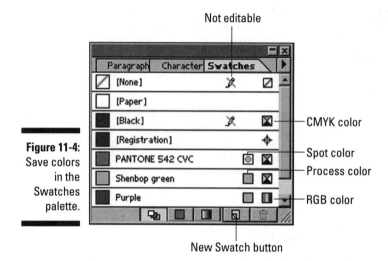

Figure 11-4:
Save colors
in the
Swatches
palette.

Not editable

CMYK color
Spot color
Process color
RGB color

New Swatch button

Here are some Swatches palette basics:

✔ To save a color to the Swatches palette, make sure the color is active in the Color palette and click on the New Swatch button at the bottom of the Swatches palette — it's the one next to the trash can. The new color is given the catchy name New Color Swatch and appears at the end of the list of swatches.

✔ You can also save and name an active color as a swatch by choosing New Color Swatch from the Swatches palette menu to display the New Color Swatch dialog box, shown in Figure 11-5. Enter a name for your new swatch in the Swatch Name option box. The Color Type and Color Mode pop-up menus display the type (as in process) and color model (as in CMYK) of your color. The color sliders and option boxes display the values for your color, as shown in Color Plate 11-1, which you can modify if you like. When you're finished, press Return or Enter to send your newly named color swatch to the bottom of the list in the Swatches palette.

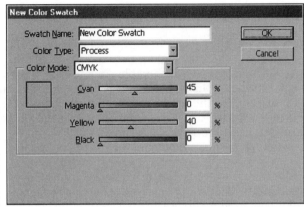

Figure 11-5:
Name your
new color
swatch
in this
dialog box.

✔ InDesign helps you keep tabs on some general info about your color swatches by displaying icons on the right side of each swatch. A square with four colored triangles in it denotes a CMYK color. A square with a red, green, and blue stripe designates an RGB color. A gray box means, hey, I'm a process color, and a box with a gray circle in it flags a spot color, which we explain shortly. A pencil with a line through it means the swatch can't be edited.

✔ To rename or readjust the color of an existing swatch, double-click on it to display the Swatch Options dialog box, which contains the same options as the New Color Swatch dialog box shown in Figure 11-5.

✔ Here's a neat trick that's especially handy when you want to create a new color in the Color palette based on an existing swatch. You can quickly check the color values of any swatch by hovering your cursor over it to display a box containing the CMYK, RGB, or Lab values for the color. Now you can enter those values in the Color palette and simply adjust them to make your new color.

✔ To create a copy of an existing swatch, select it and choose Duplicate Swatch from the Swatches palette menu. This is useful when you want to create a new swatch that's similar to an existing one.

✔ To delete a swatch, select it and drag it to the trash can icon in the bottom-right corner of the palette. You can also choose Delete Swatch from the palette menu.

Applying a color from the Swatches palette is as simple as selecting an object, clicking on the Fill or Stroke icon in the toolbox or the Color palette, and clicking on the color swatch.

Swatches are saved with the document in which you created them. If you want to use swatches that you created in one document in another document, you need to import them, as described in the next section.

Adding spot colors

InDesign also lets you add spot colors to the Swatches palette. *Spot colors* are separate inks that you can use in addition to or instead of the four basic process colors (cyan, magenta, yellow, and black). For example, if you're printing a two-color document using black and bright green, you can simply use a premixed spot color for the bright green rather than mixing four inks to achieve it. The only downside to using spot colors is that they increase printing costs because you have to pay for each spot color that you use. For this reason, most folks don't use more than one or two spot colors in a document.

To add a spot color to the Swatches palette, choose Window➪Swatch Libraries and then choose Pantone Coated or Pantone Uncoated. (Pantone, by the way, is the largest color vendor in America.) If you'll be printing your document on coated paper (for a color brochure, for example), choose Pantone Coated. If you're printing to regular old uncoated paper, choose Pantone Uncoated. Either way, the swatch library appears in a new palette window, as shown in Figure 11-6. Scroll through the list of spot colors to find one that suits you and double-click on it. The color is added to the bottom of the list in the Swatches palette. To add two or more colors at once, ⌘-click or Ctrl-click on each color you want to select. You can also Shift-click to select a consecutive range of colors. Then choose Add to Swatches from the palette menu.

As Figure 11-6 shows, Pantone colors are identified by numbers. Pantone 102, for example, is a rich yellow. If you know the number of the Pantone color you're looking for, ⌘+Option+click or Ctrl+Alt+click in the Pantone library palette and type the number. The palette will automatically scroll to and select the desired swatch.

Figure 11-6:
The Pantone
Uncoated
spot color
swatch
library.

PANTONE Uncoated	
PANTONE 100 CVU	◉ ⊠
PANTONE 101 CVU	◉ ⊠
PANTONE 102 CVU	◉ ⊠
PANTONE 103 CVU	◉ ⊠

You can also use the swatch libraries to add process colors to the Swatches palette or to import swatches from other InDesign or Illustrator files. The Pantone Process and Trumatch options in the Swatch Libraries submenu are our favorite process color libraries, but InDesign offers several others as well. To import swatches from another InDesign or Illustrator document, choose the Other

Library option from the Swatch Libraries submenu. Then locate the desired file in the dialog box that appears and double-click on it. InDesign loads the swatches into a new palette that sports the name of the file from which they were imported.

Creating tints of spot colors

A *tint* is simply a lighter version of a color. Creating tints is a great way to make variations of a spot color without having to pay the printing costs associated with using multiple spot color inks.

To create a tint of a spot color, select a spot color swatch in the Swatches palette. The Color palette displays the color and a tint slider bar, as shown in Figure 11-7. Then simply modify the intensity of the color by dragging the triangle on the slider or entering a new value in the option box.

Figure 11-7: Use the Tint slider in the Color palette to modify the intensity of a spot color.

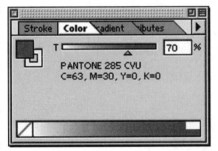

Mixing colors in overlapping objects

So what happens when you print two overlapping objects with different color fills or strokes? By default, the color of the object on top prints and the covered portion of the object on bottom doesn't. But you can tell InDesign to *overprint* overlapping colors so that they mix together. For example, you could overprint blue onto yellow to get green.

To overprint colors in selected objects, choose Window⇨Attributes to display the Attributes palette. Then select the Overprint Fill or Overprint Stroke check box to specify whether the fill or stroke colors overprint. You can't see the effects of overprinting on-screen or when you print your document on an inkjet printer for proofing, but rest assured that the colors will mix when your document is printed on an output device that supports PostScript Level 2 or higher.

You can save a tint to the Swatches palette by clicking on the New Swatch button, just as you would to save a color. InDesign adds the tint at the bottom of the list of swatches, which you can then apply to the fill or stroke of a selected object by clicking on the swatch. Tint swatches are easy to distinguish from color swatches because the percentage of the tint (such as 70%) is listed to the right of the swatch name.

Blending colors for backgrounds

Sometimes *flat fills*, such as process colors or spot colors, seem just that — flat. If you want to create a background that gives a shape, a text block, or a graphic frame a sense of depth and texture, gradients are the way to go. A *gradient* is a fill that gradually fades from one color into another. To apply a gradient fill to a selected object, click on the Fill icon in the toolbox and follow these steps:

1. **Choose Window⇨Gradient.**

    The Gradient palette appears, as shown in Figure 11-8.

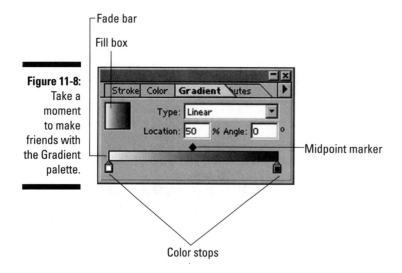

Figure 11-8: Take a moment to make friends with the Gradient palette.

2. **Click on the Fill box.**

    This specifies the gradient as the fill for the selected object.

3. **Click on the left color stop on the fade bar.**

    Both of these items are labeled in Figure 11-8. The left color stop represents the starting color of your gradient.

4. **Specify the starting color for your gradient.**

   You can create a new color in the Color palette or you can Option-click or Alt-click on a swatch in the Swatches palette. Either way, the color appears on the left color stop and on the left side of the fade bar.

5. **Click on the right color stop and specify an ending color for your gradient.**

   Select a color just as you did in Step 4.

6. **From the Type pop-up menu, choose Linear or Radial.**

   The Linear option creates a gradient in which the color transition follows a straight line. The Radial option makes a gradient that starts with a point of color and fades outward in concentric circles. Check out Color Plate 11-2 to see examples of both types of gradients.

7. **Drag the midpoint marker and color stops to change the rate and position of the fade.**

   The midpoint marker represents the spot at which the colors mix in equal amounts, and the midpoint value is measured relative to the color stop positions. Dragging the midpoint marker to the left causes the colors to fade faster; dragging the marker to the right makes them fade more slowly. The position of the color stops determines where the fade can begin and end. Color Plate 11-3 shows examples of different color stop and midpoint marker positions applied to a single gradient.

   You can also change the position of the midpoint marker or color stops by selecting a marker or a stop and changing the value in the Location option box.

8. **Adjust the angle of the gradient, if desired.**

   If you're creating a linear gradient, you can change the angle by entering a value in the Angle option box in the Gradient palette.

   You can also change the angle of a linear or radial gradient by dragging across the object with the gradient tool, which is located just above the zoom tool in the toolbox. The gradient begins at the point where you start your drag and ends where you release the mouse button. The angle of the gradient corresponds to the angle of the drag.

Here's a newsflash: Two color stops let you create a two-color gradient. But you can add as many colors as your RAM allows by adding more color stops. Just click below the fade bar to add a color stop. InDesign adds a midpoint marker between the new color stop and the existing one to its right or left. To remove a color stop, drag it down off the palette.

At this point, you can save the gradient as a swatch by clicking on the New Swatch button in the Swatches palette. Then you can apply and edit it just as you would a color or tint swatch.

Cozying Up to the Stroke Palette

We mention the Stroke palette briefly in a couple other chapters, so you might recall that it delivers the goods when you need to change the thickness of an object's outline. But the Stroke palette lets you do loads of other things as well, such as create dash patterns, change the appearance of an object's corners, and add elements to the beginning and end of a line. To begin, press F10 to display the Stroke palette, as shown in Figure 11-9.

Butt cap

Round cap

Square cap

Figure 11-9:
Modify the
stroke of a
selected
object using
the options
in the Stroke
palette.

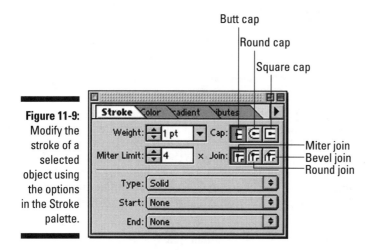

Miter join
Bevel join
Round join

To change the thickness of the stroke of a selected object, choose an option from the Weight pop-up menu or enter a value between 0 and 800 (in 0.001 increments) in the Weight option box, and then press Return or Enter. Stroke weight is measured in points, and any value smaller than 0.1 is basically invisible.

The Cap options determine the appearance of the endpoints of a stroke and are generally used for stroking lines. The Cap icons themselves show how the options affect the endpoints of a selected line. The black line that runs through the center of each icon indicates the position of the line's endpoint relative to the stroke. Notice that the stroke extends past the end of the line in the Round cap and Square cap options, which results in a longer line. The nitty-gritty details follow:

✔ **Butt cap:** The Butt cap option is the default setting and the most common line cap. The stroke ends at the endpoints and is perpendicular to the line.

✔ **Round cap:** Select the Round cap option to apply round endpoints to a selected line. In a round cap, the stroke wraps around the line's endpoints in a semicircle that is half the stroke weight. So if your stroke is 6 points, the round cap extends 3 points past each endpoint.

Use round caps to soften the appearance of thick lines so that they don't end abruptly.

✔ **Square cap:** The Square cap option works just like the round cap, except the part of the stroke that extends past the line's endpoints is square. Square caps aren't very useful, but they can come in handy when you need a little extra length to make the edges of two lines meet.

The Join options determine the appearance of a stroke at corners. As with the Cap icons, the Join icons illustrate the effect they apply. Here's how the options work:

✔ **Miter join:** If a corner has a miter join, as by default, the stroke extends to form a sharp point.

✔ **Round join:** The round join is similar to the round cap. The stroke wraps around the corner in a semicircle.

✔ **Bevel join:** The bevel join is similar to the butt cap. It chops off the stroke at the corner point to create a flat edge.

The length of a miter join grows as the line segments that meet to form the corner get closer together. This can result in long, weird looking spikes. That's why InDesign provides the Miter Limit option box to the left of the Join options. The Miter Limit value tells InDesign when to lop off miter joins that are just too long. The default value of 4, for example, tells InDesign that when the miter length reaches four times the stroke weight, InDesign should replace the miter join with a bevel join.

The top example in Figure 11-10 shows a star with a stroke weight of 6 points, the miter join option applied, and a Miter Limit value of 4. The bottom example shows the same star scaled to a little more than half its original size. Notice that the upper left and right spikes have been chopped off. Disturbing, huh? You could attempt to avoid this scenario by raising the Miter Limit to a value up to 500, but then you could end up with ridiculously long spikes. A better solution is to use round joins.

Fancy line tricks

The options in the bottom half of the Stroke palette let you change the appearance of selected lines. For example, you can turn a solid line into a dash pattern, as you might want to do to indicate a clip out coupon in an advertisement. To create a dash pattern, choose Dashed from the Type pop-up menu in the Stroke palette. This reveals six option boxes at the bottom of the palette, alternately labeled Dash and Gap. Enter values in the Dash option boxes to specify the length of the dashes, measured in points. Enter values in the Gap option boxes to indicate the length of the gaps between the dashes. That's all there is to it.

Figure 11-10:
A happy star with healthy miter joins (top) can lose its limbs when scaled (bottom).

Unless you want to vary the length of the dashes and gaps, you don't have to fill in all the option boxes. If you just enter values in the first two, InDesign ignores the empty option boxes and simply repeats the values you entered.

The Start and End pop-up menus let you add arrowheads and shapes to either end (or both ends) of a selected line. These options are especially useful for creating callouts on graphics. To apply an arrowhead or shape to a selected line, choose an option from the Start pop-up menu, or the End pop-up menu, or both menus. Press Option or Alt as you choose an option from the Start or End pop-up menu to apply the arrowhead or shape to both ends of the selected line. Which end is which depends on how you drew the line. If you can't remember, just guess. If you're wrong, press ⌘+Z on the Mac or Ctrl+Z under Windows and try again.

Figure 11-11 shows examples of several arrowhead and shape options. As you can see, the size of the arrowhead or shape depends on the stroke weight of the line.

Figure 11-11:
Some
arrowheads
and shapes
applied to
lines 1, 2,
and 4 points
thick (from
top to
bottom).

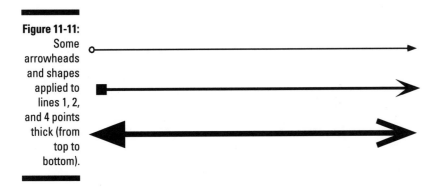

Chapter 12

Slipping an Image into a New Shape

· ·

In This Chapter

▶ Changing the shape of a graphic frame

▶ Applying corner effects

▶ Placing images in new shapes

▶ Creating and editing clipping paths

· ·

*I*f you were a child in the seventies, there's a good chance that for a few years you had a certain hairstyle called "the bowl." Now don't be embarrassed — you're not alone. In fact, back then it was all the rage. Kids everywhere from coast to coast sported the bowl. Some kids actually wore it well, while others of us swore that if we ever had children of our own when we grew up, we would never subject them to such bland conformity.

If images were children, their frames would be their hairstyles. The rectangular frame around an imported image is like the bowl — it works well for some images but not for others. That's why this chapter explains how you can give your images a haircut that suits them. You find out how to change the shape of a graphic's frame, give a frame's corners a new look, and put an image into a different shape. You also find out how to clip away unwanted backgrounds in images using clipping paths. That's right, you learn all this without attending a single day of beauty school.

Changing the Frame You're Dealt

As explained in Chapter 10, you can scale, rotate, slant, crop, and otherwise manipulate a graphic frame. But you don't have to stop there. InDesign also lets you edit the shape of a frame. Just follow these steps:

1. **Select an image with the arrow tool.**

   The frame appears with eight blue handles, each with a white dot in the center.

2. **Press A to select the hollow arrow tool.**

   The eight frame handles change to four *anchor points* (also simply called *points*), which are white with a blue dot in the center, located on the corners of the frame.

3. **Click on a point and drag in toward the center of the image.**

   In Figure 12-1, for example, we dragged the point in the lower-right corner of the image up and to the left. Notice how the adjacent points remain stationary and the segment of the frame between the point you're moving and the neighboring points shrinks or stretches to accommodate the change in distance.

   You can press the Shift key while you drag to constrain your movements horizontally, vertically, or diagonally.

   When you release the mouse button, the portion of the image you dragged over disappears. Actually, it's only hidden, just like when you crop an image with the regular arrow tool. Nevertheless, you can't see it and it won't print, so it's as good as gone.

4. **Continue dragging points to create the shape you want.**

   Feel free to fool around a little. You can always press ⌘+Z or Ctrl+Z to undo a drag and try again. In case you're curious, we fashioned a bowl to hold our gourds and squash, as shown in Figure 12-2.

Editing your brains out

Of course, with only four points to work with, your reshaping options are limited. If you want more control over the shape of the frame, you need more points. You can add points to a frame using the pen tool.

Before we proceed, we need to come clean and tell you the truth about frames and points. First, the reason why you can edit frames is because they are actually paths. In fact, anything you can draw in InDesign, including lines and shapes, is called a *path*.

Second, points are the basic building blocks of paths, and points come in two kinds: corner points and smooth points. *Corner points* represent the corner between two segments in a path, like the points located at the corners of a frame when you select it with the hollow arrow tool. *Smooth points* connect two segments in a path as a continuous curve. So the type of point you add to a frame (or any other path) determines how you can edit the frame's shape.

Figure 12-3, for example, shows both kinds of points on a graphic frame. All the points are corner points, except for the one in the middle of the top frame edge, which is a smooth point. Notice how the corner points connect straight segments, and the segments connected by the smooth point are curved.

Figure 12-1:
Drag an anchor point with the hollow arrow tool to change the outline of a graphic frame.

Figure 12-2:
You can change the shape of a frame in only one or two drags.

Pen tool   Smooth point   Control handles

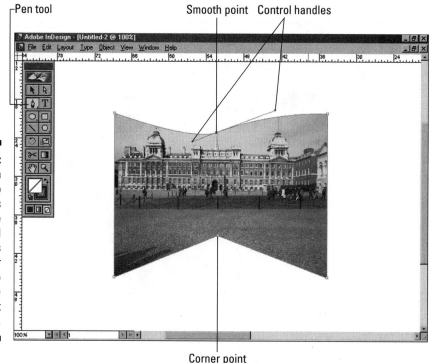

Figure 12-3:
Add smooth
points to
frames
to create
curved
segments
and corner
points to
create
straight
ones.

Corner point

To add points to a frame, you need to select the frame with the arrow tool or hollow arrow tool. Then press P to select the pen tool or click on the icon in the toolbox that looks like the tip of a fountain pen, labeled in Figure 12-3. Position the pen tool anywhere along the frame outline, *except* over an existing corner point. A little plus sign (+) appears to the right of the pen tool cursor, letting you know that it is positioned over the frame and is now in add point mode. If you see a small x next to the pen tool cursor, the tool is not positioned over the frame. Move your mouse a bit until you see a plus sign. Then proceed as follows:

✔ To add a corner point to a frame, just click on the frame with the pen tool to insert the point. Then select the new corner point with the hollow arrow tool and drag to move it as described in the preceding section. Repeat this process to create as many new corner points as you want.

✔ To add a smooth point to a frame, click and hold on the frame with the pen tool until the cursor changes to a black triangle. Then drag. "Whoa!" you shout, "what the heck are those two lines sticking out from my point?" Those lines are called *control handles* (labeled in Figure 12-3), and they allow you to create and manipulate curved frame segments. To move a control handle, select the hollow arrow tool, click on the nob at the end of a handle, and drag. Drag away from the point to increase the curvature of the segment or toward the point to decrease the curvature. As with corner points, you can also drag a smooth point with the hollow arrow tool to stretch or shrink the length of the frame segments.

We'll talk more about paths, points, and control handles later in this chapter. But the best way to learn how to use them is to use them. In other words, play around to get a feel for how they work. When you get tired of tugging and dragging points and control handles, read the next section to find out how you can jazz up your frames with a little less effort.

Making pretty corners

Another way to enhance a plain old graphic frame is to apply one of InDesign's preset corner styles. Select any frame (rectangular or otherwise) with the arrow or hollow arrow tool and choose Object➪Corner Effects to display the dialog box shown in Figure 12-4. You can also press ⌘+Option+R on the Mac or Ctrl+Alt+R under Windows.

Figure 12-4:
A corner effect can add flare to your frame.

Choose a corner style from the Effect pop-up menu. Most of the styles are straightforward: the Bevel style chops off all the corners in your frame, Inset cuts them out in squares, Rounded rounds corners off, and Inverse Rounded scoops them out in a semicircle. The Fancy style, however, isn't self-explanatory, which is why we show it in Figure 12-4.

Select the Preview check box to see the effect on-screen before you apply it. If you want to make the effect more or less pronounced, change the value in the Size option box. Larger values create bigger effects; smaller values create smaller ones. When you're happy with the way your corners look, press Return or Enter to apply the effect.

If you apply corner effects to a frame that you've reshaped using the pen and hollow arrow tools, you might get some unexpected results. For example, a corner might bulge out instead of stick in, or the corner effect might throw another layout element out of whack. The best way to avoid unwanted effects is to always preview corner styles before you apply them.

Giving an image a whole new shape

If editing the shape of a frame and applying corner effects just don't do it for you, you can ditch the frame around your graphic entirely. Simply draw a new shape, and import or copy and paste your graphic inside it.

You can either draw a shape using one of the shape tools discussed in Chapter 10, or use one of the following frame drawing tools, all of which are pictured in Figure 12-5:

- **Rectangle frame tool:** Select the rectangle frame tool by clicking and holding on the rectangle tool to display a flyout menu. Then move your cursor over the second tool on the flyout and release the mouse button. Alternatively, you can press Shift+M. Then click and drag to draw a rectangle just as you would with the regular rectangle tool. The result is a rectangle with a big x in it, as shown in Figure 12-5. The x simply marks the rectangle as a placeholder for a graphic or text.

- **Ellipse frame tool:** Select this tool by clicking and holding on the ellipse tool and choosing the second tool on the resulting flyout menu. Or simply press Shift+L. Then click and drag to draw an ellipse as shown in Figure 12-5. Again, the x just marks the shape as a placeholder frame.

- **Polygon frame tool:** We could take you through the whole flyout menu deal again, but you're probably more interested in the shortcut. Press Shift+N to select the polygon frame tool. Then — you guessed it — click and drag to draw a polygon with an x in it.

Rectangle frame tool

Ellipse frame tool

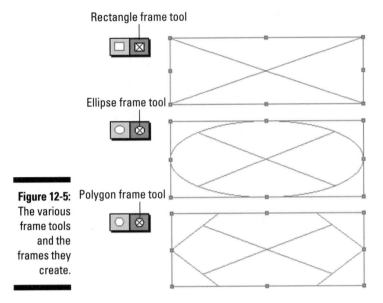

Figure 12-5:
The various
frame tools
and the
frames they
create.

Polygon frame tool

Whether you draw a shape with a regular shape tool or a frame tool, you can import a graphic into it by selecting it and using the File⇨Place command to place the graphic as described in Chapter 10. In Figure 12-6, for example, we decided to give Shenbop a new look. We drew a circle with the ellipse tool, filled it with a light blue background, and selected it. Then we chose File⇨Place and imported Shenbop directly into the circle. If you compare the graphic in the document to the original version of the graphic on the pasteboard, you'll notice that the bottom of the new graphic is cropped. (For a complete explanation of cropping, see Chapter 10.) That's because we haven't changed the shape of the graphic itself; we've changed only the shape of its frame.

You can also simply cut or copy any graphic in your document and paste it into a new shape or a placeholder frame. Select the graphic and press ⌘+X or Ctrl+X to cut it or press ⌘+C or Ctrl+C to copy it. Then select the shape or frame and choose Edit⇨Paste Into. You can also press ⌘+Option+V on the Mac or Ctrl+Alt+V under Windows.

Don't use the regular paste command to paste a graphic inside a selected shape or frame. Choosing Edit⇨Paste simply pastes the graphic on top of the shape rather than inside it.

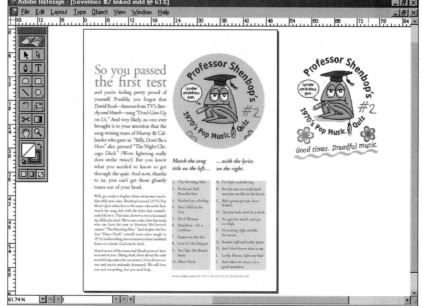

Figure 12-6:
You can
import or
paste a
graphic into
any shape
or frame.

When you import or paste a graphic into a new shape, it may not be cropped the way you want. If that's the case, select the graphic with the hollow arrow tool and drag to reposition it inside the shape.

Getting Rid of Unwanted Backgrounds

So you can change the shape of a graphic's frame in a bunch of different ways, which is great. But suppose you have an image like the one pictured in Figure 12-7. You want this songstress (we call her Sally, by the way) to belt out a few tunes in your document, but you don't want that murky gray background. What do you do? You use a clipping path to clip away the unwanted background. A *clipping path* is like a frame snuggled up against the outline of a specific portion of an image. Everything inside the clipping path appears on-screen and in your printed document. Everything that lies outside the clipping path is transparent on-screen and in print. InDesign gives you several ways to use clipping paths, and we cover them all from worst to best in the following sections.

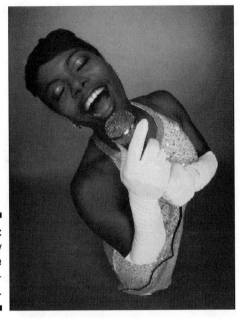

Figure 12-7:
A likely
candidate
for a clip-
ping path.

Creating clipping paths automatically

InDesign offers a Clipping Path command that lets you create clipping paths for images automatically. But the sad truth is that it's not very useful. The problem is that it works only when the subject of an image is very dark and the background is super light (like white). If you have an image that fits these criteria, follow these steps to create a clipping path automatically:

1. **Select the image to which you want to apply a clipping path.**

   Remember, for the Clipping Path command to work, the subject of the image must be dark and the background must be light. Sally the songstress in Figure 12-7, for example, is *not* a good candidate. (But don't worry, you haven't seen the last of Sally. We get back to her later.)

2. **Choose Object⇨Clipping Path.**

   This displays the dialog box shown in Figure 12-8.

3. **Select the Preview check box.**

   You'll need to experiment a little, so you should definitely preview the effects of various settings before you apply them.

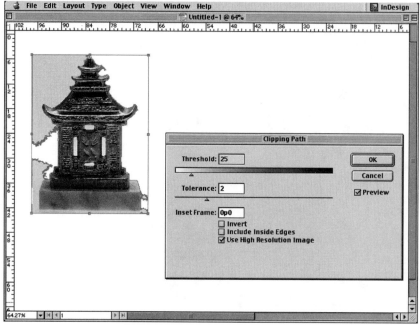

Figure 12-8:
Use the
Clipping
Path dialog
box to
create
automatic
clipping
paths for
images with
very light
backgrounds.

4. Play around with the Threshold value.

You can either type a new value in the Threshold option box or drag the triangle on the slider bar. The Threshold value defines the darkest pixel that will be clipped away, so increasing the value makes more pixels invisible. In other words, raise the Threshold value to make the clipping path remove darker colors.

Figure 12-8, for example, shows an image with the Threshold value set too low. Notice how most of the background color on the right side has been removed, while darker shades of the background on the left side remain visible.

The only way to determine the best Threshold value is to experiment. If you can't find an acceptable Threshold setting, the background of your image is probably too dark for the Clipping Path command to work.

5. Test out different Tolerance values.

You can either enter a value in the Tolerance option box or drag the triangle on the Tolerance slider bar. The Tolerance value works in tandem with the Threshold value. In general, higher values create smoother but looser clipping paths, and lower values create tighter, rougher ones. Again, the only way to find the best setting is to try out different values.

6. **Specify remaining options, if desired.**

   Here's a quick rundown on the last four options. Entering a value (measured in picas and points) in the Inset Frame option box shrinks or expands the clipping path uniformly. Negative values make the clipping path larger, and positive values make it smaller. Select the Invert check box to swap the areas inside and outside the clipping path. If your graphic contains holes that you want to make transparent (like the image in Figure 12-8), select the Include Inside Edges check box. Leave the Use High Resolution Image option turned on, as it is by default, to make sure your clipping path is based on the actual image file and not a low resolution preview.

7. **When you're finished, press Return or Enter to apply the clipping path to your image.**

   If you're not satisfied with your results, you can edit the clipping path as described later in this chapter. Or read the next section to find out about a better way to create clipping paths.

Making manual clipping paths

As much as we all prefer to ignore it, the following adage definitely applies to creating clipping paths: "If you want something done right, do it yourself." The bad news is that drawing clipping paths by hand is a lot of work and not easy. The good news is that we get to revisit two of our favorite characters from earlier in the chapter — the pen tool and Sally the songstress.

Here's the deal: To draw a clipping path, you need to trace the outline of the subject of your image by laying down points with the pen tool. To begin, press P to select the pen tool and click on a spot where the subject of the image meets the background to add a corner point. Then continue clicking and dragging along the edge where the subject and background meet to create a path composed of a series of straight and curved segments, depending on the needs of your image. Figure 12-9, for example, shows the clipping path we drew for Sally. (We removed Sally temporarily so you can see the clipping path more clearly.)

The following list explains the basic stuff you need to know to draw a clipping path with the pen tool:

✔ Just to refresh your memory, click to create a corner point and drag to create a smooth point.

✔ To draw a straight segment between two corner points, click at two different locations. InDesign connects the two points with a straight line.

✔ Drag at two different locations to create a curved segment between two smooth points.

✔ To create a curved segment after drawing a straight segment, drag from the corner point you just created to add a control handle. Then drag at a different location to append a curved segment to the end of the straight segment.

✔ To create a straight segment after drawing a curved segment, Option-click or Alt-click on the smooth point you just created to delete the forward control handle. This converts the smooth point to a corner point with one handle. Then click at a different location to append a straight segment to the end of the curved segment.

When drawing a clipping path, it often helps to zoom in on the portion of the image you're tracing. That way, you can see and avoid small gaps between your path and the edge you're tracing. Remember, you can quickly zoom in and out by pressing ⌘+plus (+) and ⌘+minus (–) on the Mac or Ctrl+plus and Ctrl+minus under Windows.

You can drag points and control handles with the hollow arrow tool to change the length, direction, and curvature of path segments.

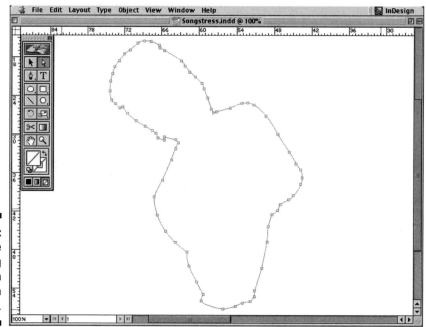

Figure 12-9:
A simple clipping path drawn with the pen tool.

Editing clipping paths

If you make a mistake or your path isn't working correctly, don't sweat it. Fortunately, paths are infinitely editable. You can add, delete, and convert points along a path you've selected with the hollow arrow tool as follows:

✔ To add a point to an existing segment, select the pen tool (that's the P key), position it over the path so that a plus sign (+) appears next to it, and click to insert a corner point or drag to insert a smooth point. (Sound familiar?)

✔ You can also add a point to a path segment by using the add point tool, labeled in Figure 12-10. Select the second icon on the pen tool flyout menu or press the plus (+) key to activate the add point tool.

Add point tool

Delete point tool

Figure 12-10:
The three
point tools
on the pen
tool flyout
menu.

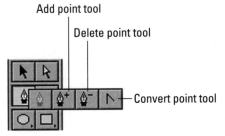

Convert point tool

✔ To close an open path (in other words, to connect two endpoints so there's no beginning or end), position the pen tool over one endpoint so that a small slash (/) appears next to it, and then click or drag. Then click or drag on the opposite endpoint to draw a segment that closes the path.

✔ To delete a point from a segment, position the pen tool over the point so that you see a minus sign (–) next to the pen tool cursor, and then click. The point disappears, but the segment remains intact.

✔ You can also delete a point by using the delete point tool, labeled in Figure 12-10. Select the third icon on the pen tool flyout menu or press the minus (–) key to select the tool.

✔ If you want to convert a corner point to a smooth point, press Shift+P to select the convert point tool, labeled in Figure 12-10. Then drag from the corner point to convert it to a smooth point with two control handles.

✔ Rather than selecting the convert point tool, you can press Option on the Mac or Alt under Windows when the pen tool is active to quickly access the convert point tool. Or if the hollow arrow tool is active, you can press ⌘+Option on the Mac or Ctrl+Alt under Windows to switch to the convert point tool.

  ✔ Just click on a smooth point with the convert point tool to convert it to a corner point.

  ✔ You can break a path anywhere you like using the scissors tool, which is located just above the hand tool in the toolbox. Just click on the scissors tool icon or press C to select the tool, and then click on a segment or a point. You can then drag the two sections apart using the hollow arrow tool.

When you're happy with your clipping path, select the image (not the path) with the arrow tool and press ⌘+X on the Mac or Ctrl+X under Windows. Yep, that's right, cut the image. It's okay, promise. Now select the clipping path with the hollow arrow tool and choose Edit⇨Paste Into, just as you would to paste an image into a new shape or frame. You might need to adjust the position of the image inside the path by dragging it with the hollow arrow tool, but otherwise you're good to go. Figure 12-11 shows our songstress nestled within her cozy new clipping path.

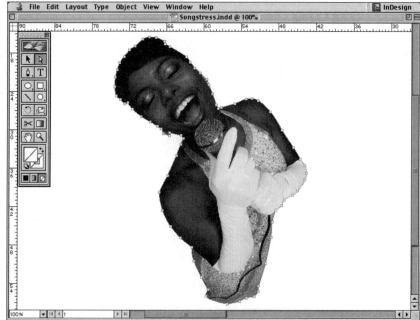

Figure 12-11:
Sally the
songstress
sheds her
dull gray
background
thanks to a
clipping
path.

Editing paths from Illustrator files

If you're familiar with Illustrator, you're no stranger to the hollow arrow and pen tools. In fact, you might have the overwhelming urge to put those tools to work editing the paths in a drawing you've imported from Illustrator. Well, unlike other page layout programs, InDesign lets you do exactly that. But for paths to remain editable in InDesign, you need to import an Illustrator file as follows: Open the file in Illustrator and choose Edit⇨Select All. Then either copy and paste or drag the drawing onto your InDesign page. You can now edit the paths in the Illustrator drawing directly in InDesign. For a pictorial representation of the whole process, see Color Plates 12-1 and 12-2.

The best clipping path of all

Although you can draw a decent clipping path with the pen tool in InDesign, the very best clipping path is the one you create in your image-editing program and import into InDesign with your image.

InDesign can import clipping paths from TIFF, EPS, and native Photoshop (PSD) files. In Chapter 10, we explain how to import images using the File⇨Place command. In that chapter, we mention the Show Import Options check box in the Place dialog box. Well, if you're importing TIFF, EPS, or PSD files with clipping paths, be sure to select that check box because otherwise InDesign won't import the clipping paths saved with your images. Figure 12-12 spotlights the clipping path import option for TIFF and PSD files. The same option appears in a different dialog box when you import EPS files with Show Import Options turned on.

Figure 12-12: Be sure to turn on the clipping path option in the Image Import Options dialog box.

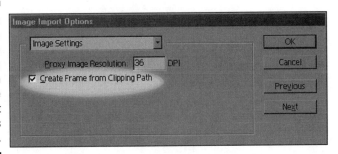

Color Plate 12-3 shows an image imported with a clipping path and placed on a gradient background that we created in InDesign.

Like clipping paths created with the Clipping Path command or drawn with the pen tool, you can edit clipping paths imported with images using the techniques described in the preceding section.

Chapter 13

A Word Is Worth a Thousand Pictures

*E*diting graphic frames, applying corner effects, drawing clipping paths — with all this primping and preening of graphics, just think how your text must feel right now. Sad, neglected, comparatively homely. Poor little guys. It's just not fair.

Well, this chapter shows you how to put things right. You find out how to whip your text into the best shape of its life, make it wrap comfortably around its graphic neighbors, and even turn it into a graphic you can edit like any other.

Doing Wacky Things to Text Frames

A simple way to give your text a little character is to dress up its frame. In InDesign, you can edit a text frame just as you would a graphic frame. For example, you can use the hollow arrow tool, pen tool, and pals to change a frame's basic shape, as explained in Chapter 12. If you're really feeling wacky, you can throw in the Corner Effects command to boot.

Putting a text block on a diet

In the following example, we put all these tools to work to give a frumpy old text block a shapely new figure. Just follow these steps:

1. **Select a plain old rectangular text block with the arrow tool.**

   For this exercise, a text block that's taller than it is wide works best.

2. **Press A to switch to the hollow arrow tool.**

   The eight frame handles are replaced by a point at each corner.

3. **Press P to select the pen tool.**

   Click in the middle of the left frame outline to insert a point. Then click on the right frame outline to insert another point opposite the first. If you want to be precise, drag from the top ruler to create a horizontal guide and position it to align with the point on the left frame outline. Then click on the spot where the guide intersects with the right frame outline to insert the second point.

   Remember, clicking with the pen tool inserts a corner point and dragging inserts a smooth point. For this technique to work, you need to use corner points. So make sure you click, not drag, on the frame outline with the pen tool.

4. **Press A to switch back to the hollow arrow tool and then Shift-drag each new point in toward the center of the text block, as shown in Figure 13-1.**

   As you can see, the farther in you drag, the more dramatic your curve will be. Note that the text adjusts automatically to accommodate changes to the frame.

   Pressing the Shift key while you drag constrains your drag horizontally.

5. **Choose Object⇨Corner Effects.**

   The Corner Effects dialog box appears, as shown in Figure 13-2. We'll use this dialog box to round off the corners of the text block's frame, as explained next.

6. **Specify Corner Effects options.**

   First, select the Preview check box so you can see the effects of your changes on-screen. Then choose Rounded from the Effects pop-up menu to round off all six corners off your text frame. Type a value in the Size option box. Larger values round off corners more dramatically; smaller values result in subtler rounding. To achieve the effect shown in Figure 13-2, we used a Size value of 2 picas.

7. **Press Return or Enter to apply the effect.**

   Get up, take out the garbage, feed your dog, and then proceed to the next step.

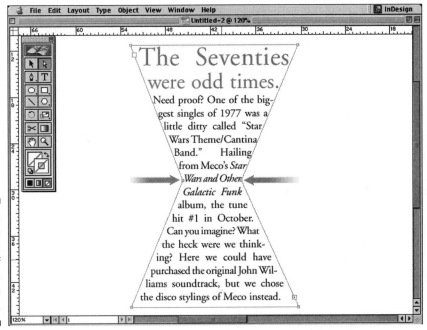

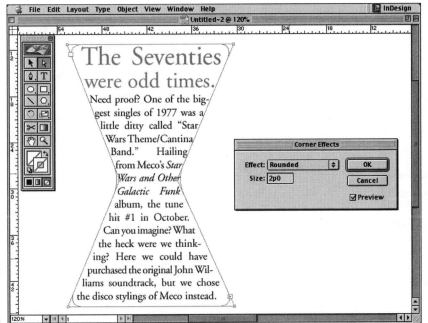

8. **Modify the shape as desired.**

   To refine your text block's new curvaceous figure, click on the frame outline with the pen tool to add points. Then drag the points with the hollow arrow tool to fine-tune the shape, as shown in the left example in Figure 13-3.

9. **Apply a stroke or a fill if you like.**

   In the right example in Figure 13-3, for instance, we applied a fill to give our shapely new text block some texture.

Wrapping Type Around Graphics

Like any page-layout program worth it's weight in motor oil, InDesign lets you wrap text around graphics. The process works as follows:

1. **Select the graphic you want to wrap text around with the arrow tool.**

   This requires a simple click of the mouse.

2. **Choose Object⇨Text Wrap to display the Text Wrap palette, as shown in Figure 13-4.**

   You can also display the palette by pressing ⌘+Option+W on the Mac or Ctrl+Alt+W under Windows.

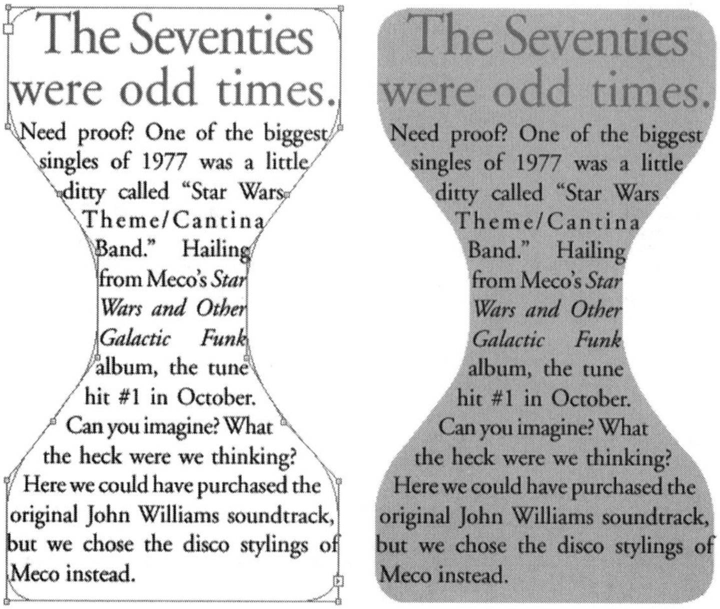

Figure 13-3: Add and drag points to fine-tune the shape of your text frame (left) and finish it off with a fill (right).

The Seventies were odd times.

Need proof? One of the biggest singles of 1977 was a little ditty called "Star Wars Theme/Cantina Band." Hailing from Meco's *Star Wars and Other Galactic Funk* album, the tune hit #1 in October.

Can you imagine? What the heck were we thinking? Here we could have purchased the original John Williams soundtrack, but we chose the disco stylings of Meco instead.

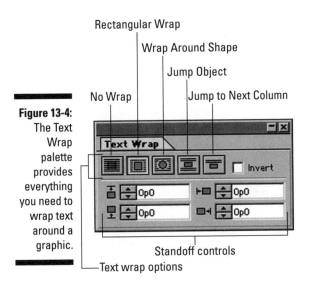

Rectangular Wrap

Wrap Around Shape

Jump Object

No Wrap Jump to Next Column

Figure 13-4:
The Text
Wrap
palette
provides
everything
you need to
wrap text
around a
graphic.

Standoff controls

Text wrap options

3. **Select a text wrap option.**

   The Text Wrap palette includes five wrap options in the form of buttons across the top of the palette. The first option is the No Wrap button, which is selected by default and means no text wrap is applied to the selected graphic. Figure 13-5 shows all the other text wrap options in action.

   Click on the Rectangular Wrap button to wrap text in a rectangle around the graphic's frame, as shown in the top left example in Figure 13-5. Click on the Wrap Around Shape button to wrap text around the graphic's shape. InDesign automatically creates a *standoff boundary* that's the same shape as the graphic's frame when it's selected with the hollow arrow tool. The standoff boundary sets the amount of space between a graphic and the text wrapped around it, as illustrated in the top right example in Figure 13-5.

   To wrap text around a graphic's clipping path, select the Wrap Around Shape option.

   You're not likely to use the last two wrap options as often as the others, but here's when you might. If a graphic takes up most of the width of a column, wrapping text around the sides of the graphic can result in very short lines, making text difficult to read. In this situation, you would want to prevent text from wrapping around the left and right sides of the graphic, which you can do by clicking on the Jump Object button. To keep text from wrapping around the left, right, *and* bottom of the graphic, click on the Jump to Next Column button. As you might have guessed, the text resumes at the top of the next column.

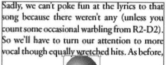

Standoff boundary

 Sadly, we can't poke fun at the lyrics to that song because there weren't any (unless you count some occasional warbling from R2-D2). So we'll have to turn our attention to more vocal though equally wretched hits. As before, your job is to match the song title in the left column with the lyrics on the right. However, this time around, the lyrics might occur anywhere in the song and do *not* immediately follow the mention of the song title. Up for the challenge? You should be able to match up half the songs easy and piece together some others by process of elimination. Get all right, and we'll have to revoke your radio privileges for a month.

Sadly, we can't poke fun at the lyrics to that song because there weren't any (unless you count some occasional warbling from R2-D2). So we'll have to turn our attention to more vocal though equally wretched hits. As before, your job is to match the song title in the left column with the lyrics on the right. However, this time around, the lyrics might occur anywhere in the song and do *not* immediately follow the mention of the song title. Up for the challenge? You should be able to match up half the songs easy and piece together some others by process of elimination. Get all right, and we'll have to revoke your radio privileges for a month.

 Sadly, we can't poke fun at the lyrics to that song because there weren't any (unless you count some occasional warbling from R2-D2). So we'll have to turn our attention to more vocal though equally wretched hits. As before,

your job is to match the song title in the left column with the lyrics on the right. However, this time around, the lyrics might occur anywhere in the song and do *not* immediately follow the mention of the song title. Up for the challenge? You should be able to match up half the songs easy and piece together some

Sadly, we can't poke fun at the lyrics to that song because there weren't any (unless you count some occasional warbling from R2-D2). So we'll have to turn our attention to more vocal though equally wretched hits. As before,

Figure 13-5:
The four different text wrap options on display.

4. Use the standoff controls to define the amount of space between the graphic and the wrapped text.

The Text Wrap palette offers four standoff option boxes, as shown back in Figure 13-4. If you selected the second text wrap option in the previous step, all four option boxes are active. Enter values in the option boxes on the left side of the palette to set the standoff for the top and bottom of the graphic. Enter values in the option boxes on the right side of the palette to specify the standoff for the sides of the graphic.

TIP

If you enter negative standoff values, the standoff boundary is positioned inside the graphic's frame, which allows text to flow over the edges of the graphic.

If you selected the Wrap Around Shape option in the preceding step, the standoff is automatically set to 10 points around the entire graphic. But you can change the standoff to any amount you like by entering a new value in the first standoff option box.

If you selected the Jump Object option, only the standoff controls for the top and bottom of the graphic are active. The other two option boxes are irrelevant because the text won't wrap around the sides of the graphic. Similarly, if you selected the Jump to Next Column option, only the first standoff option box is active because the text won't wrap around the sides or bottom of the graphic.

What standoff value should you use? One pica is generally a safe bet, but depending on the situation, you might want to go as low as 6 points or as high as 18 points. One standoff value to avoid is 0. This would let your text bump up against your graphic.

Unless your graphic included a clipping path, at this point you probably have a text wrap that looks something like the one in Figure 13-6. If that's not quite the kind of interaction between text and graphic you had in mind, not to worry. You can modify the standoff boundary to change the shape of the wrap as described next.

Adjusting the standoff

InDesign lets you edit the standoff boundary for a text wrap in the same way you edit frames and paths. You can drag the points on the standoff boundary with the hollow arrow tool and the text automatically rewraps to accommodate the changes.

Figure 13-6: A standard rectangular text wrap with a one-pica standoff boundary.

Need more points to achieve the effect you're looking for? Just click on the boundary with the pen tool to add points. Click on existing points with the pen tool to remove them, press Option or Alt and drag to convert corner points to smooth points with control handles, and Option-click or Alt-click on smooth points to convert them to corner points. Then drag the points and control handles to adjust the shape of the standoff boundary. (If you need a refresher on working with points and control handles, see Chapter 12.)

In Figure 13-7, for example, we modified the standoff boundary so that the text in the left column wraps more naturally around the shape of the graphic rather than around the graphic's rectangular frame. (To see Shenbop enjoying his new text wrap in full-blown color, take a look at Color Plate 13-1.)

While you're visiting the color section to check out Color Plate 13-1, we invite you to pass your eyes over Color Plate 13-2. This color plate has absolutely nothing to do with text wrap or any other InDesign feature. In fact, it's completely superfluous. We offer it only as evidence that Shenbop occasionally gets a break from his professorial duties and enjoys some down time at his favorite country getaway.

If you're having trouble aligning points when editing a standoff boundary, try dragging a guide from the vertical or horizontal ruler. Make sure Snap to Guides is turned on in the View menu and then drag each point to the guide.

Figure 13-7:
Add and drag points to modify a standoff boundary.

Wrapping with the best of 'em

Here are a few additional tidbits that will help you transition from new wrapper on the block to Wuf Daddy status.

✔ When you move a graphic with a text wrap applied, it retains its wrapping power, so text automatically reflows to accommodate the graphic's new position.

✔ If you mess up while editing a standoff boundary, press ⌘+Z or Ctrl+Z as many times as necessary to undo previous steps. If you *really* mess up, choose Object➪Text Wrap and click on the No Wrap button. This clears the existing text wrap. Then click on another wrap option and start over from scratch.

✔ You can apply a text wrap to multiple graphics at the same time by Shift-clicking to select the graphics and then choosing a wrap option in the Text Wrap palette.

✔ Select the Invert check box in the Text Wrap palette to flow text *inside* the standoff boundary so it overlaps the graphic.

✔ You can also wrap a text block around another text block. This can come in handy when you're creating pull quotes and other special text items that need to stand out from your body copy. Just select the text block around which you want to wrap other text and choose a wrap option from the Text Wrap palette. You can then set and edit the standoff boundary just as you would when wrapping text around a graphic.

✔ To prevent a text block from wrapping around an object with text wrap applied, click on the text block with the arrow tool and choose Object➪Text Frame Options. Then select the Ignore Text Wrap option at the bottom of the resulting dialog box and press Return or Enter. The text block will now resist the lure to wrap.

Turning Type into Graphics

When you need to create logos or other special text, perhaps for an advertisement or a brochure, you'll want to use InDesign's Create Outlines feature. By choosing Type➪Create Outlines (or pressing ⌘+Shift+O on the Mac or Ctrl+Shift+O under Windows), you can convert any text block selected with the type or arrow tool into a collection of editable paths. The top example in Figure 13-8, for instance, shows a standard text block. The bottom example shows the same text block after choosing the Create Outlines command, selecting the paths with the hollow arrow tool, and applying a fill of None.

Figure 13-8:
Select a text block (top) and choose the Create Outlines command to convert it to a collection of editable paths (bottom).

After you choose the Create Outlines command to convert type to paths, you can edit the paths using the hollow arrow and pen tools just as you would edit a frame or a clipping path. Figure 13-9, for example, shows our converted text from Figure 13-8 after a good bit of path editing. What was once Helvetica is now, well, something else.

Figure 13-9:
You can edit text converted to paths to create custom type effects.

When you convert text to paths it becomes a graphic, so you can no longer edit it with the type tool or apply text formatting attributes. But you can preserve the original editable text by pressing Option or Alt while you choose the Create Outlines command. InDesign creates a copy of the original text and converts that copy to paths. Then you can just drag the converted copy off the original text using the arrow tool.

The Create Outlines command uses font outline information from the font files to convert text to paths. Some font vendors block the outline information that InDesign needs to perform the conversion. If you try to convert text that uses such a font, you'll see a message on-screen explaining that the text can't be converted. Boo hoo.

Part IV

InDesign for Einsteins

The 5th Wave   By Rich Tennant

"...and here's me with Cindy Crawford. And this is me with Madonna and Celine Dion..."

In this part . . .

Not everyone appreciates the *...For Dummies* series. The title is a tongue-in-cheek reference to the fact that most people have neither the time nor the inclination to become computer nerds — excepting fools like ourselves, of course. Saying you're a computer dummy is like saying you don't understand the attraction of rap. You're not complaining; you're bragging.

But, alas, many misunderstand the series, both here in the United States and abroad. When translated, the title is alternatively made more or less offensive. The French *Pour Les Nuls* literally means *for the zeros,* or losers. German book covers used to feature *Für Dummies* with the *Dummies* crossed out and *Anfänger* — or *beginners* — in its place. Our favorite comes from Poland, where *Dia Opornych* translates to *for the reluctant.* There's synergy for you — being naturally lazy, we were reluctant to write this book; now they're reluctant to read it.

Well, whatever you think of the title, we call it a starting point. You begin a dummy, but you emerge a full-fledged dweeb. Now that your dummy days are behind you, it's time to move on and explore InDesign on a higher plane. Hence our book-within-a-book, *InDesign for Einsteins.* Here you'll uncover the answers to mysteries that confound ordinary dummies the world around: How do you create page numbers that automatically update? What's up with master pages? How can you manage text and graphics linked from disk? Is preflighting too cool for you? And how do you print documents in the "paperless office" of tomorrow?

You may be thinking, "I'm no Einstein! I can't handle this!" But you forget — we've seen you grow. When we met you back in Chapter 1, frankly, we didn't think you stood much of a chance. We didn't want to tell you this, but the betting pool floated your name at 22 to 1. Now look at you — such a confident expression, such agile mouse control, such a massive brain. You make Einstein look like a clueless troglodyte, a spider monkey at the zoo, or worse, one of those guys who paints his face and wears clown wigs at football games. You're so brilliant, the people around you put on UV-protected ski goggles. You, my friend, are ready for the information that awaits you. So permit us to offer these gentle words of encouragement: Whoop, whoop, whoop!

Chapter 14

Page Crazy

*I*n this chapter, we take a step back and look at the bigger picture. For once, we don't prattle on about type or graphics. Nope, this chapter is about pages, which, after all, are what a page-layout program is all about.

This is where you find out how to turn your pages into a bona fide document, complete with page numbers, sections, and multipage spreads. Okay, that might not sound as glamorous as text wraps or as sophisticated as clipping paths, but think of it like this: There comes a time in every page's life when it's ready to graduate to documenthood. Your pages yearn to make you proud, but they can't go it alone — they need a little help from you.

Say Hello to the Pages Palette

When it comes to arranging your document, the Pages palette is where it all happens. Choose Window⇨Pages or press F12 to display the palette, which is shown in Figure 14-1. As you can see, the Pages palette is divided into two parts. The bottom part is the master pages area, which happens to be the subject of Chapter 15. The top part, which is the topic of this chapter, contains icons that represent the pages in your document, as follows:

✔ By default, each page icon has the letter A on it, which indicates that the A-Master page is assigned. We explain all about master pages in Chapter 15. For now, don't worry about it.

✔ The way page icons appear in the palette depends on the number of pages in your document and whether or not you use facing (double-sided) pages. If your document contains single-sided pages, each page appears as its own icon in the palette. If your document includes an even number of double-sided pages, the first and last pages appear as single icons and all pages in-between are grouped in two-page spreads. If your document includes an odd number of double-sided pages, only the first page appears as a single icon; the rest are two-page spreads.

In case your memory about facing pages needs refreshing, here's a brief recap. Double-sided documents contain left and right pages that face each other (called a *spread*), just like the pages in an open book. The pages in a spread appear next to each other on-screen, in the Pages palette, and in your printed document.

✔ The number below each page icon indicates the page number.

✔ To quickly jump to any page in your document, double-click on a page icon. To view all pages in a spread, double-click on the page numbers below the icons. Either way, the page numbers become highlighted, indicating that the selected page or spread is currently visible on-screen.

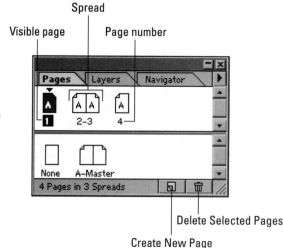

Figure 14-1:
The one, the only Pages palette.

If your document contains more than a few pages, you might need to scroll down to see all the page icons in the Pages palette. You can also drag the size box in the lower-right corner of the palette to enlarge it so that all page icons are visible.

Adding and deleting pages

When you lay out a multipage document, you need to be able to add and delete pages on the fly. Where do you go to perform such tasks? The Pages palette, of course:

✔ To add a new page at the end of your document, click on the Create New Page button in the bottom-right corner of the palette. If your document contains master pages (as described in Chapter 15), the new page will use the same master as the page that precedes it.

✔ If you want to insert multiple new pages or add a page somewhere other than at the end of your document, choose Insert Pages from the Pages palette menu to display the dialog box shown in Figure 14-2. In the Pages option box, enter the number of new pages you want to insert. Then choose an option from the Insert pop-up menu to specify where in your document the new pages should be inserted. If you choose the After Page or Before Page option, enter the number of the page you want your new page (or pages) to appear after or before, respectively. If you're using master pages, choose the master you want to apply to your new page (or pages) from the Master pop-up menu. When you're finished, click OK or press Return or Enter.

Figure 14-2:
Use this
dialog box
to specify
options for
new pages.

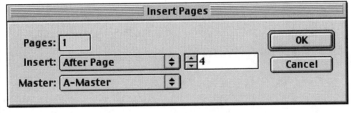

✔ You can also add one or more pages to the end of your document by choosing File⇨Document Setup and entering a new number in the Number of Pages option box. But if you don't need to change other document settings, it's faster to use the options in the Pages palette.

✔ To delete one or more pages from a document, click on the page icon for the page you want to delete, Shift-click to select multiple pages, or click on the page numbers to select a spread. Then either click on the trash can icon at the bottom of the Pages palette or drag the selected pages over the trash can and release the mouse button. InDesign serves up a dialog box asking whether you really and truly want to delete the selected page or pages. If you're sure, press Return or Enter to proceed with deletion. Otherwise, click on the Cancel button and say, "Phew! That was close."

If you don't want to be bothered with the pesky confirm dialog box, Option-click or Alt-click on the trash can icon to delete selected pages with no questions asked.

✔ But wait, you can delete selected pages in yet another way. Choose the Delete command from the palette menu. The command name changes to Delete Page, Delete Pages, Delete Spread, or Delete Spreads depending on whether you selected one or more pages or spreads.

When you delete one or more pages or spreads, InDesign preserves the links between threaded text blocks and automatically moves all subsequent pages forward in your document. For example, suppose you have a ten-page, double-sided document with a single story that flows across all pages. If you delete pages 2 and 3, InDesign reflows the text and adjusts the pages so that pages 4 and 5 become pages 2 and 3, 6 and 7 become 4 and 5, and so on.

Here's another tidbit. You can duplicate a selected spread. Just drag it to the Create New Page button or choose Duplicate Spread from the palette menu. Either way, InDesign places a copy of the spread at the end of the document.

A single page that appears at the beginning or end of a double-sided document is considered a spread, so you can make a copy of it using the Duplicate Spread command.

If you want to create a duplicate spread somewhere other than at the end of your document, just Option-drag or Alt-drag a selected spread to the desired location in the Pages palette, as described in the next section.

Rearranging pages

You can also rearrange the order of your document pages in the Pages palette. To move a page or a spread, click on a page icon or page numbers and drag. The cursor changes to a hand icon gripping a vertical black line, as shown in Figure 14-3. Position the black line at the spot where you want to move the page or spread and release the mouse button. Your page or spread now resides in its new location.

Making your spread an island

Here's a feature you might not need often, but when you do, InDesign has it covered. You know those foldout ads in magazines? They're put together as multipage spreads, otherwise known as *island spreads* in InDesign. Typically, island spreads consist of three or four pages, as in the case of a foldout advertisement. But InDesign lets you create spreads up to ten pages long if you like.

To create an island spread, double-click on a spread in the Pages palette and choose Set As Island Spread from the palette menu. The page numbers below the spread become enclosed in brackets. Then drag a page icon so that the vertical black line is positioned at the beginning, middle, or end of the spread, depending on where you want to add the page. When you release the mouse button, the page is added to the spread, as shown in Figure 14-4. You can add more pages in the same way.

Figure 14-3:
You can rearrange pages simply by dragging them in the Pages palette.

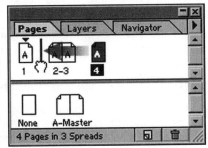

Figure 14-4:
Island spreads consist of three to ten pages.

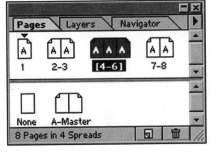

If you want to remove a page from an island spread, you need to select the spread and choose Clear Island Spread from the Pages palette menu. Then you can drag the page out of the spread.

Numbering Pages Automatically

Now that you have all your pages in order, it's time to number them. You could go and type a number on each page in your document. But in addition to being tedious, entering page numbers in this way means that if you add, delete, or rearrange pages later, you have to go through and manually renumber each page. The better way to number your pages is to use InDesign's automatic page number character, which automatically updates when you add, delete, or change the order of pages in your document.

To insert an automatic page number, double-click on a page icon in the Pages palette to go to the page you want to number. Then follow these steps:

1. **Drag with the type tool to create a text frame big enough to hold your page number and any accompanying text.**

   You'll probably want to place page numbers in the top- or bottom-right corner on right-hand pages and in the top- or bottom-left corner on left-hand pages.

2. **Type the text that you want to appear with your page number.**

   If you want to include the name of your document or any other identifying information (such as a part or chapter name), now's a good time. If you do, be sure to enter a space before or after the text to separate it from the page number.

3. **Click at the spot in the text block where you want to insert the page number.**

   On a left-hand page, for example, you probably want the page number to appear before any accompanying text. On a right-hand page, it usually appears after the text.

4. **Choose Layout⇨Insert Page Number.**

   You can also press ⌘+Option+N on the Mac or Ctrl+Alt+N under Windows. InDesign inserts the correct page number. You can then select the number and format it as you would any other text. For example, you might want to left-align page numbers on left-hand pages and right-align them on right-hand pages using the alignment options in the Paragraph palette.

Now that you've numbered one page, the next step is to number all the other pages in your document. You can do this in a few different ways. If you're creating a double-sided document, you can place the automatic page number character on one left-hand page and one right-hand page and then copy and paste them on the rest of your left- and right-hand pages, respectively. Or if you're using master pages, as explained in Chapter 15, you can enter the character on your left and right masters and call it a day.

If you add page numbers to master pages, you see the letter of the master (as in A-Master) instead of the actual page number. But the pages in your document will carry the correct page numbers.

By default, when you insert the automatic page number character, InDesign places an arabic numeral — the standard 1, 2, 3, and so on. But you can change the default numbering scheme using the Section Options command in the Pages palette.

To change the numbering scheme for your document, double-click on the first page icon in the Pages palette and choose Section Options from the palette menu. Then choose a numbering scheme from the Style pop-up menu in the resulting dialog box. In addition to arabic numerals, you can choose uppercase or lowercase Roman numerals or letters. After you make your choice, press Return or Enter. InDesign automatically updates all the page numbers in your document to use your new style of numbers (or letters, should you choose).

Using different numbering schemes is especially useful when you're creating a document with more than one section, as discussed next.

Dividing Documents into Sections

Long documents are often divided into sections that are numbered independently. For example, the pages that precede the first chapter in a book (called *front matter*) are usually numbered using lowercase roman numerals, and the rest of the book carries arabic page numbers. Along the same lines, newspapers are generally divided into lettered sections (the Sports section is often letter C, for example), which are numbered separately from each other.

To create a new section in your document, double-click on the icon in the Pages palette for the page where you want the new section to begin. Then choose Section Options from the palette menu to display the dialog box shown in Figure 14-5. Here's how the options work:

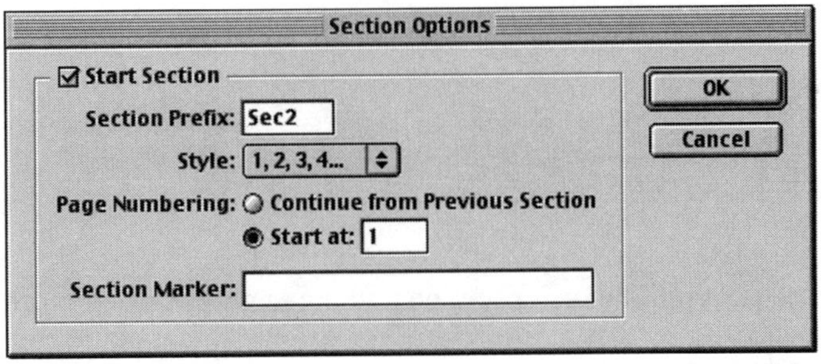

Figure 14-5:
Specify options for a new document section in this dialog box.

```
┌──────────────── Section Options ─────────────────┐
│ ┌─ ☑ Start Section ──────────────────┐           │
│ │                                     │  ┌──OK──┐ │
│ │   Section Prefix: Sec2              │  └──────┘ │
│ │                                     │ ┌─Cancel─┐│
│ │          Style: 1, 2, 3, 4...  ▢    │ └────────┘│
│ │  Page Numbering: ○ Continue from Previous Section│
│ │                  ◉ Start at: 1      │           │
│ │   Section Marker: [              ]  │           │
│ └─────────────────────────────────────┘           │
└───────────────────────────────────────────────────┘
```

✔ The Start Section check box, which is selected by default, tells InDesign to begin a new section at the selected page.

✔ In the Section Prefix option box, you can enter a prefix for your section. The prefix can be from one to five characters and appears before the page number in the page box at the bottom of the document window. For example, you might type *Intro* as a prefix for a document's introduction.

✔ From the Style pop-up menu, choose a page numbering scheme, as explained in the preceding section.

✔ If you want the page numbers in the new section to continue from the previous section, select the Continue from Previous Section radio button. Otherwise, select the Start At radio button and enter the number you want to appear on the first page of the new section.

TIP

✔ To make a new section start on a left-hand page, you need to enter an even number in the Start At option box. To start a section on a right-hand page, enter an odd number. Figure 14-6 shows examples of both scenarios.

Sections starting on right-hand page

Section starting on left-hand page

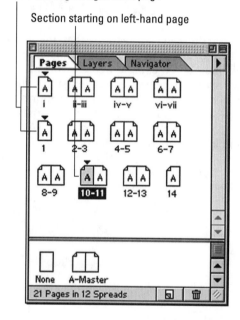

Figure 14-6:
Little black arrows mark the begin-ning of each section in your document.

✔ In the Section Marker option box, you can enter one or more words to accompany your page numbers. For example, you could type the word *Introduction* to appear along with the page numbers in the introductory section of your document. To add a section marker next to a page number in your document, you need to click with the type tool at the spot where you want to insert it. Then Control-click on the Mac or right-click under Windows and choose Insert Special Character⇨ Section Marker.

In the publishing world, copy appearing with a page number at the top of pages is called *running heads* and at the bottom of pages is referred to as *running feet*.

When you're finished, press Return or Enter to put your new section into effect. A little black down-pointing arrow appears above the first page of the section in the Pages palette. Figure 14-6 shows a document with three sections as it appears in the Pages palette.

If you want to modify or remove an existing section, select the first page in the section and choose Section Options to redisplay the Section Options dialog box. Make any changes or deselect the Start Section check box to remove the section settings, and press Return or Enter.

You can quickly access the Section Options dialog box by double-clicking on the black down-pointing arrow above the first page in the section.

If you want to see the total number of pages in a long document with many differently numbered sections, choose File⇨Preferences⇨General to display the General panel of the Preferences dialog box. Then choose Absolute Numbering from the View pop-up menu and press Return or Enter. All pages appear numbered sequentially from 1 on in the Pages palette. To return the page icons to their real page numbers, just press ⌘+Z or Ctrl+Z to undo the Preferences setting.

Chapter 15

The Masters Are Your Slaves

*I*f you had to choose your favorite thing about working on a computer, what would it be? Okay, not counting games. Keeping in touch with friends through e-mail doesn't count either. No, not shopping on the Web. Oh, never mind. Here's what we're getting at: Most of the time, computers help us do our work better and faster. If they didn't, we'd all still be laying out pages the traditional way.

Nevertheless, sometimes we feel like slaves to our computers, slowly plodding away at even the most rudimentary tasks. The beauty of working with a page-layout program such as InDesign, however, is that you can offload on your software many repetitive and mundane layout tasks by learning to use master pages. In a little while, you'll be laying out your pages faster and more consistently. And don't let the name *master pages* intimidate you. As you'll soon see, it's easy to turn any master into a willing slave.

Meeting the Masters

Master pages are like style sheets (described in Chapter 9) for entire pages. Just as you can set up styles to automate text formatting tasks, you can set up master pages to automate certain layout chores.

When you place an element on a master page, that element appears on every page that has that master applied. For example, in a single-sided document, you might want to put a page number in the top-right corner and a company logo at the bottom of each page. If you use a master page, you don't need to go through and insert the page number and logo on every page; you simply place them on the master.

In a double-sided document, you would create two master pages — one for the left page and one for the right. Any elements you place on the left master page appear on left-hand document pages, and those you place on the right master show up on right-hand document pages.

So what should you put on a master page? Prime candidates for a master page are elements that appear in the same position on many document pages. These elements commonly include layout tools such as columns, guides, grids, and empty text and graphics frames, and repeating text and graphic elements such as running heads, page numbers, logos, and ornaments.

Making Master Pages

Everything you need to make, apply, and modify master pages is located in the Pages palette, which you can display by pressing F12. The bottom part of the palette contains master page icons. If your document is double-sided, you'll see a master spread called A-Master, as shown in Figure 15-1. If your document is single-sided, the A-Master appears as a single page icon.

Figure 15-1:
The bottom portion of the Pages palette holds your master pages.

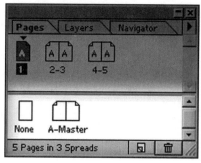

Setting up your first master page

To set up elements on a master page in a new document, double-click on the left or right A-Master page icon in the Pages palette to display the left or right master on-screen. (Of course, if your document is single-sided, you have only one A-Master page icon, so double-click on that.) You'll notice that the master page contains the margins and column guides you specified in the New Document dialog box. But any other items you may have placed on your document pages do not appear on the master.

Now all you need to do is place any elements that you want to appear on all left- or right-hand pages in your document, depending on which master you selected. In Figure 15-2, for example, in addition to margins and column guides, we included empty frames as placeholders for text and graphics, ruler guides, and page numbers. If you've already started setting up your document pages, you can even copy and paste items from those pages onto your master. When you've finished setting up the left or right master in a double-sided document, double-click on the other page icon in the A-Master spread and set up that master as well.

To return to your layout, double-click on a document page icon in the top part of the Pages palette. The items you placed on your left and right master pages now appear on the left- and right-hand pages in your document.

If you don't see the master page items on your document pages, choose View⇨Display Master Items to enable the command. You can also press ⌘+Y on the Mac or Ctrl+Y under Windows.

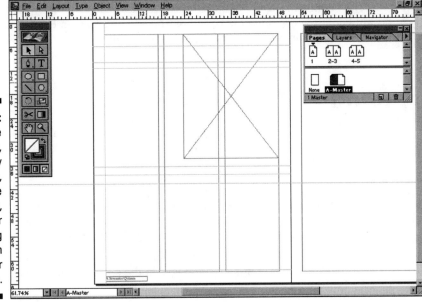

Figure 15-2:
Place guides, empty frames, page numbers, and other repeating elements on master pages.

Making more masters

You now know how to set up your default master pages — which are applied to your document pages automatically — but if your document contains multiple sections, the default masters alone won't cut it. For example, the first page in each section might have a different layout from the rest of the pages. In such a case, you'll want to create an additional master page that you can apply to each section opener.

If you want to create a new master page from scratch, ⌘-click or Ctrl-click on the Create New Page button at the bottom of the Pages palette. (Remember, that's the little page icon next to the trash can.) A new master page or spread called B-Master appears next the A-Master in the palette and is displayed in the document window. Just set up the new master as you normally would. You can create additional masters — named C-Master, D-Master, and so on — in the same way.

You can also create a new master based on an existing document page or spread by dragging it from the top part of the Pages palette to the master page area at the bottom of the palette. Alternatively, you can click on a document page or spread and choose Save As Master from the Pages palette menu. Either way, InDesign creates a new master that contains all the objects on the selected document page or spread.

If the document page you use to create a new master already has a master applied, the new master is based on the existing master. Huh? Not to worry. We explain this phenomenon later in the chapter.

Applying and Removing Master Pages

As mentioned earlier in this chapter, InDesign automatically applies default master pages (the A-Master) to all your document pages. So to use another master on a particular page, you need to apply it, as follows:

✔ To apply a master to a single page, drag the name of the master from the bottom portion of the Pages palette and position it over the page icon in the top part of the palette. When the page becomes surrounded by a black box, as shown in Figure 15-3, release the mouse button.

✔ To apply a master to a spread, drag the name of the master so that the black box surrounds all the pages in the spread. Then release the mouse button.

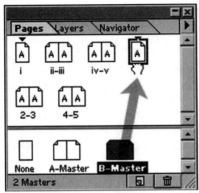

Figure 15-3:
Apply
masters to
document
pages
simply by
dragging.

✔ If you want to apply a master to multiple pages at once, choose Apply Master to Pages from the Pages palette menu to display the dialog box shown in Figure 15-4.Choose the name of the master you want to apply from the Apply Master pop-up menu. In the To Pages option box, type the page numbers or range of pages to which you want to apply the master. Press Return or Enter to apply your changes.

Figure 15-4:
Apply
masters to
multiple
pages at the
same time
using this
dialog box.

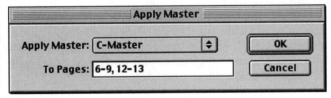

✔ You can avoid all this dragging and dialog box stuff. To quickly apply a master to one or more pages, click to select a single document page or Shift-click to select multiple pages in the Pages palette. Then Option-click or Alt-click on a master page icon to apply the master to the selected pages.

Whenever you apply a new master to one or more pages, any default master page settings for the affected pages are overridden and the letter on each page icon changes to reflect the newly applied master.

If you want to remove all master page elements from a document page, apply the None master to the page in the same way you would apply any other master in the Pages palette. In other words, you can drag the None master over the page icon, choose Apply Master to Pages from the palette menu and then choose None from the Apply Master pop-up menu, or select the desired page icon and Option-click or Alt-click on the None master icon.

To delete a master page from your document, double-click on the name of the master in the Pages palette, and then choose Delete Master Spread from the palette menu or click on the trash can icon at the bottom of the palette. A dialog box appears asking whether you really want to delete the master. Press Return or Enter to proceed with deletion. If the deleted master was applied to pages in your document, InDesign automatically applies the None master to those pages.

Modifying Masters

Suppose you've laid out your document and applied its master pages. You're feeling proud, relaxed, and altogether on top of things. Just when you're about to wrap up and head home early, you sense that annoying guy who sits in the cubicle next to yours leaning over your shoulder. "Wrong logo," he says, as if he's pleased to have created more work for you. Determined not to let him have fun at your expense, you double-click a master page icon in the Pages palette and replace the wrong logo with the right one. Then you sit back and smile as the annoying guy watches you flip through your document pages, which now have the proper logo in place.

If you're lucky enough to have your own office instead of a cubicle, you might not have problems with the annoying guy. But the point of our little story still applies: You can edit master page items to automatically update any document pages that have that master applied.

Changing master items on document pages

Sometimes, you might want to change a master page item on a document page. For example, you might need to reposition a text or graphic frame on a particular page or spread, but you don't want to change the applied master because that would affect other document pages as well. Fortunately, you don't have to create a new master or change or remove the existing master to make the adjustment. You can simply change the offending master item on the document page, as follows:

1. **Select the master item on the document page.**

   To select a master item on a document page you need to press ⌘+Shift on the Mac or Ctrl+Shift under Windows as you click on the item.

2. **Change the item.**

   You can move the item, delete it, or make any other you changes you like. When you change a master item on a document page, the item loses its link to the master page. (InDesign calls this process *overriding*.) So if you change the same item on the master page later, it *won't* be updated on the document page on which you changed it.

3. **Select and modify other master items as desired.**

   You can override as many master items as you want in the same way.

If you change your mind after overriding a master item on a document page, you're out of luck. Just kidding! Click on the item on the document page to select it, and then choose Remove Selected Local Overrides from the Pages palette menu. This reinstates the link between the item and the master page. To restore all objects on a selected page or spread to master item status, choose Edit⇨Deselect All to make sure no items are selected, and then choose Remove All Local Overrides from the palette menu.

Making masters that affect other masters

InDesign offers a master page feature you won't find in other page-layout programs. Because we know that InDesign is a family-oriented program, the concept behind the feature should seem familiar. In Chapter 9, we explain how to create styles that are based on other styles and share a parent/child relationship. Change the parent style, and the corresponding attributes in the child style change as well. InDesign lets you do the same thing with master pages. After you set up one master page or spread (the *parent*), you can create as many variations (or *children*) of that master as you like. Here's how:

1. **Choose New Master from the Pages palette menu.**

   The New Master dialog box appears, as shown in Figure 15-5.

Figure 15-5: Specify options for a new master page in this dialog box.

New Master

Prefix:	B		OK
Name:	Master		Cancel
Based on Master:	A-Master		
Number of Pages:	2		

2. Specify settings in the New Master dialog box.

In the Prefix option box, type a letter or a number to identify the master on the page icons in the Pages palette. If you want to give your master a name, enter it in the Name option box. Now for the most important step: Choose an existing master page or spread from the Based on Master pop-up menu. This master will serve as the parent for your new master. Finally, in the Number of Pages option box, type a number to specify how many pages you want in your new master spread.

3. Press Return or Enter.

Your new master appears selected in the bottom of the Pages palette, as shown in Figure 15-6. Notice that it carries the prefix of the master page on which it is based. In Figure 15-6, for example, we based the B-Master on the A-Master, so the page icons of the B-Master carry the letter *A*. Also note that your new master contains all the elements of the master page on which it is based — you can see that the two masters are related.

4. Set up any additional elements on your new master page.

You're finished.

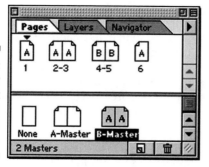

Figure 15-6: The new master that is selected is the Pages palette.

You can also base an existing master on another existing master. In the Pages palette, just drag the name of the master you want to be the parent over the icon of the master you want to be the child and release the mouse button. Alternatively, you can double-click on the parent master name and then Option-click or Alt-click on the child master. Any pre-existing margins and columns on the child master are replaced by those on the parent master. All other parent master elements are simply added to the existing elements on the child master.

You can use any of these methods to create as many child masters based on a single parent as you like. And when you make changes to the parent master, any elements that also appear on the child masters are automatically updated as well.

Saving Time with Libraries

With all this talk about master pages, we can't resist telling you about another great timesaving layout feature, called libraries. *Libraries* are storage areas for text and graphics you use frequently. If you do a lot of work for the same client, for example, you probably use certain elements — such as logos, taglines, and that sort of thing — over and over in different documents. Rather than navigating through multiple folders and files every time you need to place one of these elements in a document, you can simply put them in a library and access them on the fly.

Creating libraries

To create a new library, choose Window⇨Libraries⇨New to display the New Library dialog box. Type a name for your library and choose the folder in which you want to store it. Then press Return or Enter. A palette window appears with a palette tab sporting the name of your library, as shown in Figure 15-7. Now you can add elements to the library in any of the following ways:

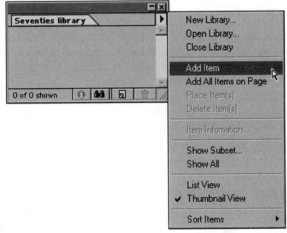

Figure 15-7:
A sad, empty Library palette with its palette menu displayed.

- ✔ Select an object in your document and drag it to the Library palette. When you release the mouse button, the object is added to the palette.

- ✔ Select one or more objects in your document, and click on the little page icon at the bottom of the Library palette.

- ✔ You can also add a selected object to a library by choosing Add Item from the Library palette menu. To add all the objects on the current page, choose Add All Items on Page from the palette menu.

No matter how you add an object, it appears as a thumbnail with the file name below it in the Library palette, as shown in Figure 15-8. If you add an embedded graphic (as explained in Chapter 16) or text block, it's given the oh-so-descriptive name *Untitled*. To give an untitled element a name that's a little more meaningful, double-click on the item in the Library palette to display the Item Information dialog box. Enter a name in the Item Name option box, type a description in the Description option box if you like, and press Return or Enter.

Figure 15-8:
Library items appear as thumbnails in the Library palette.

When you add an object to a library, all of the object's attributes are preserved. For example, text retains its formatting, images keep their colors, and grouped objects remain grouped.

To delete an item from a library, click on the item to select it. Then click on the trash can icon at the bottom of the Library palette or choose Delete Item from the palette menu. A dialog box pops up asking you to confirm your decision to delete. Press Return or Enter to proceed.

When working with libraries, keep in mind that you can't undo many of the operations you're likely to perform in the Library palette — such as deleting stuff. So be extra careful when you're making changes.

Finding and placing library items

The whole point of creating libraries is so you can quickly find and use the items in them. If the library you want is not displayed on-screen, choose Window⇨Libraries⇨Open to display the Open a Library dialog box. Locate the library file and double-click on it to open it. (Under Windows, library files carry the extension *.indl*.)

If the library doesn't include many items, you can just scroll through the Library palette to find a particular item. For bigger libraries, however, the following is a much better way to find stuff:

1. Choose Show Subset from the Library palette menu.

You can also click on the binocular icon at the bottom of the Library palette. Either way, you get the Subset dialog box shown in Figure 15-9.

2. Select a search option.

Select the Search Entire Library radio button to search all items within the library. Select the Search Currently Shown Items option to refine a previous search.

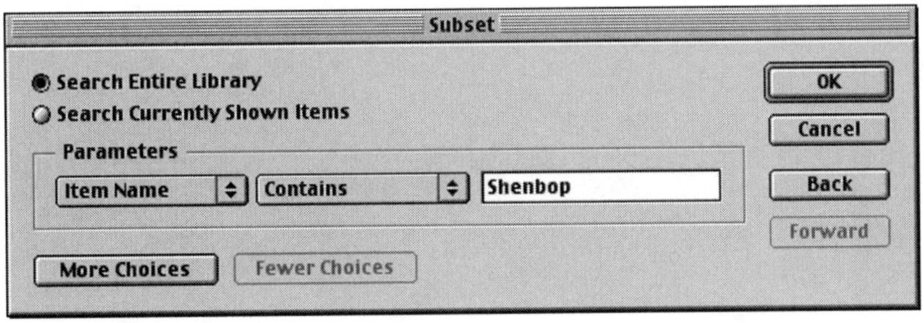

Figure 15-9:
Use this dialog box to specify how you want to search for library items.

Subset	
● Search Entire Library	OK
○ Search Currently Shown Items	Cancel
┌ Parameters ───────────────	
Item Name ⬍ Contains ⬍ Shenbop	Back
	Forward
More Choices Fewer Choices	

3. Define the parameters of your search.

The options in the Parameters section of the dialog box all work together to define your search. For example, if you choose Item Name or Description from the first pop-up menu, you can type a word or phrase in the option box on the far right. Then choose Contains from the second pop-up to search for the word or phrase, or choose Doesn't Contain to search for everything that doesn't include the word or phrase. You can also search by Creation Date or Object Type (such as Image, EPS, Text, and so on) by choosing these options from the first pop-up menu.

4. Click on the More Choices button to add more search criteria.

Each time you click on the More Choices button, the dialog box expands to let you specify additional search parameters. You can click the button up to five times. If you want to find only items that match all search criteria, select the Match All radio button. To find items that match any of the search criteria, select the Match Any One radio button.

5. Press Return or Enter to begin your search.

The Subset dialog box disappears and the Library palette displays only those items that met the search criteria. If no items matched your search request, the palette appears empty. To redisplay all the items in the Library palette, choose Show All from the palette menu.

Whew! That was a lot of work. Fortunately, the next step is much simpler. To add a library item to your document, just drag the item from the Library palette to the desired location in your document and release the mouse button. And that, friends, is all there is to it.

Chapter 16

Tinkering with Links

*H*ave you ever wondered what really goes on inside InDesign when you place a text or graphic file on a page? Well wonder no longer. Here's the straight scoop:

A cowboy lurks inside every copy of InDesign. He spends most of his time strumming a six-string beside a campfire and, oddly enough, singing '70s tunes. But when you choose File⇨Place, he goes to work. He grabs an invisible magic rope, called a *link*, and lassos the text or graphic file you requested. (That's what cowboys do after all.) Then with amazing speed and dexterity, he cinches the other end of the rope around your document. Now because the rope is magic, it can transport a replica of the text or graphic into your document without disturbing the original file in the least. At this point, the cowboy's job is finished. He hands over the reins to you through the Links palette and heads back to the campfire for a few more ditties.

Okay, so the story is a big lie. But the parts about the link and the Links palette are true. And as luck would have it, they're the subject of this chapter.

What Are Links?

Whether or not cowboys are involved, when you place a graphic on a page in an InDesign document, the graphic is not copied into the document. Rather, InDesign places a low-resolution version of the graphic on the page and creates a link to the original file on disk. Why? Well, one reason is that storing graphics outside a document keeps the document's file size smaller. Another reason is that linking to graphics makes it easy to update them in your document when you make changes to the original file.

But just because a graphic is linked by default doesn't mean it has to stay that way. When you place graphics that aren't likely to change — such as a company logo — or if you simply don't want to hassle with linked files, you can *embed* them in your document using the Links palette, as described later in this chapter. Embedding a graphic unlinks it and stores a copy of the original file inside your document.

Graphics under 48K (that's K for *kilobytes*) are an exception to the no-storage/low-resolution rule. When you import a graphic that's less than 48K, InDesign stores a copy of the file in the document and displays the graphic at full resolution on screen. InDesign still creates a link to the original file, but it's not required for printing.

Imported text files are linked the same way graphics are. But unlike graphics bigger than 48K, copies of linked text files are always stored in your InDesign document.

Looking at Links

All linked graphics and text files are listed by their file names in the Links palette, which you can display by choosing File⇨Links. You can also just press ⌘+Shift+D on the Mac or Ctrl+Shift+D under Windows. Either way, the Links palette appears with a list of all the links in your document, as shown in Figure 16-1.

Page numbers

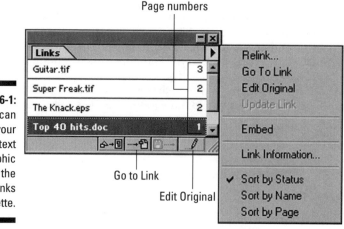

Figure 16-1:
You can view all your linked text and graphic files in the Links palette.

Go to Link

Edit Original

Here's a quick rundown of some basics:

- ✔ The number to the far right of each file name indicates the page on which the linked item appears. If a graphic appears on more than one page — as a logo might, for example — each occurrence is listed separately in the Links palette.

- ✔ If your document contains lots of links, you might need to scroll to see them. You can also resize the palette to display more links by dragging the size box in the bottom-right corner.

- ✔ To quickly jump to any linked file in your document, click on the link to select it. Then click on the Go to Link button along the bottom of the palette or choose Go to Link from the palette menu. InDesign automatically selects the graphic or text block and positions it front and center in the document window.

  You can also just press and hold the Option key on the Mac or the Alt key under Windows and double-click on a link to select and center a graphic or text block in the document window.

- ✔ You can change the order in which links are displayed in the palette by choosing a Sort option from the palette menu. By default, links are sorted by status, which means any links with problems (as discussed in the next section) appear at the top of the palette and the rest of the links are listed in reverse order of creation. In other words, the item you placed most recently appears at the top of the palette and the one you placed before that appears below it, and so on. You can also sort links alphabetically by name or sequentially by the page on which the linked items are placed.

- ✔ To edit the original of a linked text or graphic file, click on the link and then click on the Edit Original button at the bottom of the Links palette. You can also choose Edit Original from the palette menu. In either case, the application in which you created the file launches in front of the document window, and the original file is opened. You can then make changes to the file, save it, and close it. When you return to your InDesign document, you'll notice a little icon that looks like it deserves your attention. (It's next to the link's name in the Links palette.) Well, that icon does deserve your attention, and we explain how to attend to it in the next section.

- ✔ You can quickly access the Edit Original command for a linked graphic without bothering with the Links palette at all. Select the graphic with the arrow tool. Then Control-click or right-click on the graphic and choose Graphic⇨Edit Original from the resulting pop-up menu.

  If the Edit Original options appear dimmed, you don't have the application that created the original file for the selected link installed on your computer. You might still be able to edit the file by opening it in a similar program, but you can't get there from InDesign.

Dealing with scary looking icons

We don't know about you, but when we see a sign warning us about falling rocks, grizzly bears, possible encounters with Bigfoot, or some similar danger, we want to know what's up. If you're the take heed sort, you're sure to be curious about a few icons the Links palette serves up on occasion, like those in Figure 16-2.

Modified icon

Missing icon

Figure 16-2:
The Links palette with alarmist icons and the buttons that can make them go away.

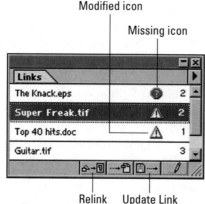

Relink   Update Link

If you see a yellow triangle containing an exclamation point to the right of a link name, that means the original text or graphic file has been modified since you placed it. In other words, the text or graphic in your document is not the most recent version. Maybe you used the Edit Original command to make some changes to an image in Photoshop, for instance. Or maybe some editor type revised some copy in a Word file.

Whatever the case may be, you need to decide whether or not you want to update the linked text or graphic to reflect the changes made to the original. Before you make any decisions about updating a text link, remember this: When you update a linked text file, any edits or formatting you applied to the text in InDesign are lost. Gone, kaput. So if the changes to the text file are minor, you're probably better off just entering them directly in your InDesign document.

In general, decisions on updating graphics are more straightforward. If the original graphic file has been changed, you want to update it in your document. Whether you're updating a graphic or text, all you need to do is click on the link for the modified file to select it. Then either click on the Update Link button at the bottom of the Links palette or choose Update Link from the palette menu. If you're updating a text link, you'll see the dialog box shown in Figure 16-3. Press Return or Enter to proceed with updating the file.

Figure 16-3:
This dialog
box warns
you that
changes
made to text
in InDesgin
will be lost
when you
update a
text link.

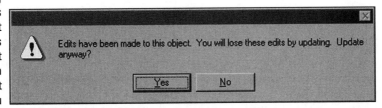

Edits have been made to this object. You will lose these edits by updating. Update anyway?

Yes   No

InDesign swaps out the old version of the graphic or text file in your document and replaces it with the updated one. It even preserves any transformations (such as rotating, scaling, or skewing) that you may have applied to the graphic or text block. The Modified icon disappears from the Links palette as well.

If your document has many modified links, you can update them all at once. Just click somewhere outside the Links palette to deselect all links and then click on the Update Link button.

If you see a little red icon that looks like a stop sign with a question mark in it, that means InDesign can't find the original text or graphic file for the link. In other words, the original file has been moved, so the link is broken or missing. To reestablish the link, click on the link in the Links palette. Then choose Relink from the palette menu or click on the Relink button at the bottom of the palette. The dialog box shown in Figure 16-4 appears. Click on the Browse button to display the Locate File dialog box. Use the pop-up menu at the top of the dialog box to find the folder that contains the file. Then double-click on the file to reestablish the link.

Figure 16-4:
Use this
dialog box
to locate
files for
broken links.

Relink

Location: ZIP-100:Desktop Folder:Seventies 2:The Knack.eps

Browse...   Cancel   OK

You can also use the Relink button or palette menu command to replace an existing graphic in your document. Just click on the link for the graphic you want to replace, and then click on the Relink button. When the Relink dialog box appears, click on the Browse button and locate the graphic file you want as a replacement for the current graphic.

By the way, if a link name has no accompanying icon, your link is happy, healthy, and ready for action.

Getting the lowdown on your links

If you want more information about a file before deciding whether to update or replace it, double-click on the link in question to display the Link Information dialog box shown in Figure 16-5. This dialog box contains tons of information about your link, including its name, status, the creation date of the original file, the file size, and whether or not it has been edited.

Link Information	
Name: Top 40 hits.doc	**OK**
Status: ⦿ Missing	**Cancel**
Date: Thu, Jun 10, 1999, 6:06 PM	
Size: 71 K	**Prev**
Page: 1	**Next**
Edited: No	
Link Needed: No	
Color Space: NA	
Profile: NA	
File Type: Microsoft® Word 97/98	
Location: ZIP-100:Desktop Folder:Seventies 2:Top 40 hits.doc	

Figure 16-5: Look here to find out everything you ever wanted to know about your links.

Figure 16-5 shows the information for a missing text link. Notice that even though the link is broken, the Link Needed entry displays the word No. That's because you don't have to link text to its source file — it's automatically stored in your document.

Embedding graphics

Previously in this chapter, we told you that you can embed graphics in your documents. Here's where we explain why and how.

The primary advantage to embedding graphics is that you don't need to bother with links and source files. If you lose the original files, you have a copy stored in your document that you can use for printing.

But embedding graphics always increases the size of your document file, and if you have lots of large graphics, your document can get huge fast. Plus, when you embed a graphic, it's no longer listed in the Links palette. If you need to edit and update the graphic, you have to locate the original file, open it, edit it, and then re-import it into your document.

You need to consider all these factors, and then decide whether or not to embed graphics on a case-by-case basis. For example, if you plan to e-mail documents to clients or a service bureau, you might want to set a file size limit of, say, 1 – 2 MB. If your document is only one page, you could probably embed several or even all graphics. If your document is longer, you could embed some. If file size isn't an issue and you don't expect to have to edit any graphics, you can embed to your heart's content.

To embed a graphic, click on the link for the graphic you want to embed and choose Embed from the Links palette menu. A dialog box like the one shown in Figure 16-6 appears to let you know how much your document's file size will increase as a result of embedding the graphic.

Figure 16-6:
This dialog
box alerts
you to the
conse-
quences of
embedding
a graphic.

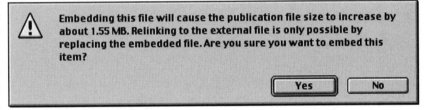

Embedding this file will cause the publication file size to increase by about 1.55 MB. Relinking to the external file is only possible by replacing the embedded file. Are you sure you want to embed this item?

Yes   No

Press Return or Enter. The graphic is embedded in your document and disappears from the Links palette.

Chapter 17

When Page Hits Paper

*I*f you're accustomed to printing documents you create in a word processor, you might be thinking, "What's to know about printing? I just choose File⇨Print, click OK, and walk over to the printer to pick up my pages. Right?"

Unfortunately, printing an InDesign document isn't quite that simple. Whether you're printing a one-page advertisement or a 100-page report from a Macintosh or a PC, you need to make some basic decisions, set up a bunch of options, and adequately prepare your document to print it accurately and reliably. But, hey, don't sweat it. Our mission — should we choose to accept it — is to take you by the hand and lead you through the printing process, so you can sleep soundly knowing all is well in Printville. Uh, hmm, er, okay — we accept.

Going PostScript Professional-Quality

The first decision you need to make is where you will print your document. If you just want to proof a draft, you might want to use an inkjet printer. But when it comes time to print the final document, you should always use a PostScript printer (also called an *output device*) to achieve high-resolution, professional-quality results. Because you'll ultimately print to a PostScript output device, that's what we explain how to do in this chapter.

If you're printing to an inkjet printer, much of the process is similar. You just won't have to bother with all the PostScript options we describe.

We begin with a few assumptions:

✔ You have a PostScript printer and the required printer driver — Adobe PS 8.6 on the Mac, Adobe PS 5.1 under Windows NT, and Adobe PS 4.3 under Windows 98 — and *PostScript printer description* (PPD) file installed on your computer.

In case you're curious, the PPD file contains a bunch of information InDesign needs to know about your printer.

If you don't have the necessary printer driver or PPD, you can find them both on the InDesign CD. Adobe, the inventor of PostScript, also has many PostScript printer drivers and PPDs available on its Web site at *www.adobe.com.*

✔ Your operating system (Macintosh or Windows) knows that your printer exists.

✔ You know that your printer exists.

If you have all that covered, you're good to go.

Setting Up Your Pages

Just as you specify the size and orientation of pages when you first create a document, you need to specify the size and orientation of the paper on which the pages will print. You can accomplish these basic tasks using the Page Setup dialog box on the Mac or the Properties dialog box under Windows.

On the Mac, choose File➪Page Setup or press ⌘+Shift+P to display the Page Attributes panel of the Page Setup dialog box, as shown in Figure 17-1. If more than one printer is connected to your computer — as is likely if you're part of an office network — choose the name of a PostScript printer from the Printer pop-up menu.

Under Windows, choose File➪Print or press Ctrl+P to display the Print dialog box. Then choose a printer from the Name pop-up menu and click on the Properties button. The Paper panel of the Properties dialog box appears, as shown in Figure 17-2.

Because of differences between operating systems, the various page setup options are in different locations on the Mac and PC. We call out differences wherever they occur, but you might want to pay close attention to our references to Mac and Windows throughout the chapter.

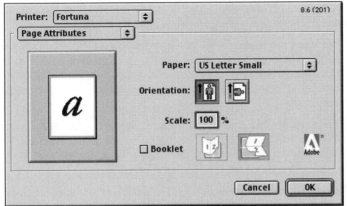

Figure 17-1:
On the Mac,
you specify
page
size and
orientation
here.

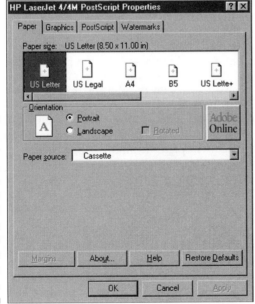

Figure 17-2:
Under
Windows,
you choose
page
size and
orientation
settings
in the
Properties
dialog box.

The options in the Page Setup and Properties dialog boxes vary slightly depending on your printer, but here are the basics:

✔ **Paper (Mac):** Choose an option from this pop-up menu to specify the size of the paper on which you want to print. Generally, the size should match the page size you chose in the New Document dialog box when you created your document. Specify a larger paper size, however, if your document will include printer's marks or a bleed, which print outside the page area (as discussed later in this chapter).

✔ **Paper Size (Windows)**: Same deal. Click on an icon to choose a paper size.

The paper size options in the Page Setup and Properties dialog boxes list only the paper sizes available for your printer, based on the active PPD. You may or may not see a custom option in the Paper pop-up menu or Paper Size area. If you do, you can choose that to set up a custom paper size.

✔ **Orientation:** Click on an icon on the Mac or a radio button under Windows to select the orientation (portrait or landscape) at which your document will be printed. Again, this setting should match the one you chose in the New Document dialog box.

✔ **Paper Source (Windows):** If you intend to manually feed special paper into the printer, choose the Manual Feed option from this pop-up menu. Otherwise, you can leave it set to Cassette, as it is by default.

✔ **Paper Source (Mac):** This option is located in the Print dialog box, which we discuss in detail later in this chapter. For now, just click OK to exit the Page Setup dialog box and choose File➪Print or press ⌘+P to display the Print dialog box. Select the All Pages From radio button if you want to print your entire document from the printer's paper tray or manual feeder. Then choose the appropriate option from the corresponding pop-up menu. If you want to print the first page on letterhead or other paper you manually feed into the printer, select the First Page From radio button and choose Manual Feed from the corresponding pop-up menu. Then choose Cassette from the Remaining From pop-up menu to print all subsequent pages from the paper tray.

On the Mac, you'll see a few additional options on the Page Attributes panel. Just ignore them. You'll specify these settings elsewhere, as explained shortly. In fact, both Mac and Windows folks can pretty much ignore all the other panels in the Page Setup and Properties dialog boxes. Most of the controls are of little use, and changing them might result in printing errors. So click OK or press Return or Enter to put your page settings into effect and exit the dialog box.

Printing Your Pages

Now that you've established your basic page settings, it's time to head to the Print dialog box. Choose File➪Print or press ⌘+P on the Mac or Ctrl+P under Windows. If you're using a Mac, you'll see the dialog box shown in Figure 17-3. Windows users get the big honkin' dialog box shown in Figure 17-4.

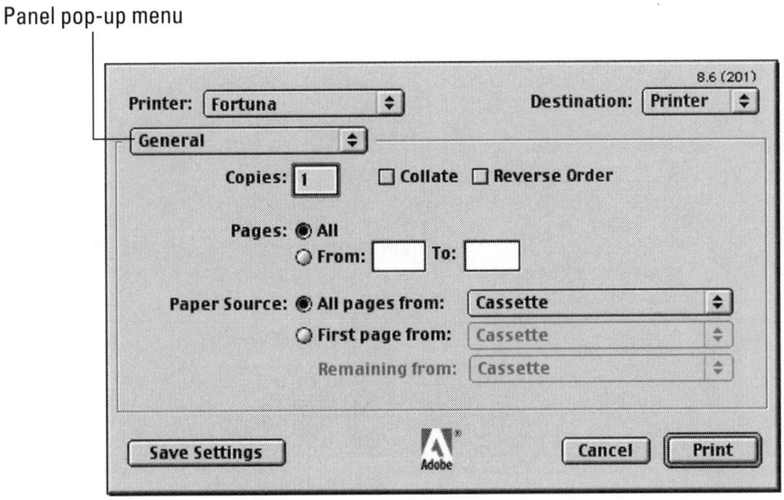

Panel pop-up menu

Figure 17-3:
The mild-
mannered
Print dialog
box on
the Mac.

If you take a gander at Figure 17-4, you'll notice several tabs across the middle of the Windows Print dialog box. These tabs lead to scads of other printing options on different panels. On the Mac, these additional options are accessible from the panel pop-up menu labeled in Figure 17-3. We discuss many, but not *all*, options on these panels in this chapter. Why don't we explain all of them? Frankly, you probably won't ever need to bother with some of them. Besides, you'd surely get bored, toss the book aside, and flip on the TV — and we can't have that. For the lowdown on the most essential options, read the following few sections.

Choosing which pages to print

Your first order of business in the Print dialog box is choosing which pages you want to print, in what order, and how many copies you want:

- **Copies:** Enter a value in this option box (called Number of Copies under Windows) to specify how many copies of your document you want to print.

- **Collate:** Select this check box if you're printing more than one copy of your document and want to print each copy in order. If you don't select this check box, InDesign prints all copies of page one, then all copies of page two, and so on.

- **Reverse Order (Mac only):** If you check this option, the last page is printed first, then the second-to-last page is printed, and so on.

Panel tabs

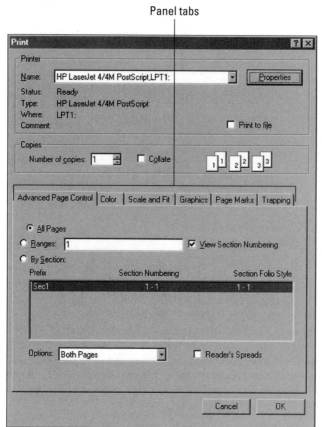

Panel tabs

Figure 17-4:
The big and
burly Print
dialog box
under
Windows.

✔ Choosing File from the Destination pop-up menu in the Mac Print dialog box or selecting the Print to File check box in the Windows Print dialog box allows you to print a PostScript version of a document to a file on disk. You might want to do this if you'll be submitting your document to a service bureau or commercial printer for high-resolution printing. This way, the technician can't modify (and possibly mess up) the document before printing.

✔ **Paper Source (Mac only):** If you haven't already specified the paper source for your printer, as explained in the previous section, do it now.

That's it for the general Print dialog box options. Now if you're on a Mac, choose the Advanced Page Control panel from the panel pop-up menu in the top-left corner of the Print dialog box. This panel is displayed by default under Windows, as you can see in Figure 17-4. Both the Mac and Windows panels contain the same options.

- ✔ **All Pages:** Not surprisingly, this option tells InDesign to print every page in your document.

- ✔ **Ranges:** Select this radio button if you want to print a range of pages. Then enter the numbers of the pages you want to print in the Ranges option box. You can mix individual pages and ranges of pages. For example, if you want to print pages 1, 2, 3, 5, 7, and 9, type **1-3, 5,7,9**. If you want to specify ranges using the section numbering in your document, select the View Section Numbering check box. Then type the range using a colon between the section prefix and the page number. For example, you might type **Sec1:1-Sec2:9** to print from page one of section one to page nine of section two.

- ✔ **By Section:** Enabling this option lets you select entire sections in your document to print. Shift-click to select a range of consecutive sections from the list. ⌘-click on the Mac or Ctrl-click under Windows to select nonconsecutive sections.

- ✔ **Options:** If your document contains two-page spreads and you want to print both pages, choose Both from this pop-up menu. You can also choose Even Pages Only or Odd Pages Only to print only even or odd numbered pages, respectively.

- ✔ **Reader's Spreads:** This option tells InDesign to print spreads together on the same sheet of paper, as if they were being bound. If the spread is larger than the selected paper size, only the part that fits on the paper will be printed.

When printing reader's spreads in a portrait-oriented document, you might want to change your page orientation to landscape to fit multiple pages on a single sheet. You can also make InDesign fit the entire spread on a single page by selecting the Scale to Fit option on the Scale and Fit panel of the Print dialog box, as described next.

Printing oversized documents

Picture two average-sized U-Haul trucks stacked one on top of the other. That's about the size of the largest document you can create in InDesign — 18 by 18 feet to be exact. Although you might never have occasion to print a document that big, you will likely need to print proofs of documents with page sizes larger than your standard desktop printer can handle. InDesign gives you two ways to do it, both of which are accessible by choosing the Scale and Fit panel of the Print dialog box shown in Figure 17-5.

You can use the Style options to scale your document to fit the selected paper size. To manually scale your document, enter values from 1 to 1000 in the Width and Height option boxes to enlarge or reduce the document by a specific percentage. Values higher than 100 enlarge your document; values lower than 100 reduce it. If you want to maintain the proportions of the document, select the Constrain Proportions check box and just enter either a Height or a Width value — the other is updated automatically. You can also

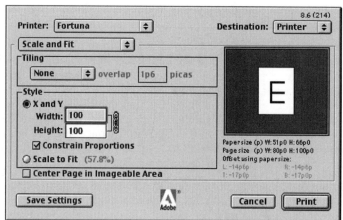

Figure 17-5:
Use the
Scale and
Fit panel of
the Print
dialog box
to print
oversized
documents
on a
desktop
printer.

click on the Scale to Fit radio button to proportionally scale the document to fit the paper size automatically. The value in parentheses next to the radio button shows the percentage at which the document was scaled.

Scaling a document does not actually change the size of your document in the InDesign file. It affects only the printed document.

Another alternative is to use *tiling*, which divides the pages in your document into sections that your printer can print. You can tell InDesign to tile your document automatically by choosing Auto from the Tiling pop-up menu. Then enter an overlap value to specify the minimum amount you want the tiles to overlap. InDesign calculates the number of tiles it will take to print your document and displays that information below the page icon on the right side of the dialog box.

The overlap value should always be greater than the margin value for your printer. Otherwise, you'll get gaps between the tiles when you assemble them after printing.

To tile a document manually, open the document and drag the ruler origin point so that the zero point is positioned at the upper-left corner of the tile you want to print. Leave a little room for overlap and page marks, if you're using any. Then choose File⇨Print, choose the Scale and Fit panel of the Print dialog box, and choose Manual from the Tiling pop-up menu. Click on the Print button to print the first tile. Repeat the process until you've printed all the tiles.

Printing in full-blown color

When you're printing a color document, you need to tell InDesign whether you want to print a composite or color separations. If you're simply printing a proof of your document on an office printer, you can print a *composite*, in which all elements and colors in your document print on one page. But if you're sending your document to a commercial printer for reproduction, you need to print *color separations*, one page for each of the process color primaries — cyan, magenta, yellow, and black — or for each spot color used in the document.

To print color separations, follow these steps:

1. **In the Print dialog box, choose Color from the panel pop-up menu on the Mac or click on the Color tab under Windows.**

   Figure 17-6 shows the options available on the Color panel, which are the same on both the Mac and Windows.

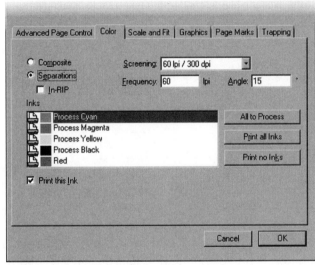

Figure 17-6:
The color printing options on display.

2. **Click on the Separations radio button.**

   The scrolling list below the Separations option lists all the inks used in your document. By default, InDesign creates a separation for all inks. Most of the time, you'll want to create separations for only the primary process colors, which you can do by clicking on the All to Process button.

3. **To prevent printing a separation for an ink, double-click on it.**

   An X appears on the printer icon to the left of the ink name, indicating that a separation will not be created for that ink.

4. **Press Return or Enter to print the separations.**

If you just want to print a composite of your document for proofing, select the Composite radio button and move on.

Color Plate 17-1 shows the cyan, magenta, and yellow separations for a graphic and how they each mix with black to take on greater detail. It also includes examples of how colors combine during the commercial printing process.

Dealing with graphics and fonts

The Graphics panel of the Print dialog box, shown in Figure 17-7, includes options that control how graphics print and how fonts are downloaded to your printer.

Figure 17-7:
Specify how images are printed and fonts are downloaded here.

The Send Image Data pop-up menu lets you set the resolution at which images are printed. If you're printing your final document, go with the All option — which is selected by default — to send all image data to the printer. The Optimized Subsampling option tells InDesign to send just enough image data to print the graphic at the best resolution the printer can achieve. This option can be useful when you're printing a proof copy of your document from a low-resolution printer. If you're just printing a draft to proof your layout (and not images), you can reduce printing time by choosing Low Resolution (72 dpi), which sends screen resolution versions of images to the printer.

To reduce proof printing time even more, select the Proof Print check box to remove all graphics and replace them with empty frames when you print.

The Font Downloading section of the Graphics panel lets you specify how fonts are downloaded to your printer. The Subset option, which is selected by default, tells InDesign to download only those characters used in your document once per page. In most cases, you should leave this option on. If you select the Complete radio button, InDesign downloads all your document's fonts once per page, which generally isn't necessary and can slow down printing.

When you are 100 percent sure your printer has all the fonts you've used, select the None radio button. If in doubt, don't select this option because it can really mess up your print job if you're wrong.

Adding special printer's marks

The Page Marks panel of the Print dialog box, shown in Figure 17-8, lets you add special marks that a commercial printer will use when printing your document. Here's how they work:

Page preview

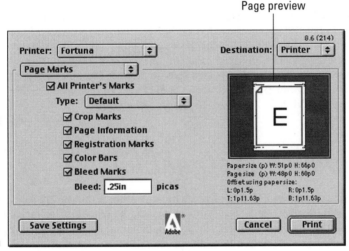

Figure17-8:
The Page
Marks panel
lets you add
printer's
marks to
pages.

 ✔ **Crop Marks:** Selecting this option adds hairline rules at the corners of your pages to indicate where the page should be trimmed. Crop marks are also called *trim marks*.

 ✔ **Page Information:** Click on this check box to tell InDesign to print the file name, page number, and current date and time in 8-point Helvetica (Mac) or 8-point Arial (Windows) in the lower-left corner of each page.

 ✔ **Registration Marks:** Select this option to add registration marks outside the page area to be used for aligning color separations.

 ✔ **Color Bars:** Click on this option to add a bar composed of color and grayscale squares at the top of pages. Printers use these color bars to make sure the colors in your document are registering properly.

✔ **Bleed Marks:** Select this option to insert at the corners of pages hairline rules that mark the edge of the bleed area, as described next.

✔ **Bleed:** Enter a value in this option box to specify the size of a bleed. The term *bleed* refers to an image or text that intentionally runs off the edge of a page. Because pages can slip while printing, you need to specify about ¼-inch bleed area beyond the edge of the page so that the bled image or text prints outside the page boundary.

If you want to add all these printer's marks to your printed pages, select the All Printer's Marks option. InDesign automatically inserts all selected printer's marks 3 points beyond the edge of the specified bleed or 3 points beyond the edge of the page boundary if no bleed is specified. That means there needs to be enough room on the paper to print them.

To see how printer's marks will affect your printed page, check the page preview area on the right side of the Page Marks panel, labeled in Figure 17-8. The blue box inside the page area indicates the page boundary. More importantly, you can tell whether or not printer's marks will fit on the printed page by looking at the Offset information below the preview area. If the offset values appear in red type, printer's marks won't fit. In that case, you have a few options. You can define a custom paper size if your printer allows it, choose a larger predefined paper size, or reduce the size of your page so that it fits on the paper by selecting the Scale to Fit option in the Scale and Fit panel of the Print dialog box.

Flying through Preflighting

Before you print your document or send it off to a commercial printer or other service provider, it's a good idea to make use of InDesign's Preflight command to check that everything is in order. *Preflighting* is what publishing folks call the process of checking the components of a document before printing. The purpose is to catch any problems that might prevent a document from printing correctly. A good idea, don't you think?

To perform a preflight check of an open document, choose File⇨Preflight to display the Summary panel of the Preflight dialog box, as shown in Figure 17-9. You can also press ⌘+Shift+Option+F on the Mac or Ctrl+Shift+Alt+F under Windows. The panel lists information on the status of all the fonts, links, images, colors, and inks used in the document.

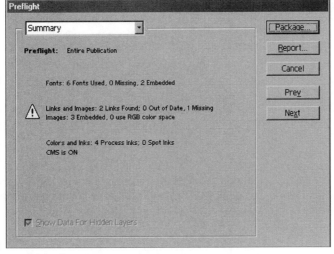

Figure 17-9:
Use the
Preflight
dialog box
to check
your docu-
ment for
problems
before
printing.

If you see a yellow triangle containing an exclamation point next to a category of information, a problem needs your attention. Choose the name of the
troublesome category (Fonts, Links and Images, or Colors and Inks) from the
pop-up menu at the top of the dialog box to access a panel with more detailed
information on the problem. In Figure 17-9, for example, we were missing a
link, so we chose Links and Images from the pop-up menu to display the
panel shown in Figure 17-10.

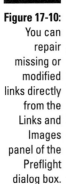

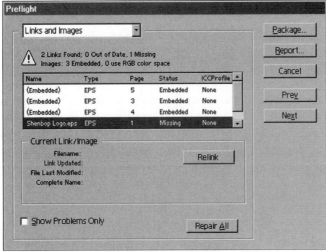

Figure 17-10:
You can
repair
missing or
modified
links directly
from the
Links and
Images
panel of the
Preflight
dialog box.

The center of each panel contains a scrolling list of all fonts, links, inks, or print settings and their status, if any. If you click on an item in the list on the Fonts or Links and Images panel, InDesign gives you more details about the item in the area below the list. In the case of a missing or outdated link, you can click on the Relink or Update button to correct the problem without accessing the Links palette.

To display only problem items in the scrolling list on the Fonts or Links and Images panel, select the Show Problems Only option at the bottom of the dialog box.

If the Fonts panel reports that fonts are missing, they're not installed on your computer. You need to either install the missing fonts or verify that they're installed on the output device on which you will be printing your document. If both these options fail, change the offending font in your document to one that's installed on your computer.

InDesign uses your document's print settings and ink list to check for duplicate spot colors. If it finds any, it lists them in the scrolling list on the Colors and Inks panel. To remove duplicate spot colors, click Cancel to close the Preflight dialog box. Then return to your document and delete the duplicate spot colors in the Swatches palette.

If you want to view all preflighting information without having to move between panels in the Preflight dialog box, click on the Report button to create and save a text file containing all current information. When the Save As dialog box appears, enter a name for the file and press Return or Enter. Then you can open the resulting file in SimpleText on the Mac or Notepad under Windows.

Packaging Your Stuff

When it comes time to send your document to a commercial printer for printing, you need to gather up all your files for hand off. Once again, InDesign provides a convenient command that does everything for you. Follow these steps:

1. **Choose File⇨Package.**

   If you still have the Preflight dialog box open, you can just click on the Package button. Alternatively, you can press ⌘+Shift+Option+P on the Mac or Ctrl+Shift+Alt+P under Windows.

   If a dialog box appears telling you that problems were detected, click on the View Info button to access the Preflight dialog box and repair the problems, and then choose the Package command again. If you see a dialog box saying you need to save your document, press Return or Enter to oblige. The Printing Instructions dialog box appears, as shown in Figure 17-11.

2. **Fill in the printing instructions.**

The information you enter in the Printing Instructions dialog box becomes part of a report — saved as a text file — that will accompany all your document files. Enter a file name, contact information, and any special instructions for the printer.

3. **Press Return or Enter.**

This leads you to the Create Package Folder dialog box, shown in Figure 17-12, on the Mac or the Package Publication dialog box under Windows. Both dialog boxes contain the same options.

4. **Enter a name for your package folder.**

Type a name in the Name option box on the Mac or the Folder Name option box under Windows.

5. **Specify packaging options.**

Several check boxes appear selected by default in the bottom part of the dialog box, which is the way you should leave them. The Copy Fonts, Copy Output Profiles, and Copy Linked Graphics options tell InDesign to copy all the fonts, color management profiles, and graphics used in your document. The Update Graphic Links in Package option changes all the graphic links in your document to the package folder you're creating.

Figure 17-11:
Enter contact information and printing instructions in this dialog box.

Printing Instructions	
Filename: Seventies Music Quizzes	Continue
Contact: Professor Shenbop	Cancel
Company: Shenbop, Inc.	
Address: Somewhere in	
Froggyville, USA	
Phone: 1-800-Shenbop	**Fax:** I don't fax
Email: shen@bop.com	
Instructions: Please be kind to my files	

In case you're wondering, text files are not relinked because they don't need to be. If you want to relink text files, you need to do it manually in the Links palette.

If you want to open your printing instructions report immediately after creating your package, click on the View Report button. If you want to edit the printing instructions before packaging, click on the Instructions button.

6. Click on the Package button.

You'll probably see a Font Alert dialog box telling you a bunch of stuff about license agreements for fonts. Press Return or Enter to make it disappear. InDesign chugs away for a few seconds, and then your package is complete.

If you go to the folder you named in Step 4, you'll find a copy of your document file, a text file with printing instructions, and folders that contain your fonts, links, and output profiles. Not bad for a few minutes of work. Now you can hand off the package folder to your commercial printer with confidence.

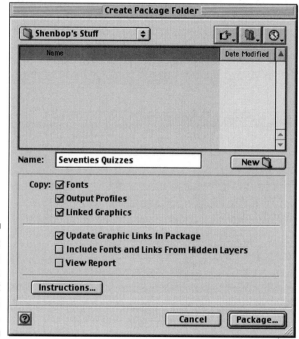

Figure 17-12:
This is where you select packaging options.

Chapter 18

The Best Printer Is No Printer at All

In This Chapter

▶ Deciding when to use HTML and PDF

▶ Setting up HTML export options

▶ Creating and viewing an HTML file

▶ Choosing PDF export options

▶ Exporting and viewing a PDF file

A s any tree would gladly confirm, the road to publishing isn't always paved with paper. No doubt, you're familiar with a little thing called the Web. (Shoot, you couldn't avoid it if you tried.) And you're likely well versed in the joys of sharing documents by e-mail.

How does InDesign let you take advantage of these online methods of distributing documents? We reveal the answers in this chapter.

HTML or PDF?

When you want to create a paperless version of your document, you need to decide first which format to use. And that decision depends on what you plan to do with the document and how you want it to be viewed.

When to use HTML

If you want to post your document as a Web page, you need to export it as a *Hypertext Markup Language* (HTML) file. HTML is the authoring language used to create documents on the Web. It consists of a set of tags for adding elements such as italics, boldface, images, and hyperlinks to Web pages. But you don't need to bother with these tags. Instead, InDesign lets you export documents directly to HTML files, as explained shortly. Then you can open and view those files in a Web browser such as Microsoft Internet Explorer or Netscape Navigator.

Sounds great, huh? Well, it is. But you must keep the following in mind before you start repurposing all your documents as Web pages:

- ✔ Folks will likely be viewing your pages on a computer monitor with a screen size of 8.33 x 6.25 or 11.11 x 8.33 inches. So a document you design to print on, say, letter-size, portrait-oriented paper (that's 8.5 x 11 inches) will not span the width of the screen and will also require readers to scroll down to see the whole page. The solution? Change your page size and orientation.

  To get a head start on modifying your layout to suit your new page size dimensions, choose Layout➪Layout Adjustment and select the Enable Layout Adjustment check box. (For more details on using this feature, see Chapter 4.)

- ✔ To ensure that your document's colors are displayed consistently across platforms and different Web browsers, you need to use the Web-safe colors in the Web swatch library, which you can access by choosing Window➪Swatch Libraries➪Web. If you don't use Web-safe colors, the colors in your HTML files may appear different depending on the platform and browser on which they are viewed.

- ✔ Because of the limitations of HTML and the differences between Web browsers, you have limited control over formatting. Symbols, kerning, hyphenation, justification, tabs, and other elements aren't preserved when you convert a document to HTML. The solution? Well, you can't do a whole lot about some formatting limitations, but it helps to keep your formatting simple.

When to use PDF

If the thought of losing even one tab in your document sends you into a fit of hysteria, you're probably more of a *Portable Document Format* (PDF) kind of person. PDF is a file format developed by Adobe that preserves the exact look of your original document, including fonts, images, layout, formatting, and colors. When you export an InDesign document to PDF, as we explain later, you're creating an exact electronic rendition of your printed document. Anyone with Adobe Acrobat or Acrobat Reader (available on the InDesign CD and as a free download from Adobe's Web site at *www.adobe.com*) can open and view a PDF document.

So what can you do with PDF files? For one, they're perfect for sending documents to clients or colleagues for review. You don't need to bother making and mailing multiple printouts (which can get pretty darn expensive). You just create one PDF file, and e-mail it to as many people as you like. Recipients can open, view, and even print the document exactly as you created it — with no hassles.

Here's another scenario. Suppose you have a full-color product brochure that you're printing and mailing to select customers. But you also want to make it more widely available electronically. You can post a PDF version of it on your Web site so all your customers can view it on-screen or print it on their desktop printers.

If you're still not sure whether you want to export an InDesign document to HTML or PDF, take a look at Color Plate 18-1 to see a full-color example of the kind of results you can expect from each format.

Exporting Documents to HTML

So you've considered your options, and you want a Web page, darn it. Enough said. Choose File⇨Export or press ⌘+E on the Mac or Ctrl+E under Windows. If you're using a PC, you'll see the Export dialog box shown in Figure 18-1. (On the Mac, your Export dialog will look a little different, but the basic options are the same.) This is where you choose the HTML export option and specify a name and location for your new file.

Figure 18-1:
In this dialog box, you specify the name, location, and format to which you want to export your document.

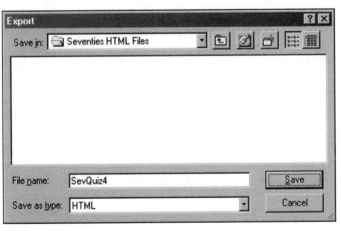

Choose the folder in which you want to store your file from the pop-up menu at the top of the dialog box. Then choose HTML from the Formats pop-up menu on the Mac or the Save As Type pop-up menu under Windows. Last but not least, enter a name for your HTML file in the Name option box on the Mac or in the File Name option box under Windows. Then press Return or Enter to display the Documents panel of the Export HTML dialog box.

Setting up document options

The Documents panel, shown in Figure 18-2, lets you specify whether you want to create a single HTML file for your entire document or separate files for each page. Here's how the various options work:

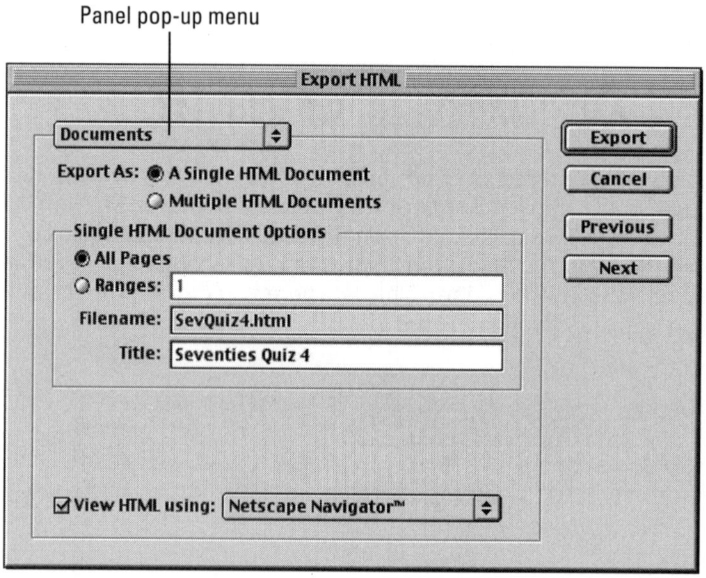

Panel pop-up menu

Export HTML

Documents

Export As: ● A Single HTML Document
○ Multiple HTML Documents

Single HTML Document Options
● All Pages
○ Ranges: 1
Filename: SevQuiz4.html
Title: Seventies Quiz 4

Export
Cancel
Previous
Next

☑ View HTML using: Netscape Navigator™

Figure 18-2:
Use the
Documents
panel to
export
document
pages to
multiple
HTML files.

✔ The A Single HTML Document radio button, which is selected by default, creates a single HTML file. If you want that file to include every page in your document, select the All Pages radio button. If you want to include only certain pages, click on the Ranges option and type the page numbers, or range of pages (or both) in the option box that you want to include.

Generally, you should avoid exporting a multipage document as a single HTML file for a couple reasons. First, you end up with one long Web page that might require lots of scrolling to get through. Second, InDesign inserts a gray horizontal rule that's supposed to separate each page when viewed in a Web browser. The problem is that the rule often ends up overlapping page elements, which is likely to drive you bonkers.

✔ To export each page in your document as a separate HTML file, select the Multiple HTML Documents option. This displays a scrolling list of every page in your document. If you want to exclude a page from being converted to HTML, just click on the check box next to the page name to deselect that page.

✔ The Title option box lets you specify a title for your HTML file, which will appear in the title bar at the top of most Web browsers. When you're exporting to multiple files, you can enter a separate title for each page. Simply click on the page entry in the scrolling list and type a title in the Title option box, and then repeat the process for each page.

✔ Select the View HTML Using check box and choose a browser from the corresponding pop-up menu. If your browser isn't listed in the pop-up menu, choose the Other option and locate the browser in the resulting dialog box. This option prompts InDesign to automatically display your HTML file in the selected Web browser after you export the file.

Choosing basic formatting options

When you've finished specifying the settings in the Documents panel, click on the Next button or choose Formatting from the panel pop-up menu labeled back in Figure 18-2. This displays the Formatting panel of the Export HTML dialog box, shown in Figure 18-3. Here you can do three things: specify how text with special formatting will be displayed; change the color of all regular text; and choose a background color or graphic for your Web page.

If your document includes text blocks that you've skewed, rotated, scaled, or edited with the hollow arrow tool, choose Appearance from the Maintain Non-Standard Text pop-up menu to preserve the appearance of those elements in the HTML file. When this option is selected, InDesign automatically converts any text with these attributes to a GIF image. This means your text won't be editable after conversion, but it will look the way you want it to. If you choose Editability from the pop-up menu, InDesign strips away any special formatting and leaves you with plain old HTML text.

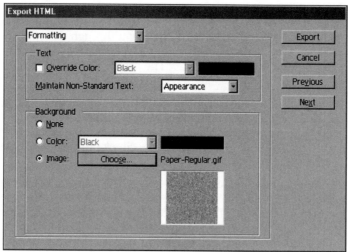

Figure 18-3:
The
Formatting
panel lets
you convert
text with
special
formatting
to GIF
images.

If for some reason you want to change the color of all the text in your HTML file, click on the Override Color check box and choose a color from the corresponding pop-up menu. The color swatch to the right of the pop-up menu shows a preview of the color you choose. If you're not fond of any of the choices InDesign provides, choose the Custom option or double-click on the color swatch to choose a color from the Color Picker on the Mac or the Color dialog box under Windows.

The bottom half of the Formatting panel lets you specify a background for your Web page. The None option, which is selected by default, leaves the background of your page as it appears in your InDesign document. To apply a color background, select the Color radio button and choose an option from the Color pop-up menu. Choose the Custom option or double-click on the color swatch to choose a color from the Color Picker on the Mac or the Color dialog box under Windows.

If you want to use an image as the background for your page, select the Image option and click on the Choose button. Locate and select the GIF or JPEG image you want to use from the Open an Image File dialog box that appears. When you press Return or Enter, you return to the Formatting panel to find a preview of the image in the box to the right of the Choose button.

If the background image you choose isn't large enough to fill an entire Web page, the image is *tiled*. In other words, it's copied and repeated as many times as needed to fill the page.

When you've finished choosing formatting options, click on the Next button to move to the Layout panel and read on.

Reproducing your layout

The Layout panel of the Export HTML dialog box is muy importante. This is where you tell InDesign whether or not to maintain the position of elements in your InDesign document on your Web page. In almost every instance, you'll want to preserve your layout as much as possible, so leave the default Positioning option — Best CSS-1 — as is. Presumably, you designed your document the way you want it to appear in your HTML file. But if for some reason you want InDesign to change your layout so that all text flows in a single column with graphics set alone as if they were paragraphs, by all means choose the None option.

From the InDesign Margins pop-up menu, select Maintain if you want your HTML file to use the same margins as your InDesign document. If you select None, your Web page will use the default margins of the browser in which it is viewed.

When you're exporting a document as multiple HTML files, you can tell InDesign to add navigational links that allow people to move from page to page. Choose Top, Bottom, or Both from the Navigation Bar pop-up menu to tell InDesign where to insert the links. If you don't want InDesign to put any links on your pages, choose None from the pop-up menu.

Specifying how graphics are converted

To specify how graphics in your InDesign document will be converted in your HTML file, choose Graphics from the panel pop-up menu at the top of the Export HTML dialog box. The panel shown in Figure 18-4 appears.

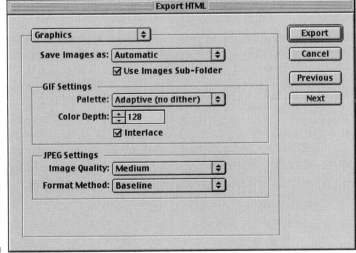

Figure 18-4:
Use this panel to specify how graphics will be converted.

Here's the skinny on the options:

- ✔ In most cases, you'll want to leave the default option — Automatic — selected in the Save Images As pop-up menu. This option lets InDesign automatically choose the best format for each graphic in your document, selecting GIF or JPEG on a case-by-case basis. If you want to convert all graphics to one format or the other, choose the GIF or JPEG option.

- ✔ Leave the Use Images Sub-Folder check box selected to let InDesign create a folder named Images within the folder that will contain your HTML file. InDesign will store all converted graphics in that folder. If you deselect this option, converted graphics are stored in the same folder as your HTML files.

- ✔ The GIF graphic format is limited to 256 colors. So if your document contains images with *more* than 256 colors, and those images may be converted to the GIF format, choose the Adaptive (no dither) option from the Palette pop-up menu. Otherwise, choose Exact to tell InDesign to create a palette using the existing colors in your graphics.

- ✔ Choose the Web option if you want InDesign to use only Web-safe colors when converting graphics to GIF format.

- ✔ If you choose the Adaptive (no dither) or Exact option, you can specify the number of colors (up to 256) that will be used in all GIF files. Lower numbers produce smaller image file sizes but may cause less than desirable color results.

- ✔ Select the Interlace option if you want GIF images to display gradually as they are downloaded to a Web browser. If you don't select this option, a GIF image will not appear on-screen until the entire graphic has been downloaded.

If you chose JPEG from the Save Images As pop-up menu, you don't need to specify GIF settings because all your images will be converted to JPEG. Similarly, you can ignore the JPEG settings (described next) if you chose GIF from the Save Images As pop-up menu.

- ✔ Choose an option from the Image Quality pop-up menu to specify how much compression will be applied to JPEG images. Low produces the smallest file sizes but the poorest image quality, and Maximum produces the largest file sizes with the highest image quality. In general, choosing Medium or High will yield an acceptable tradeoff between quality and size.

- ✔ If you want JPEG images to appear gradually as they download to a Web browser, choose Progressive from the Format Method pop-up menu. Choose Baseline if you want JPEG images to appear only after they are completely downloaded.

Initiating export and viewing your HTML file

Now that you have everything set up, it's time to click on the Export button. InDesign begins exporting away. Completing the process takes a few moments — or more than a few for large documents. If you enabled the View HTML Using option back in the Documents panel of the Export HTML dialog box, InDesign automatically launches the Web browser you specified and opens your new HTML file, as shown in Figure 18-5. If you didn't select the View HTML Using option, just double-click on the HTML file to open it in your default browser.

Your HTML file will look different depending on the browser and platform (Mac or Windows) on which you view it. Be sure to proof your Web page in both Microsoft Internet Explorer and Netscape Navigator. And do so on both platforms if you can. If you find problems with your HTML file, you can either edit it in an HTML editor, such as Adobe GoLive or NetObjects Fusion, or make changes in your original InDesign document and re-export it.

You can download Navigator from Netscape's Web site at *www.netscape.com* and Internet Explorer from Microsoft's site at *www.microsoft.com*.

Figure 18-5:
An InDesign document repurposed for the Web, exported to HTML, and viewed in Internet Explorer.

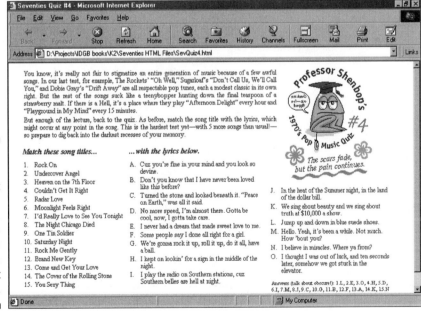

Exporting Documents to PDF

The biggest drawback to exporting documents as HTML files is that you can't preserve your print layout, colors, and formatting. You need to redesign your documents to accommodate the limitations of HTML and Web browsers, and even then the results are sometimes disappointing. If you want to distribute a document electronically *and* preserve your print layout, colors, and formatting, exporting to PDF is the way to go.

If you're accustomed to converting QuarkXPress or PageMaker documents to PDF files, you'll be pleasantly surprised by how easy it is to create PDF files from InDesign documents. Most notably, you don't need Acrobat Distiller because you can export to PDF directly from InDesign. And InDesign supports PDF version 1.3, which is currently the latest version.

To export an InDesign document to a PDF file, choose File⇨Export to display the Export dialog box pictured back in Figure 18-1. Choose a folder and enter a file name just as you would when exporting to HTML. Then choose Adobe PDF from the Format pop-up menu on the Mac or the Save As Type pop-up menu under Windows and press Return or Enter. The Export PDF dialog box appears with the PDF Options panel displayed, as shown in Figure 18-6.

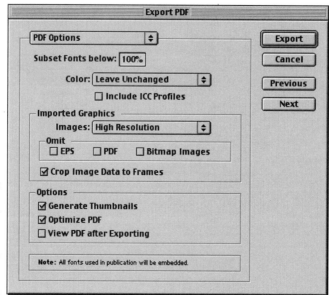

Figure 18-6:
The PDF Options panel of the Export PDF dialog box.

Controlling fonts, images, and display

You probably won't often need to change most of the default settings in the PDF Options panel of the Export PDF dialog box. But the following list highlights several options you should pay attention to:

- ✔ **Subset Fonts Below:** This option controls the point at which an entire font is embedded in the PDF file. A value of 25 percent, for example, tells InDesign to embed an entire font only if more than 25 percent of the font's characters are used in the document. Otherwise, only the individual characters used are embedded. The default value of 100 percent embeds just the individual characters used in the document.

- ✔ **Include ICC Profiles:** This option is available only if your document uses color management, in which case you should click on this check box.

- ✔ **Images:** If you plan for readers to view your PDF file on-screen, choose Low Resolution from this pop-up menu to place screen resolution (72 dpi) versions of images in the file. If you expect readers to print the PDF file, leave the High Resolution option selected. But be aware that this may increase the size of your file dramatically.

- ✔ **Crop Image Data to Frames:** This option reduces the file size by exporting only the visible portion of cropped images to the PDF file. Make sure this option is checked.

- ✔ **Optimize PDF:** This option prepares PDF files for page-at-a-time downloading from a Web server and reduces file size. If your document is bound for the Web, leave this option selected.

- ✔ **View PDF After Exporting:** Select this option to open the PDF file in Acrobat Reader (available on the InDesign CD) immediately after export.

Compressing graphics

Choose Compression from the panel pop-up to display the Compression panel, shown in Figure 18-7, which provides compression options for color, grayscale, and black-and-white images.

You can leave all the default settings as they are, with the following exceptions:

- ✔ If you expect readers to view the PDF file on-screen only, enter 72 in all three DPI option boxes. If you plan for readers to print the PDF file from a desktop inkjet or laser printer, change the DPI value for color and grayscale images to 300 and the DPI value for monochrome images to 600.

- ✔ Choose Medium or High from the two Quality pop-up menus. This will help reduce file size while maintaining an acceptable image quality.

Export PDF

| Compression | ▼ |

Color Bitmap Images

| Downsample to | ▼ | 300 | DPI |

Compression: | Automatic | ▼ |

Quality: | Maximum | ▼ |

Grayscale Bitmap Images

| Downsample to | ▼ | 300 | DPI |

Compression: | Automatic | ▼ |

Quality: | Maximum | ▼ |

Monochrome Bitmap Images

| Downsample to | ▼ | 1200 | DPI |

Compression: | CCITT Group 4 | ▼ |

☑ Compress Text and Line Art

[Export]
[Cancel]
[Previous]
[Next]

Figure 18-7:
Use this panel to specify compression settings for graphics.

Choosing which pages to export

To select the pages in your InDesign document that you want to include in your PDF file, choose Pages and Page Marks from the panel pop-up menu at the top of the Export PDF dialog box. This brings up the Pages and Page Marks panel, shown in Figure 18-8.

You can ignore the Page Marks options in the bottom half of the dialog box — they're relevant only if you're preparing a PDF file for high-resolution output from a commercial printer.

If you want to export your entire document, leave the All Pages radio button selected, as it is by default. Select the Ranges radio button to export one or more ranges of pages. Then in the Ranges option box, type the numbers of the pages you want to export. To export entire sections of your document, select the By Sections radio button. Then Shift-click to select a range of consecutive sections from the list. To select nonconsecutive sections, ⌘-click on the Mac or Ctrl-click under Windows.

To export facing pages so that they appear as two-page spreads in the PDF file, click on the Reader's Spreads check box.

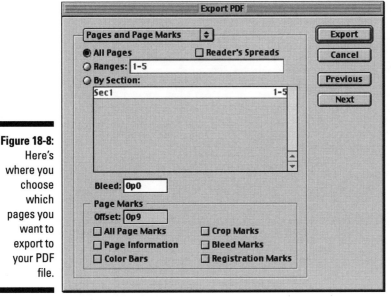

Figure 18-8:
Here's
where you
choose
which
pages you
want to
export to
your PDF
file.

Protecting your PDF file against intruders

An added perk to distributing documents as PDF files is that you can password-protect them so that only intended recipients can open them. To add security options to your file, choose Security from the panel pop-up menu to display the Security panel, shown in Figure 18-9.

Select the Use Security Features check box to make all the security options active. In the Open Document option box, type a password that users will need to enter to open the PDF file. In the Change Security option box, type a password that users will have to enter to change any security options.

If you're feeling really protective, you can select options in the Do Not Allow area to prevent people from doing things such as printing, changing, or copying the contents of the PDF file.

Making and viewing the PDF file

When you've finished setting up all your options, click on the Export button to get the export process underway. It may take awhile; a progress bar appears on-screen to let you know that InDesign is working on it. When the progress bar disappears, InDesign is finished.

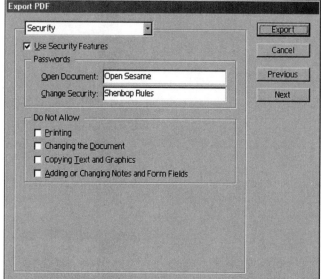

Figure 18-9:
Keep your
PDF file
from falling
into the
wrong
hands by
using the
options in
the Security
panel.

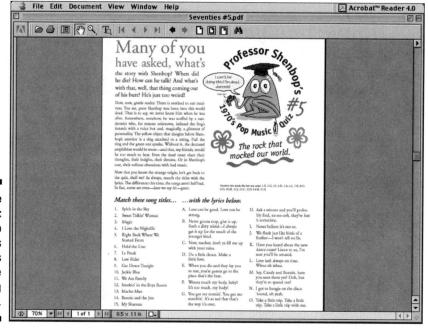

**Figure
18-10:**
Shenbop
and his
Seventies
songs are
looking
good in PDF.

The next step is to see how your new PDF file looks. If you selected the View PDF After Exporting option back in the PDF Options panel of the Export PDF dialog box, InDesign automatically launches Acrobat Reader (or Acrobat, if you have it installed on your system) with your new PDF file displayed, as shown in Figure 18-10. If you didn't select the View PDF After Exporting option, just double-click on the PDF file icon to open it in Acrobat 4, if you have it, or Acrobat Reader 4.

If you plan to e-mail your PDF file to colleagues or clients, you need to watch out for large file sizes. As a general rule, 1 to 2MB is about the maximum acceptable size. To check the file size on the Mac, Control-click on the PDF file icon, press ⌘+I, and check the Size value. Under Windows, right-click on the PDF file icon, choose Properties from the resulting menu, and check the Size value. If the file size exceeds 2MB or so, you should re-export your InDesign document to multiple PDF files.

Part V
The Part of Tens

"THAT'S A LOVELY SCANNED IMAGE OF YOUR SISTER'S PORTRAIT. NOW TAKE IT OFF THE BODY OF THAT PIT VIPER BEFORE SHE COMES IN THE ROOM."

In this part . . .

Believe it or not, "The Part of Tens" is a section in virtually every ...*For Dummies* book. It's what the publisher calls a brand element, so it has to be there. Hundreds and hundreds of ...*For Dummies* titles are on the market, each with its own "The Part of Tens" and each with a unique "The Part of Tens" introduction.

So we thought, rather than writing yet another brain-dead introduction to "The Part of Tens" — after all, it's just a bunch of top ten lists, so what's to introduce? — we'd reserve this space for listing the top ten themes of "The Part of Tens" introductions found inside other ...For Dummies books. According to our 5-minute survey of 2,359 ...*For Dummies* books, the top ten themes are:

10. Gee whiz, everybody sure loves a good old-fashioned Top Ten list.

9. Moses brought forth the Ten Commandments, and who are we to go against such a solemn tradition?

8. Have you ever seen David Letterman's Top Ten list? It's quite the crack up.

7. A carton has ten eggs — at least by the time we get home.

6. Moses called down the Ten Plagues upon Pharaoh, and who are we to go against such a grisly tradition?

5. Another rib-tickling reference to Dave Letterman, only not so clever.

4. Moses had ten toes and ten fingers, and who are we to go against such a traditional tradition?

3. In Base 12, the number 10 stands for a dozen, so on Planet Nerd, a carton really does have 10 eggs!

2. Some talk-show host on late-night TV does a regular top ten list. At least, that's what we hear. Our moms don't let us stay up that late.

And the number-one theme for the introduction of "The Part of Tens" in a ...For Dummies book is:

1. The publisher told us to do it, and we're so sick of writing by this point in the book that we'll do anything to get it over with.

Chapter 19

Ten Shortcuts Everyone Should Know

Do you get visibly irritated when it takes more than two minutes to get a Whopper at your local Burger King? Do you wave your fists in fury if a motorist pauses when it's his or her turn to go at a four-way stop? Do you start docking a waitress' tip by one percent for every minute you have to wait for the check after finishing a meal?

If you answered yes to any of these questions, you definitely value your time. (Some might argue you *over*value it, but that's not for us to say.) And if you value your time, you definitely need to read this chapter. You, friend, are the reason we wrote it. So enjoy.

Opening, Closing, and Other Vital Tasks

⌘+N or Ctrl+N

To create a new document based on your default settings (that's one page and letter sized, if you haven't changed InDesign's defaults), press ⌘+N on the Mac or Ctrl+N under Windows. Then press Return or Enter.

⌘+O or Ctrl+O

To open a document you've saved to disk, press ⌘+O on the Mac or Ctrl+O under Windows.

⌘+S or Ctrl+S

To save an open document, press ⌘+S on the Mac or Ctrl+S under Windows.

⌘+W or Ctrl+W

To close an open document, press ⌘+W on the Mac or Ctrl+W under Windows.

⌘+Q or Ctrl+Q

To quit InDesign and call it a day, press ⌘+Q on the Mac or Ctrl+Q under Windows.

Displaying and Hiding the Toolbox and Palettes

Tab

Press Tab to hide all open palettes and the toolbox. Press Tab again to redisplay them. Press Shift+Tab to hide or display palettes but leave the toolbox on-screen.

If a text insertion point is visible, or text is selected, or a dialog box is open, or an option box in a palette is active, pressing the Tab key affects the text, dialog box, or palette option. After you deselect text, or close the dialog box, or press Return or Enter to apply the palette option, the Tab key regains its control over the visibility of the toolbox and palettes.

⌘+T or Ctrl+T, ⌘+M or Ctrl+M

Press ⌘+T or Ctrl+T to display or hide the Character palette. Then you can click on the Paragraph palette tab or press ⌘+M or Ctrl+M to display the Paragraph palette.

F5 – F12

Press the following keys to hide or display the corresponding palettes: F5 for Swatches, F6 for Color, F7 for Layers, F8 for Align, F9 for Transform, F10 for Stroke, F11 for Paragraph Styles, Shift+F11 for Character Styles, and F12 for Pages.

Scrolling and Switching Pages

Spacebar, Option-click or Alt-click

Press the spacebar to temporarily access the hand tool when any other tool is selected. Then while holding down the spacebar, drag to scroll your document.

If a text insertion point is visible, pressing the spacebar enters spaces in your text, so you need to press Option or Alt and click to temporarily access the hand tool.

Shift+Page Up, Shift+Page Down

To move to the preceding page in your document, press Shift+Page Up. To move to the next page, press Shift+Page Down.

⌘+Page Up or Ctrl+Page Up, ⌘+Page Down or Ctrl+Page Down

Press ⌘+Page Up on the Mac or Ctrl+Page Up under Windows to go back to the page you last viewed. To move forward one page in the sequence of pages you've viewed, press ⌘+Page Down on the Mac or Ctrl+Page Down under Windows.

Zooming by Keys and Clicks

⌘+spacebar or Ctrl+spacebar, ⌘+Option+spacebar or Ctrl+Alt+spacebar

To get the zoom in cursor when another tool is selected, press ⌘+spacebar on the Mac or Ctrl+spacebar under Windows. Pressing ⌘+Option+spacebar on the Mac or Ctrl+Alt+spacebar under Windows displays the zoom out cursor. So you can magnify your view at any time by ⌘+spacebar+clicking on the Mac or Ctrl+spacebar+clicking under Windows. To zoom out, ⌘+Option+spacebar+click on the Mac or Ctrl+Alt+spacebar+click under Windows.

⌘+plus (+) or Ctrl+plus, ⌘+minus (−) or Ctrl+minus

You can also zoom in and out from the keyboard. Press ⌘+plus on the Mac or Ctrl+plus under Windows to zoom in. Press ⌘+minus or Ctrl+minus under Windows to zoom out.

Double-click on the zoom tool, ⌘+1 or Ctrl+1

To quickly change the magnification to 100 percent, double-click on the zoom tool. You can also press ⌘+1 on the Mac or Ctrl+1 under Windows.

Viewing and Hiding Layout Elements

Most of the time, you'll want to be sure your margins, columns, ruler guides, and frame outlines are visible on-screen. But sometimes you'll want to switch these items off so you can see how your document is shaping up without a bunch of distracting lines cluttering your view. The following shortcuts let you quickly switch these items on and off.

⌘+semicolon (;) or Ctrl+semicolon

To hide or display all margin, column, and ruler guides, press ⌘+semicolon on the Mac or Ctrl+semicolon under Windows.

⌘+H or Ctrl+H

Press ⌘+H on the Mac or Ctrl+H under Windows to hide or display all frame edges.

If a frame is selected with the arrow or hollow arrow tool, it can't be hidden. So you might want to press ⌘+Shift+A on the Mac or Ctrl+Shift+A under Windows to deselect everything before hiding frames.

Selecting Selection, Shape, and Type Tools

V, A

Press V to select the arrow tool. Press A to select the hollow arrow tool.

When another other tool is active, you can temporarily access the last used selection tool (arrow or hollow arrow) by pressing the ⌘ key on the Mac or the Ctrl key under Windows. As long as you hold the ⌘ or Ctrl key, the last-used selection tool remains active.

T

Press T to select the type tool.

L, Shift+L, M, Shift+M, N, Shift+N

Press L to select the ellipse tool. Press Shift+L to toggle between the ellipse and ellipse frame tools. To select the rectangle tool, press M. Press Shift+M to toggle between the rectangle and rectangle frame tools. Press N to activate the polygon tool. And here's a shocker, press Shift+N to toggle between the polygon and polygon frame tools.

None of the tool keyboard shortcuts work when a text insertion point is visible because pressing a letter key types a letter.

Undoing and Redoing Stuff

⌘+Z or Ctrl+Z

Press ⌘+Z on the Mac or Ctrl+Z under Windows to undo the last operation you performed. To undo several past actions, press ⌘+Z or Ctrl+Z several times.

⌘+Shift+Z or Ctrl+Shift+Z

To redo something you've just undone, press ⌘+Shift+Z on the Mac or Ctrl+Shift+Z under Windows. Again, you can redo several undone operations by pressing ⌘+Shift+Z or Ctrl+Shift+Z several times.

Nudging and Duplicating

Arrow key, Shift+arrow key

To nudge a selected object by 1 point, press an arrow key. Press Shift plus an arrow key to nudge a selected object in 10-point increments.

⌘+C or Ctrl+C, ⌘+X or Ctrl+X, ⌘+V or Ctrl+V

To copy selected text or a selected graphic to the Clipboard, press ⌘+C on the Mac or Ctrl+C under Windows. To cut selected text or a selected graphic and transfer it to the Clipboard, press ⌘+X on the Mac or Ctrl+X under Windows. To paste the contents of the Clipboard into your document, press ⌘+V on the Mac or Ctrl+V under Windows.

⌘+Option+D or Ctrl+Alt+D

To duplicate a selected graphic or text block and offset it from the original, press ⌘+Option+D on the Mac or Ctrl+Alt+D under Windows.

Option-drag or Alt-drag

You can also press and hold the Option key on the Mac or the Alt key under Windows while you drag a graphic or text block. Each time you release the mouse button, the graphic is duplicated.

Filling and Stroking from the Keyboard

X, Shift+X

Press X to toggle between the Fill and Stroke icons in the toolbox. Press Shift+X to swap the current fill and stroke colors.

D

To return to the default fill and stroke colors, press the D key.

Comma (,), period (.), slash (/)

To apply the last used color to the fill or stroke (depending on which is active) of a selected object, press the comma (,) key. Press the period (.) key to apply the last used gradient to the fill or stroke. To remove a fill or stroke applied to a selected object, press the slash (/) key.

Formatting Text

InDesign gives you loads of ways to change the formatting of text from the keyboard. Here are a few of the shortcuts you're likely to use often.

⌘+Shift+< or Ctrl+Shift+<, ⌘+Shift+> or Ctrl+Shift+>

To reduce the type size of selected text in 2-point increments (assuming you haven't changed the default Size/Leading value in Preferences), press ⌘+Shift+< on the Mac or Ctrl+Shift+< under Windows. Press ⌘+Shift+> on the Mac or Ctrl+Shift+> under Windows to increase the type size by 2 points. Throw in the Option or Alt key to reduce or enlarge type size by five times that amount. For example, press ⌘+Shift+Option+< on the Mac or Ctrl+Shift+Alt+< under Windows to reduce the type size of selected text by 10 points.

Option+left arrow or Alt+left arrow, Option+right arrow or Alt+right arrow

To kern two letters closer, click between them with the type tool and press Option+left arrow on the Mac or Alt+left arrow under Windows. Press Option+right arrow on the Mac or Alt+right arrow to kern the letters apart.

⌘+Shift or Ctrl+Shift plus B, I, or Y

Press ⌘+Shift+B on the Mac or Ctrl+Shift+B under Windows to make selected text bold. Press ⌘+Shift+I on the Mac or Ctrl+Shift+I under Windows to apply italics to selected text. To return to the normal type style, press ⌘+Shift+Y on the Mac or Ctrl+Shift+Y under Windows.

These keyboard shortcuts apply only to typefaces that include bold or italic font definitions.

⌘+Shift or Ctrl+Shift plus L, C, R, J, or F

To change the alignment of a selected paragraph on the Mac, press ⌘ and Shift plus the first letter of the alignment. Under Windows, press Ctrl and Shift plus the letter. For example, press ⌘+Shift+L or Ctrl+Shift+L to left align a selected paragraph. Center aligned is ⌘+Shift+C or Ctrl+Shift+C. Right is ⌘+Shift+R or Ctrl+Shift+R. Justified is ⌘+Shift+J or Ctrl+Shift+J, and force justified is ⌘+Shift+F or Ctrl+Shift+F.

Chapter 20

Ten Hidden Tricks Even Einstein Didn't Know

Some folks say, "The devil's in the details." If that's true, we should all grow horns and run around with pitchforks. We're not really evil, mind you. It's just that when it comes to designing pages, it's the details that can turn an ordinary document into an extraordinary one, or simply make your job a little easier. That's where this chapter comes in. The next several pages contain an assortment of tips and tricks that will help you make the most of those devilish details.

We're fairly certain that nothing in the following pages poses the least threat to your spiritual well being, when read as written. But we make no guarantees about what you might find if you read this chapter backwards at half-speed.

Creating Killer Fractions

With a little help from the Baseline Shift option in the Character palette, you can turn a feeble fraction such as 56/332 into the real deal — $^{56}/_{332}$. Just click inside a text frame with the type tool and follow these steps:

1. **Type a number for the numerator.**

   Any number will do. And just in case you need a discreet reminder, the numerator is the top number in a fraction.

2. **Choose Type⇨Insert Character.**

   The dialog box shown in Figure 20-1 appears.

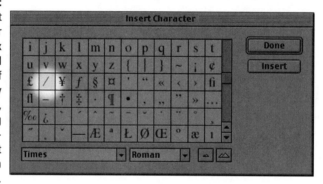

Figure 20-1: The Insert Character dialog box includes all kinds of shady characters, including the all-important fraction symbol.

3. **Select the special fraction symbol and click on the Insert button.**

   The fraction symbol is the one that looks like a skinny slash, as spotlighted in Figure 20-1.

4. **Type the denominator.**

   Psst. That's the bottom number.

5. **Select the numerator and make it about half the current type size.**

   For example, if the current type size is 30 points, change the numerator to about 15 points.

6. **Enter a Baseline Shift value equal to about one-third the original type size.**

   For example, if the original type size was 30 points, type **10** in the Baseline Shift option box.

7. **Select the denominator and change its type size to match that of the numerator.**

   Leave the Baseline Shift value for the denominator at 0. The result is a beautifully formatted fraction. Darn, you're good.

Making Type Show What It Means

You can also use baseline shift to create special type effects, like the one shown in Figure 20-2. Just select one or more characters with the type tool and press Shift+Option+up arrow or Shift+Option+down arrow on the Mac to raise or lower (respectively) the selected characters from the baseline in 2-point increments. Under Windows, press Shift+Alt+up arrow or Shift+Alt+down arrow. Figure 20-2 includes baseline shifts ranging from –12 points to 12 points.

Figure 20-2:
Don't stare
at this text
too long
unless
you've taken
Dramamine.

FEELING SEASICK

Ending a Story with Justified Flare

One way to wrap up a story with some style is to add a special ornamental character at the end, as shown in Figure 20-3. If you're wondering how we aligned the flower character — which is from the Zapf Dingbats typeface, by the way — flush right, the answer is that we used a flush space in a fully justified paragraph. Follow these steps:

1. **Click with the type tool at the end of the last paragraph in your story.**

   No mysteries here.

2. **Press ⌘+Shift+Option+J on the Mac or Ctrl+Shift+Alt+J under Windows to insert a flush space.**

   You won't be able to see the space yet, but it's there.

3. **Click on the last alignment icon in the Paragraph palette to justify all lines in the paragraph, if you haven't already.**

   Or press ⌘+Shift+F on the Mac or Ctrl+Shift+F under Windows.

4. **Choose Type⇨Insert Character, select a character from the Insert Character dialog box, and click on the Insert button.**

   This inserts the character that will appear at the end of your story.

5. **Then click on the Done button to exit the dialog box.**

Your special character now appears flush right with the flush space fill-ing the gap between it and the period at the end of the paragraph.

"Scientists Reveal Veggies Feel Pain!" Who could resist such a headline? Not Suzy, so she read on. "When you steam broc-coli, you're literally torturing it."

Being a long time vegetarian, Suzy was understandably shaken. After a moment, she collected herself and sighed, "Oh well, I guess it's back to bacon double-cheeseburgers." ❋

Figure 20-3: Witness the power of a flush space.

When a Tab Doesn't Cut It. . .

Use an em space instead. Tabs are great for aligning columns of data and cre-ating bulleted and numbered lists, but as Figure 20-4 shows, they're not ideal for elements such as run-in heads. In the two left paragraphs, the words *Friday* and *Saturday* (the *run-in heads*) are separated from the ensuing text by tabs. As the dotted line shows, the tabs line up, which results in a gap after the word *Friday*. To get an equal amount of space between run-in heads and text, as shown in the two right paragraphs in the figure, don't use tabs. Click after each run-in head with the type tool and press ⌘+Shift+M on the Mac or Ctrl+Shift+M under Windows to insert em spaces.

Figure 20-4: Run-in heads separated by tabs (left) and em spaces (right).

Friday Take out the garbage. Call mom. Wash the car.

Saturday Do the three things you forgot to do yesterday.

Friday Take out the garbage. Call mom. Wash the car.

Saturday Do the three things you forgot to do yesterday.

Making the Most of Layers

In Chapter 10, we talk about using layers to keep elements such as graphics organized. But that's not all you can do with layers. They're also a great way to manage multiple versions of a document. For example, suppose you're creating an advertisement that your client wants to use in the United States, United Kingdom, and Australia. The basic layout is the same for all three, but each needs to contain different information on pricing and availability. Rather than having to deal with creating and managing three different files, you can simply put each version of the ad on its own layer in the same file. Then you can just click on the View icon box next to the layer names in the Layers palette (that's F7) to quickly switch back and forth between versions.

Engraving Text

Everyone likes a cool text effect, so here's one to add to your quiver. You can easily give text an engraved look, as shown in Figure 20-5. First, Option-drag or Alt-drag a text block with the arrow tool just slightly up and to the right, or down and to the left, or whatever direction you prefer. Then release the mouse button. Now you have two overlapping versions of your text block. Select the text in the top text block with the type tool and apply a fill of white.

Figure 20-5:
Copy a text block and fill the text in front with white to create an engraved effect.

To adjust the effect, select the top text block and nudge it by pressing the arrow keys. To make the effect more pronounced, you might want to also draw a rectangle or some other shape around the text and fill it with a light color, as we did in Figure 20-5. Then send the rectangle to the back of the stacking order by choosing Object⇨Arrange⇨Send to Back.

Making Pretty Tables with Rules

You can use paragraph rules to turn dull and dusty tables into a visual delight. Select your table heading with the type tool and choose Paragraph Rules from the Paragraph palette menu. Click on the Preview check box and select Rule On. In the Weight option box, type a value that's equivalent to the size of the selected text plus about 4 points. In Figure 20-6, for example, our table heading is set in 14-point Helvetica Bold, so we typed **18pt** in the Weight option box to extend the rule a few points above and below the text. Then choose a color for the rule from the Color pop-up menu. (Remember, only colors in the Swatches palette are available.)

Figure 20-6:
Use para-
graph rules
to separate
rows in
tables.

Stevie's Seventies Superstore	
Bell bottoms	$8.00
Platform shoes	$6.50
Leisure suits	$9.99

For regular text, you'll need to use a fairly light color so that the text will show up. If you want to use a dark color or black, you can fill the table heading text with white or some other light color, like we did in Figure 20-6.

Use the Offset value to position the rule over the text. If you need to move it up to center it on your table heading, enter a positive value; if you need to move it down, enter a negative value. When you're happy with the size and position of the rule, press Return or Enter to make your rule a reality. You can create rules for other rows in your table in the same way.

Creating Type that Fades

Here's a simple trick. You can quickly create fading type using gradients, as shown in Figure 20-7 and in the top example in Color Plate 20-1. With the type tool, select the text you want to fade. Click on the Gradient button in the toolbox to apply a gradient fill, and then choose Window⇨Gradient to display the Gradient palette. Create a gradient using two or more colors, as described in Chapter 11. Just make sure the colors go from light to dark or dark to light. (Otherwise, the fading effect won't work.)

Figure 20-7:
Use
gradients to
achieve
fading type.

With your text still selected, click on the gradient tool in the toolbox and drag across the text to set the beginning and ending points of the gradient. The direction you drag determines the direction of the fade. The example in Figure 20-7, for instance, shows a two-color gradient that fades from left to right. But you can make your text fade from right to left, top to bottom, bottom to top, or diagonally.

Slipping an Image Inside Type

If you've ever thought, "Gee, I'd sure like to fill that type with an image," you'll be tickled some shade of red to discover that in InDesign you can. If you don't believe us, just take a look at Figure 20-8. Or if you prefer, flip to the middle example in Color Plate 20-1.

Figure 20-8:
An image
placed
inside type
that's been
converted to
paths.

Here's how you do it. Select some type with the type or arrow tool and choose Type➪Create Outlines to convert the text to paths. Select the converted type with the hollow arrow tool. Then either import an image directly into the selected paths using the File➪Place command or copy an existing image in your layout, select the paths with the arrow or hollow arrow tool, and choose Edit➪Paste Into. Either way, the image appears inside the paths. Then you can drag the image with the hollow arrow tool to change the portion displayed in the converted type outlines.

You can also place an image in text that's been converted to paths to create a translucent type effect, as shown in the bottom example in Color Plate 20-1. Drag with the type tool to create a text frame over an image and type some text. Convert the text to paths and select the paths with the hollow arrow tool. Then prepare a lighter version of the original image in your image-editing program and save it as a separate file. (To create the effect in Color Plate 20-1, for example, we adjusted the output levels in Photoshop.) Return to InDesign and import the light version of the image into the selected text paths. Finally, drag with the hollow arrow tool to position the light image so that it overlaps the original image exactly. Now you have the appearance of see-through type.

Jumping around in a Story

If your document contains multiple stories that don't all flow in consecutive columns, it can be a drag having to remember which pages a story appears on when you're trying to make changes. Fortunately, InDesign provides a few hidden shortcuts that let you move quickly between the text blocks in a story. First, select a text block with the arrow tool and then do any of the following:

✔ To move to the next text block in a story, press ⌘+Option+Page Down on the Mac or Ctrl+Alt+Page Down under Windows. If the last text block in a story is already selected, this shortcut doesn't do a darn thing.

✔ Press ⌘+Option+Page Up on the Mac or Ctrl+Alt+Page Up under Windows to move to the previous text block. Like the preceding shortcut, this one doesn't work if the first text block in a story is selected.

✔ To jump to the first text block in a story, press ⌘+Option+Shift+Page Up on the Mac or Ctrl+Alt+Shift+Page Up under Windows.

✔ Bet you can guess what's coming next. That's right, press ⌘+Option+Shift+Page Down on the Mac or Ctrl+Alt+Shift+Page Down under Windows to go to the last text block in a story.

Chapter 21

Ten Terrific Typeface Families

*I*f you're new to page design, one of your first questions will probably be: "What typefaces should I use?"

The answer is, "Why, whatever you think looks good."

Then you say, "But I have no taste."

"Yes you do," we respond, "You just need to have more faith in yourself. Try experimenting with a few fonts to see how they look together, and build your library based on that."

"No, you don't understand," you protest. "I still wear leisure suits and drive a Gremlin."

"Uh oh, this is worse than we thought."

For those who need a little help — taste or no taste — we offer this chapter. Keep in mind that selecting typefaces is a subjective task. Therefore, rather than throwing out our hit parade of favorites, we'll steer you toward a few tried and true solutions that have been around long enough to find mainstream acceptance.

We selected these fonts from the Adobe Typeface Library because it's one of the most established. Adobe also licenses its fonts from the source, which means you get the font as it was originally designed. See, you can copyright only a typeface's name — not the typeface itself. So if some other font manufacturer sees a typeface it likes, they can copy it as long as they name it something different, such as Missive instead of Mistral. As your grandpappy told you, life ain't always fair.

The upshot is that Adobe's fonts are of the highest quality. They're readily available at your local service bureau or commercial printer but they're also expensive, roughly $100 to $200 per family of four type styles. For that same price, you can get 100 fonts from a knockoff vendor. Either way, you'll get basically the same font.

Here goes — the ten best typefaces in all creation coming at you!

Helvetica

If we were to conduct a scientific survey to determine the most legible font at all type sizes, Helvetica would probably come out the winner. Sure, it's kind of boring and it appears in just about every desktop-published document in the Western world, but it epitomizes stability and flexibility.

Helvetica's no-nonsense approach seems to provide type designers with constant inspiration. It's sort of the Cher of fonts, readily lending itself to one makeover after another. Since its debut in 1957, Helvetica has been the subject of countless stylistic variations, just a few of which are shown in Figure 21-1. The Adobe Type Library alone contains nearly 100 styles of the font, including outline, condensed, expanded, and rounded. Our recommendation: Buy all the Helveticas you can get your hands on.

Antique Olive

If you're looking for a sans serif face with a little more flair than Helvetica, you can't go wrong with Antique Olive. Although its name might conjure up images of Popeye's girlfriend in a retirement home, it's a highly distinctive font, sporting angular terminals — the ends of the characters — and variable-weight strokes, as demonstrated by the variations shown in Figure 21-2.

Helvetica
Helvetica Light
Black Oblique
Helvetica Condensed
Condensed Bold Oblique
Helvetica Extra Compressed
Neue 23 Ultra Light
Extended
Neue 56 Italic
**Neue 107 Extra Black
Condensed**
Neue 75 Bold Outline
*Helvetica Rounded
Bold Oblique*
Fractions ½ ¾ $^{56}/_{78}$ $\frac{3}{8}$ $7\frac{5}{16}$
Bold ½ ¾ $^{56}/_{78}$ $\frac{3}{8}$ $7\frac{5}{16}$

Figure 21-1:
These are
but a few of
the half
billion
variations
on
Helvetica.

If you want to add a little attitude to your sans serif text, use Antique Olive. And if Antique Olive isn't quite your cup of tea, try out Optima, Stone Sans, Eras, or Franklin Gothic, each of which offers its own flair. They all prove that sans serif fonts don't have to be as boring or dated as the PostScript standard Avant Garde Gothic.

Antique Olive
Antique Olive Italic
Antique Olive Light
Antique Olive Bold
Antique Olive Black
Antique Olive Nord
Nord Oblique
Antique Olive Compact
Antique Olive Bold Condensed

Figure 21-2: Antique Olive shows that sans serif fonts can be as individual and as stylish as their serifed cousins.

Baskerville

We're sorry, but we hate Times, the common serifed typeface provided with just about every personal computer ever sold. It's the Yugo of fonts, cheesy, scrawny, and unsuitable to most design terrains. Okay, if you're typesetting a paperback novel — particularly one devoid of intellectual merit (our favorite kind!) — Times is ideal. But for anything else, forget it.

The font that should have found its way onto the world's PCs is Baskerville. Ultimately a conservative and symmetrical face, Baskerville is at the same time stylish and versatile, as shown in Figure 21-3. In other words, it has all the advantages of Times and none of the deficits.

Berthold Baskerville
Baskerville Italic
Baskerville Medium
Medium Italic
Baskerville Bold
Baskerville Book
Baskerville Book Italic
Book Medium
Book Medium Italic
New Baskerville Roman
New Baskerville Italic
New Baskerville Bold
Bold Italic 1234567890
SMALL CAPS &
OLD STYLE 1234567890
Bold Ital OS 1234567890

Figure 21-3: Some of the many variations available for Baskerville, including a special small caps style.

Garamond

Claude Garamond designed type in the 16th century and is considered by many to be the father of modern typography. His primary legacy is a font named for him but based on a recutting made by contemporary Jean Jannon and wrongly ascribed to Garamond around the turn of the twentieth century. Meanwhile, the italics came from Robert Granjon, a friend of Garamond's who helped divide the labor. Still, the modern font looks a lot like the stuff Claude carved, so the name stuck.

You'd think after that introduction that Garamond would be a dusty relic, of interest only to type historians and wholly illegible by modern standards. But as Figure 21-4 shows, this is anything but the case. Garamond is perhaps the most widely available, modified, and remodified typeface short of Helvetica. At last count, the Adobe Typeface Library contained 14 complete families of Garamond. And unlike Helvetica, the font lends itself to small cap and ornamental variations, such as the Swash Italic pictured in Figure 21-4. You can even use a multiple master version based on the design from the eminent ITC type foundry.

For other serifed typefaces with an historic appeal, try out Bembo — based on the first roman typeface designed by Aldus Manutius — Granjon, Galliard, and Caslon. The last of these was based on the 18th-century designs of William Caslon and was, according to type historian Douglas C. McMurtrie, "as good a book type as has ever been produced." He wrote that in 1938, before most of the fonts in this chapter had been produced, but it's still one heck of a recommendation.

Adobe Garamond
Garamond Italic
Garamond Semibold
Garamond Bold
GARAMOND SMALL CAPS
Italic Old Style 1234567890
G. Italic Alternate QvNstZ
Berthold Garamond
Medium Condensed
G. Swash Italic 123456789
Stempel Garamond
SMALL CAPS 1234567890
Simoncini Garamond Italic
ITC Garamond Multiple Master
300 Light Italic 440 Narrow
595 Bold 625 Normal
775 Ultra 400 Condensed
Handtooled Bold

Figure 21-4:
Garamond and its many variations are based on some of the oldest roman type designs in existence.

Palatino

Is all this history making you thirsty for something more modern? Well, look no further than Palatino. Created by modern type wiz Hermann Zapf, Palatino is a modernization of the age-old designs of Garamond and gang. The font features chiseled terminals, sculpted transitional strokes, and calligraphic italics, all of which appear in Figure 21-5.

Palatino Roman
Palatino Italic
Palatino Light
Palatino Light Italic
Palatino Medium
Palatino Medium Italic
Palatino Bold
Bold Italic 1234567890
Palatino Black
Palatino Black Italic
PALATINO SMALL CAPS
& OLD STYLE 1234567890
Bold Ital OS 1234567890

Figure 21-5: Modern PostScript printers come equipped with Palatino's roman, italic, bold, and bold italic styles.

The best news about Palatino is that — like Times and Helvetica — four of its styles are built into all PostScript printers. This means you'll never have problems printing the font (as long as you're careful to steer clear of the TrueType version of Palatino that comes with all Macs). If you want to expand your Palatino collection, you can add light, black, and small cap styles. Ironically, Zapf created Palatino exclusively for headlines and logos, but it caught on for body text as well. To complement Palatino, Zapf created a lighter font called Aldus that looks better at very small type sizes, such as 9 points and smaller.

Bodoni

The Didots were an illustrious family of French printers from the late 18th century. We are told that François Ambroise Didot tutored Benjamin Franklin's grandson in the art of typography. Ironically, the most famous creator of so-called Didone fonts was an Italian named Giambattista Bodoni. Some say he got in cheap by lifting Didot's style. Some say he *perfected* it. All we know is that he ended up creating something along the lines of the styles shown in Figure 21-6.

Bodoni Roman
Bodoni Italic
Bodoni Book
Book Italic 1234567890
Bodoni Bold
Bodoni Bold Italic
Bodoni Bold Condensed
Bodoni Poster
Bodoni Poster Compressed
Bauer Bodoni Roman
Bodoni Black Italic
Bodoni Black Condensed
Bodoni Small Caps
Italic Old Style 123456789
Berthold Bodoni Antiqua
Antiqua Light Italic
Bold Condensed Italic
Bodoni Old Face
Old Face Ital Small Caps

Figure 21-6: The Bodoni family includes dozens of variations, including the ultra-heavy Bodoni Poster.

Like all Didone styles, Bodoni features very thick vertical strokes and hairline horizontal strokes. This radical contrast between neighboring stems makes for a highly stylized font that works well at larger sizes, say, 12 points and up. Other Didone styles include New Caledonia and, to a lesser extent, New Century Schoolbook. The latter is built into PostScript laser printers.

American Typewriter

If you want to impart a typewriter look to your pages, avoid the ubiquitous Courier, the *monospaced* font in which all characters — from the *i* to the *M* — are the same width. Instead, try out American Typewriter, shown in Figure 21-7. It's just the thing for that "Extra, extra, read all about it!" look.

American Typewriter falls into a category of type called *slab serifs*, which gained momentum during the Industrial Revolution of the 1800's. The difference between Typewriter and other slab serifs — such as Clarendon and Melior — is that the stroke weight of Typewriter characters is uniform throughout. In other words, the serifs are just as thick as the stems, perfect for hearty text that reproduces well even at small sizes.

Figure 21-7: American Typewriter reproduces well regardless of how many times you photocopy it.

American Typewriter
Typewriter Light
Typewriter Bold
Typewriter Medium
Condensed (eR$&)
Typewriter Light Condensed
Bold Condensed
Typewriter Condensed
Alternate (eR$&)

Script and Calligraphic

Having the gang over for a few hands of pinochle? Thinking of getting hitched and want to create you own invites? Well, then, you'll need some *script faces*. As shown in Figure 21-8, script characters typically join together, just like cursive handwriting. Script faces that don't join together — such as Medici Script and Poetica Chancery pictured in the figure — are sometimes called *calligraphic*.

Mistral (123&xyz?)

Künstler Script Bold (123&xyz?)

Wiesbaden Swing (123&xyz?)

Dorchester Script (123&xyz?)

Caflisch Script Multiple Master

Medici Script (123&xyz?)

Ruling Script Two

Boulevard (123&xyz?)

Brush Script (123&xyz?)

Shelley Volante Script

Poppl-Residenz (123&xyz?)

Charme (123&xyz?)

Poetica Chancery IV (123&xyz?)

Linoscript (123&xyz?)

Figure 21-8:
Text set in script faces generally look like they were written in one continuous stroke.

When working with script faces, don't kern them or change the letter spacing. This means you can't justify the text. If you do, you'll change the amount of space between neighboring characters and they'll no longer join correctly.

Display Faces

One thing you may have noticed about the fonts we've discussed so far is that they're not wacky. That's because wacky fonts — like the ones shown in Figure 21-9 — aren't particularly legible at small sizes. Can you imagine reading a whole paragraph set in Arnold Böcklin? Only a unicorn could put up with that font for more than a few words. Although unsuitable for body text, these *display faces* are great for headlines, logos, and other large type — typically 18 points or larger.

Figure 21-9:
Thousands
of display
faces are on
the market
and most
look much
goofier than
these.

Arnold Böcklin (123&?)

Cooper Black Italic

MACHINE MEDIUM (123&?)

TRAJAN (123&?)

Serpentine Oblique

BEES KNEES (123&?)

Wilhelm Klingspor Gotisch

Lo-Type Med. Italic

Litterbox (123&xyz?)

BANCO (123&XYZ?)

Goudy Text Lombardic Caps

Paisley (123&xyz?)

Mezz Multiple Master (123)

Block Berthold Condensed

Friz Quadrata (123&xyz?)

It's good to have an arsenal of display faces at your fingertips. Why? Because you can't use them often. They're so distinctive that your readers will notice if you use them over and over. For example, you might set the headline for a monthly column about World War I paraphernalia in the Wilhelm Klingspor Gotisch font. But if you did, you wouldn't want to use that font anywhere else in your newsletter. It's just too obvious.

Zapf Dingbats and Other Symbols

The last font on my hit parade is Zapf Dingbats (Figure 21-10), another font built into PostScript printers. Rather than being composed of letters, Dingbats comprises more than 250 symbols. You'll find check marks, crosses, stars, flowers, arrows, and a bunch of other doohickeys. Some are a little dated — Hermann Zapf created the font in the glorious Seventies — but you can find all sorts of useful stuff if you search around.

Figure 21-10: A smattering of the many characters available in Zapf Dingbats, Symbol, and several other symbol fonts.

In addition to Zapf Dingbats, Figure 21-10 features other useful symbol fonts, including the aptly named Symbol (built into all PostScript printers), Carta (a map font), Linotype Game Pi, Universal News, and Minion Ornaments.

On the Mac, many characters from Symbol get mixed in with other typefaces. For example, suppose you're using Helvetica Black Oblique. Pressing Option+5 produces the infinity character (∞). The weird thing is that the infinity symbol appears neither bold nor slanted. That's because it comes from the Symbol font. This means it doesn't match Helvetica Black Oblique and looks bad with it. The same goes for Option+period (.) for greater than or equal ($\geq$), Option+P for pi (π), and Option+J for delta (Δ). As a general rule of thumb, if a character isn't pictured in Figure 6-7 back in Chapter 6, it's part of the Symbol font.

This is not a problem with Windows. On the PC, characters might be harder to access, but you can bet that they all come from the same font.

More Fonts!

By limiting ourselves to ten (or so) fonts, we don't even begin to scrape the surface of what's out there. If you're feeling ambitious, here are some more faces we suggest you look into:

- **Melior**. Featured at the top of Figure 21-11, Melior is Deke's favorite font, bar none. Its squarish forms make it highly readable at very small sizes. He particularly likes the screen font on the Mac, which he uses religiously when writing.

- **Berkeley Oldstyle**. Armed with unusual diagonal crossbars, angled vowels, and calligraphic italics, this face hearkens back to the first roman typefaces. Based on a design for the University of California Press created by the father of American typography, Frederic W. Goudy, this is one of our favorites.

- **Souvenir**. Okay, it's been called the smiley face of type, but we just love the sloping letterforms and plastic transitions of Souvenir. In fact, we're big fans of all of Ed Benguiat's stuff, including Korinna, Tiffany, and of course, Benguiat.

- **Tekton**. Invented by Adobe's type staff, this face is based on the meticulous hand lettering of architect Francis Ching, complete with little balls at the terminals of the letters. It's great for architectural drawings and other plans.

- **Minion**. The second of Adobe's multiple master typefaces, right after Myriad, Minion provides three axes — Weight, Width, and Optical Size — perfect for use with InDesign. There's also a multiple master version of Tekton, incidentally, as well as the script face Caflisch and the display face Mezz.

Melior *Italic* **Bold** *Italic*

Berkeley Old Style *Italic* **Bold** Book *Black Italic*

Souvenir *Italic* **Medium Demi** *Bold Italic*

Tekton *Oblique* LightCondensed *Bold Cond.Oblique* Extended

Minion M. Master *Italic* **Semibold Condensed Bold** SMALL CAPS *ITALIC 1234567890*

Figure 21-11: Although these fonts don't share Garamond's rich history or Helvetica's wealth of style, they rank among our favorites.

Tons more fonts are out there, but we're afraid that if we continue like this, we'll reveal ourselves as the type dweebs we really are. So to finish things off, we'll stop telling you which fonts we like and focus some attention on the ones we *don't* like:

- ✔ **Wood Type.** These display faces hearken back to the woodcut letters of the Old West. As illustrated by Rosewood in Figure 21-12, Wood faces are kind of fun in moderation but get old fast. Honestly, how many wanted posters and hoedown leaflets are you going to typeset?

- ✔ **Zapf Chancery.** This font has become synonymous with cheesy restaurant menus. Thanks to the fact it's installed in all PostScript laser printers, Zapf Chancery is absolutely the most over-used calligraphic face in existence. And — with all due respect to Mr. Zapf — it's ugly to boot. What gives?

✔ **Courier**. Your computer is not a typewriter.

✔ **Futura**. We keep thinking we'll warm up to this font, but it always leaves us cold. Perhaps the least interesting sans serif font on the planet, Futura features miserable little lowercase letters and overly geometric letterforms. Futura Condensed is a marked improvement; at large sizes, it can even look stylish.

Of course, these are just our personal pet peeves. You might love all these fonts. But if you use them, keep in mind that at least a couple of snooty typeface aficionados out there are looking at your document and saying, "Yuck."

Figure 21-12: Okay, so there's no such thing as a bad font. But if we never saw these again, we wouldn't miss them.

Index

• E •

• F •

Notes

Notes

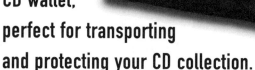

Discover Dummies Online!

The Dummies Web Site is your fun and friendly online resource for the latest information about ...*For Dummies*® books and your favorite topics. The Web site is the place to communicate with us, exchange ideas with other ...*For Dummies* readers, chat with authors, and have fun!

Ten Fun and Useful Things You Can Do at www.dummies.com

1. Win free ...*For Dummies* books and more!
2. Register your book and be entered in a prize drawing.
3. Meet your favorite authors through the IDG Books Author Chat Series.
4. Exchange helpful information with other ...*For Dummies* readers.
5. Discover other great ...*For Dummies* books you must have!
6. Purchase Dummieswear™ exclusively from our Web site.
7. Buy ...*For Dummies* books online.
8. Talk to us. Make comments, ask questions, get answers!
9. Download free software.
10. Find additional useful resources from authors.

Link directly to these ten
fun and useful things at
http://www.dummies.com/10useful

For other technology titles from IDG Books Worldwide, go to
www.idgbooks.com

Not on the Web yet? It's easy to get started with *Dummies 101*®: *The Internet For Windows*®*98* or *The Internet For Dummies*®, 6th Edition, at local retailers everywhere.

Find other ...*For Dummies* books on these topics:
Business • Career • Databases • Food & Beverage • Games • Gardening • Graphics • Hardware
Health & Fitness • Internet and the World Wide Web • Networking • Office Suites
Operating Systems • Personal Finance • Pets • Programming • Recreation • Sports
Spreadsheets • Teacher Resources • Test Prep • Word Processing

IDG BOOKS WORLDWIDE
BOOK REGISTRATION

Register This Book and Win!

We want to hear from you!

Visit **http://my2cents.dummies.com** to register this book and tell us how you liked it!

- Get entered in our monthly prize giveaway.

- Give us feedback about this book — tell us what you like best, what you like least, or maybe what you'd like to ask the author and us to change!

- Let us know any other ...*For Dummies*® topics that interest you.

Your feedback helps us determine what books to publish, tells us what coverage to add as we revise our books, and lets us know whether we're meeting your needs as a ...*For Dummies* reader. You're our most valuable resource, and what you have to say is important to us!

Not on the Web yet? It's easy to get started with *Dummies 101*®: *The Internet For Windows*® *98* or *The Internet For Dummies*®, 6th Edition, at local retailers everywhere.

Or let us know what you think by sending us a letter at the following address:

...*For Dummies* Book Registration
Dummies Press
7260 Shadeland Station, Suite 100
Indianapolis, IN 46256-3917
Fax 317-596-5498

...FOR DUMMIES™

BESTSELLING BOOK SERIES